RESEARCH IN MARITIME HISTORY
NO. 38

TRADE, MIGRATION AND URBAN NETWORKS IN PORT CITIES, C. 1640-1940

Edited by
Adrian Jarvis and Robert Lee

International Maritime Economic History Association

St. John's, Newfoundland
2008

ISSN 1188-3928
ISBN 978-0-9738934-8-9

Research in Maritime History is available free of charge to members of the International Maritime Economic History Association. The price to others is US $25 per copy, plus US $5 postage and handling.

Back issues of *Research in Maritime History* are available:

Research in Maritime History would like to thank Memorial University of Newfoundland, National Museums Liverpool and P.H. Holt Trust for their generous financial assistance in support of this volume.

Table of Contents

ABOUT THE EDITORS

ADRIAN JARVIS < Adrian.jarvis@liverpool.ac.uk > is an Honorary Fellow of the University of Liverpool, before which he was for fifteen years Curator of Port History at Merseyside Maritime Museum, a post in which he was able to spend most of his time on research and publication, working chiefly on the huge Mersey Docks and Harbour Board collection in the Museum's Maritime Archives and Library. He was also Co-director of the Centre of Port and Maritime History, a joint initiative of the University and the Maritime Museum. His particular interests have hinged on the machinery of management and the engineering of the port, and he has published extensively in these and other areas. As well, with Robert Lee he was one of the initiators of the Mercantile Liverpool Project. He served as a Senior Editor of the *Oxford Encyclopaedia of Maritime History* and has written many articles in that and other reference works. His major project at the moment is to complete a new general history of the Port of Liverpool.

ROBERT LEE < W.R.Lee@liverpool.ac.uk > is Chaddock Professor of Economic and Social History at the University of Liverpool and Co-Director of the Centre for Port and Maritime History. Professor Lee, who has held the Chaddock professorship since 1989, has been instrumental in developing a wide range of research initiatives and has over twelve major publications to his name. Recent research activity has included projects on official statistics and the development of population science in Germany; the Liverpool merchant community, 1800-1914; and the social and economic history of parks and open spaces.

CONTRIBUTORS

CÁTIA ANTUNES < c.a.p.antunes@hum.leidenuniv.nl > teaches history at the University of Leiden in the Netherlands. A specialist in urban, port and business history since 1500, she recently spent a year at Yale University as a Fulbright Research Fellow and is currently conducting research on cross-cultural business networks in the Atlantic world during the early modern period. Her recent publications include *Globalisation in the Early Modern Period: The Economic Relationship between Amsterdam and Lisbon* (Amsterdam, 2004); and "The Commercial Relationship between Amsterdam and the Portuguese Salt-Exporting Ports: Aveiro and Setubal, 1580-1715," *Journal of Early Modern History*, XII, No. 1 (2008), 25-53.

IDA BULL < ida.bull@hf.ntnu.no > has been Professor of History at the Norwegian University of Science and Technology (NTNU) since 1998. Her main research interests include social, economic, local, regional and women's history in the early modern and modern periods. Among her many publications are *Thomas Angell: kapitalisten som ble hjembyens velgjører* (Trondheim, 1992); *De trondhjemske handelshusene på 1700-tallet; slekt, hushold og forretning* (Trondheim, 1998; and "Handelskapitalismens tid 1650-1850," in Bull, *et al.* (eds.), *Trøndelags historie, Vol. 2* (Trondheim, 2005).

CHRIS EVANS < cevans3@glam.ac.uk > teaches history at the University of Glamorgan. He is the author, with Göran Rydén, of *Baltic Iron in the Atlantic World in the Eighteenth Century* (Leiden, 2007); and *The Industrial Revolution in Iron: The Impact of British Coal Technology in the Atlantic World in the Eighteenth Century* (Aldershot, 2007).

ATHANASIOS GEKAS < Athanasios.Gekas@EUI.eu > teaches the history of globalization and Mediterranean History at the University of Manchester. He has taught Economic History at the London School of Economics and Political Science and was a Max Weber Fellow at the European University Institute. His research interests include the economic and social history of eastern Mediterranean ports, and he has published on the business and social history of Corfu and other Greek ports during the nineteenth century.

HILDE GREEFS < hilde.greefs@ua.ac.be > works at the Centre for Urban History at the University of Antwerp. She is a specialist on the social and economic behaviour, strategies and networks of the business elite in Antwerp during the nineteenth century and is interested in nineteenth-century social and urban topics.

SARI MÄENPÄÄ < Sari.Maenpaa@nba.fi > was employed as a Research Associate in the Mercantile Liverpool Project at the School of History at the University of Liverpool until 2005. She is now working as a Curator at the Maritime Museum of Finland in Kotka.

JAN PARMENTIER < janvangent@telenet.be > is a part-time lecturer in Overseas and Maritime History at Ghent University and a researcher at the Museum aan de Stroom, a new city museum in Antwerp. His recent publications focus on Irish mercantile networks in the seventeenth and eighteenth centuries and on the maritime history of the Scheldt delta from the fifteenth to the nineteenth centuries.

GÖRAN RYDÉN < goran.ryden@ekhist.uu.se > is Professor of Economic History at the Institute of Housing and Urban Research at Uppsala University. He is the author, with Chris Evans, of two books: *Baltic Iron in the Atlantic World in the Eighteenth Century* (Leiden, 2007); and *The Industrial Revolution in Iron: The Impact of British Coal Technology in the Atlantic World in the Eighteenth Century* (Aldershot, 2007).

OLIVER SCHULZ < schulzol@yahoo.de > teaches in the Department of Contemporary History at Düsseldorf University. A specialist on Bulgarian history, his most recent publication is "Grenzziehung und Identität in einem Yielvölkerreich: Bessarabien unter russischer Herrschaft, 1812-1917/18," in Christophe Duhamelle, Andreas Kossert, and Bernhard Struck (eds.), *Grenzregionen: ein europäischer Vergleich vom 18. bis zum 20. Jahrhundert* (Frankfurt am Main, 2007), 333-360.

Trade, Migration and Urban Networks, c. 1640-1940: An Introduction[1]

Adrian Jarvis and Robert Lee

This is a book about merchants and their activities, an historiography which still has many gaps. The merchant is by definition a middleman. He neither produces nor consumes but makes his money by operating a sort of marriage bureau serving lovelorn producers and consumers. As modern shoppers, tempted to the local trading estate by promises that "we cut out the middleman," may come to realize, merchants also provide many other services. If you want a few 7/16-inch Whitworth nuts you will not find them in a do-it-yourself store, because "odd sixteenths" sizes became difficult to get long before metrification. An old-style engineer's merchant saw it as his business to find some for you. They would cost more than the metric equivalent but his expertise would find what you wanted. That is how he made his profit: effectively through a trade network which allowed him to know who had, or could get, what. But how long should he continue to supply a niche market for obsolete threaded fasteners? Stocking such items on the assumption that the market would survive was a risky business. Investing time in fulfilling a trivial order for something abstruse in the hope that the customer would value the effort and recognize it with an order for several million ten-millimetre nuts is an example of accepting an avoidable risk.

The business of the merchant has long been, and remains, one of risk. When he enters into a contract to supply goods, every stage of the process has its hazards. As the simplest example, goods obtained for onward sale may not be of the quality represented by the vendor, and until recently legal redress in such matters could be difficult or impossible to obtain in many parts of the world, including Britain. Yet Britain was able to build a world domination in mercantile activities at a time when even positive white-collar crime was but sketchily delineated,[2] and the grey areas at the edges of legality were both ex-

[1]Publication of this volume was substantially assisted by grants from National Museums Liverpool and the P.H. Holt Trust.

[2]George Robb, *White Collar Crime in Modern England: Financial Fraud and Business Morality, 1845-1929* (Cambridge, 1992), was the pioneer in the field.

tensive and even more vague.[3] That this could happen indicates that extralegal methods of limiting fraud and other risks had either evolved or been invented, and there is no reason to suppose that such limitations were peculiar to, or originated in, Britain.

Some forms of risk reduction have no place in this volume. The natural hazards of the sea, which broke Shakespeare's Antonio and countless others since, were greatly diminished over the course of the nineteenth century, largely by the application of new technology and in some cases by the application of science. Steel vessels, designed with the aid of a greatly increased understanding of both the strength of materials and the best structural form for ships' hulls, were far safer than either wooden or iron ones.[4] The great steel four-masters of ocean-going sail's last hurrah could and did safely negotiate seas so large as to have their jib-boom, which in port would be about sixty feet above water, plunging into the waves shortly before most of the deck disappeared under "green water" only to rise again to meet the next swell. Steam propulsion is usually considered only in terms of its improved transport efficiency, but engines gave the steamer captain a storm-survival method denied to sailing ships: he could keep the ship's head to the weather.[5] By 1914 he also had the means to avoid storms as weather reports became available by "wireless telegraphy."[6] After all, the best storm-survival strategy is to be somewhere else when the weather turns bad.

The origins of the lighthouse are lost in classical antiquity, and merchants trading around Britain, whether coastwise or ocean-going, had their risks reduced by the construction of dozens of these beacons.[7] Those along the

---

[3]The notion of shady commercial practice as the equivalent of crime seems to date, in Britain at least, only from Lord Lytton's highly controversial novel *Paul Clifford*, first published in 1830.

[4]This was in large part to the credit of the early members of the Institution of Naval Architects, established in 1860.

[5]This tactic could only deal with very bad, not extreme, conditions: see Alexander McKee, *The Golden Wreck* (London, 1961), which provides a detailed account of the wreck of *Royal Charter* on 26 October 1859. The vessel was driven ashore at Moelfre Bay, Anglesey, by weather so violent that its engine was insufficient to save it.

[6]"WT" was invented by Oliver Lodge, first Professor of Physics at Liverpool University, but the man who saw its potential – and packaged and marketed it – is the one usually credited with its invention. By no means were all ships fitted with WT by 1914; Marconi had such efficient means of extracting money from shipowners that many simply took the risk of doing without.

[7]Books on lighthouses tend to be hagiographies of their builders, which is perhaps not surprising considering the difficulties they overcame. Bella Bathurst, *The*

stormy and rocky coasts in the southwest and north of Scotland were probably the most important in saving lives and cargoes. In other danger spots around the British coast, harbours of refuge were constructed, which might be home to a little fishing or trading activity but were primarily there to provide a sheltered anchorage or mooring in stormy weather. There were exceptions, such as the London North and Western Railway's steamers, operating out of Holyhead, competed with Liverpool in the Irish passenger trade. All these safety initiatives were more important around Britain than in most other European countries because of the frequent high winds and large tidal variations. Those disadvantages gave a proportionately greater importance to hydrography and the production of tide tables in Britain.[8]

It will be immediately apparent that these risks are different from commercial ones. In some cases – such as those of ship technology – they might be under the complete or partial control of merchants or shipowners, whether individually or collectively. But in general, the adoption or otherwise of safer technology was reactive. A new technique might have been designed specifically to benefit them, but except in the cases of express passenger liners the initiative usually came from naval architects or builders in the expectation that a better product would command a higher price.[9] Above all, however, the difference is that shipwrecks and cargo jettison or spoilage are insurable risks, while being cheated is not.

There is some debate about the origins of marine insurance, but it seems fairly clear that the system known as "bottomry" was a recognizable forebear of modern methods and that it was in use in Phoenicia by about 1200 BC. Atle Thowsen has suggested that the origin of the modern system, where the premiums provide the funds to pay on a loss, was to be found in Venice in

---

Lighthouse Stevensons (London, 1999), is no exception, but it does have a good bibliography.

[8]Liverpool was a leader here through Dockmaster William Hutchinson. In 1764 he began recording the times and heights of tides at the entrance to the Old Dock, thus beginning the second-longest sequence of tidal data in the world. From these and other data Richard and George Holden published acceptably accurate (and improving) tide prediction tables from 1770 onwards, making a considerable contribution to the safety of shipping in the port and establishing a pattern for the rest of the world. For further information, see P.L. Woodworth, "Three Georges and One Richard Holden: The Liverpool Tide Table Makers," *Transactions of the Historic Society of Lancashire and Cheshire*, CLI (2002), 19-51.

[9]For example, the first steel cargo vessels, the specialist blockade runners of the American Civil War, adopted steel for lightness and speed and were based on existing steam yacht design, where for a time the principal design parameter was that the new yacht should be faster than anyone else's.

1255.[10] The extent to which insurance cover has been available for war risks or against piracy has varied with place and time, but it is clear that great seaborne trading states like late medieval Venice, the seventeenth-century Netherlands or nineteenth-century Britain have felt it necessary to maintain powerful navies to protect that trade, often considered as a form of insurance in which the naval costs are the premium. Some high-value, long-distance trades which operated between Europe and one or more of its colonies were considered so important that monopoly companies were established with the right to maintain private armies and navies.[11] This again might be taken as a kind of quasi-insurance.

Down to the time of effective steam fire pumps, the loss of or damage to cargo by fire, whether afloat or ashore, was an ever-present risk. It is probably the case that more harm was done by frequent minor fires which went largely unnoticed by historians than by the spectacular ones, but the single year of 1842 saw fires in both Liverpool and Hamburg which each levelled many acres of warehousing.[12] After those events, merchants in both ports were prepared to surrender some of their autonomy to the enforcement of higher standards of fire resistance in warehouse buildings. Other warehousing hazards included damp, rats and insects. Anywhere there was a warehouse there was the risk of theft, and if it was a bonded warehouse, there was the danger of smuggling as well. Smuggling was not always, as it might appear, a victimless crime, harmless to the trader, because one favourite ploy was to falsify the case markings on the paperwork so that a merchant wishing to withdraw his fifteen cases of fine cigars might discover that his boxes contained something very cheap which had about the same density. The cigars had gone out on the false paperwork.[13] It was not only distressing to the consignee, it was difficult for him even to prove that it had happened, never mind who did it. While the

---

[10]For a masterly summary of the history of marine insurance, see Atle Thowsen's article in the *Oxford Encyclopaedia of Maritime History* (New York, 2007). For more recent periods, old encyclopaedias are often a surprisingly good source, giving clear outlines of contemporary practice and written to be comprehensible to the non-specialist reader.

[11]The largest and most famous were the English and Dutch East India companies, but there were many others.

[12]Such events feature prominently in the local newspapers of most port cities, and major ones appear in effectively international organs such as *Lloyds List*.

[13]For some idea of the things found abandoned in warehouses, see Adrian Jarvis, "The Effective Size of Port Facilities," in Jarvis (ed.) *Foul Berths and French Spies* (Liverpool, 2003).

prevention of smuggling was the concern of the state, pilferage in large ports could reach levels that indicated a need for a dedicated port police.[14]

These last-mentioned hazards are peculiar to ports, and of course there were many others. Collisions and groundings within ports were frequent for the very obvious reason that large numbers of ships were in close proximity both to each other and to immovable objects like quaysides.[15] The risk of contracting freshly-imported infectious diseases was not insignificant. There were exaggerated financial hazards as well in that port cities tended to have rather narrowly-based economies, so that a financial panic might be proportionately worse than in other places, particularly when one or more local bank failures were involved.

If the merchant could reduce the first group of risks by taking out adequate insurance, it would be preferable if some could be reduced in other ways. The risk of physical damage to a vessel or its cargo could be reduced by the provision of pilotage services in ports or the appointment of a harbourmaster to maintain some element of control over ship movements.[16] That, however, merely poses the further question of who is going to appoint and pay the pilots and the harbourmaster or impose penalties on ships' masters who do not comply with instructions. The generic answer is, obviously, that a port authority will do this. While these may take a variety of forms, all have it in common that they are constituted by or for those whose interests will be served by applying resources to the reduction of damage to ships and their cargoes – in short, to the fostering of trade. This may imply the municipality, a single large-scale landowner, and later perhaps a railway company or an elected body of commissioners, but the principle remained the same. It was worth spending money on port dues and surrendering a certain amount of freedom of action to

---

[14]The words of Arthur Hugh Clough, "Thou shalt not steal, a pointless feat, when it's much easier to cheat," were of wide application. As the son of a Liverpool cotton merchant, Clough may have had insider knowledge. Not much has been published on port police, but Rachel M. Mulhearn, "Police and Pilferers at the Port of Liverpool, 1800-1850," *International Journal of Maritime History*, XI, No. 1 (1999), 149-161, provides a useful start.

[15]Adrian Jarvis, "Safe Home in Port? Shipping Safety within the Port of Liverpool," *The Northern Mariner/Le Marin du Nord*, VIII, No. 4 (1998), 17-33.

[16]In ports which depended mainly or wholly on impounded docks it was essential to appoint a harbourmaster to determine the times at which the gates were opened or closed before opening for business at all. The urgency or otherwise of the need for pilotage depended on the quality of the approach channels and the size of the vessels using them, and therefore varied very widely with time and place.

reduce trading risks for everyone. The same applied, albeit less directly, if these elementary port facilities were provided by the state.[17]

So it was as well with the framing and enforcement of further fire precautions, whether aimed at the cabin stoves and oil lighting of vessels tied up in port or at practices which might cause fires starting on quaysides and spreading to vessels or warehouses. Prior to the container age, most quays were cluttered with dunnage timber and mats, odd ends of rope and the like for stowing a cargo tightly; these things also burned quite well. Such fires as those in Liverpool and Hamburg caused enormous destruction, and the provision of the rudiments of what we now call a fire brigade, in some cases specifically for the port area only, follows the rule above.[18] Nor was all change necessarily for the better: a steel steamship might be less of a fire risk than a wooden sailing vessel, but some of the new trades in which it engaged, notably the carriage of petroleum, introduced new hazards.

The question of port health was much thornier, particularly before the nature of infectious diseases was properly understood. But by about 1850 it was fairly widely recognized that the cleaner and tidier a port city was – and the better supplied with fresh water and drained – the less likely the spread of waterborne diseases. The "miasmic theory of disease" might have been scientific nonsense, but the actions it suggested were often the right ones. As with improvements in port safety, at least part of the solution was simple: all it needed was a constitutional and financial organization to implement it. Merchant enthusiasm for universal quarantine regulations (commonplace since their adoption in fifteenth-century Venice and remaining so until the late nineteenth century) was, however, distinctly limited because they had awful effects on cash flow, cost extra money in port dues for their enforcement, extra expense in feeding crews during quarantine and, as the nineteenth-century cholera pandemics proved, they did not work. All the second group of risks, however, could be controlled more-or-less effectively either by state or local government intervention or by merchants acting collectively in the shape of a port authority. Obviously, the degree of merchant control of that authority would vary between nearly complete in the case of a body of elected port commissioners and limited only to (possibly quite high-powered) lobbying in the case of a state facility.

---

[17]For an attempt at evaluating different forms of port management, see Adrian Jarvis, "Managing Change: The Organisation of Port Authorities at the Turn of the Twentieth Century," *The Northern Mariner/Le Marin du Nord*, VI, No. 2 (1996), 31-42.

[18]Liverpool was not alone in having a separate municipal water system specifically for supplying fire mains, hydraulic power to the docks and fresh water to ships. The horror stories of minimal one hour per day supply to the hovels of the underclass were true – but only with regard to the underclass.

The situation regarding fraud was completely different. In the first place, it was extremely diverse. A merchant could be defrauded by misstatement as to the quantity, quality, origin, condition or location of goods which he either owned or was being offered for sale. An extreme case, related by Morier Evans in 1854, involved a consignment of copper lying on a London quay. It had been sold and resold several times, and all its documentation from manufacture to the time in question was in order; the only problem was that no actual copper belonging to this paperwork could be found.[19] At a less dramatic, more prosaic level, an unfortunate failure to clear a consignment of cotton from the quayside on a wet day could increase its weight considerably: just how "unfortunate" the rain was depended upon whether you were buying or selling. It was possible to insure cotton against fire or theft but not against a mysterious decrease in weight (as it dried out) after it had been delivered and paid for.

Merchants have from time to time been portrayed as essentially unskilled men whose low cunning could enable them to gain rather than earn large sums of money. Cobbett and Carlyle, despite their obvious differences on some subjects, both wrote a great deal on the sanctity of work, and it is clear that they did not regard commerce as coming within the meaning of the word "work" at all. Work meant (chiefly) primary production, with some rather reluctant recognition of manufacturing, which might be evil work, but it was work of a kind, as distinct from stock-jobbing and other "squalid" occupations which were not.[20] In the evidence presented to Parliament in the three bills for the Manchester Ship Canal, there are endless complaints about the profits made by Liverpool merchants, as if they were unnecessary parasites.[21] In fact, as Sari Mäenpää's contribution to this volume shows, they needed long training to develop their considerable skills and a vast amount of knowledge of (for example) conditions in the areas of origin of the goods in

[19]D. Morier Evans, *Facts, Failures and Frauds* (London, 1859; reprint, New York, 1968), chapter 5. The old ones are the best; a cargo surveyor of my acquaintance recently uncovered a similar fraud involving purely imaginary cocoa beans supposedly warehoused in Hamburg to the value of several million pounds. Their paperwork was impeccable as well.

[20]It is, of course, legitimate to question whether the production of their various trades constituted noble and honest work. Cobbett certainly knew one end of a shovel from the other, but it is doubtful that Carlyle did.

[21]The merchants are robustly defended by Neil McKendrick, "Literary Luddism and the Businessman," in the introduction to Peter N. Davies, *Sir Alfred Jones: Shipping Entrepreneur Par Excellence* (London, 1978).

which they were trading. Buying or selling at the wrong time could bring speedy ruin, as could trusting the wrong people.[22]

The papers in this volume extend from Norway to Greece and over four centuries, but one common mercantile method of risk reduction is noticeable in all of them. It may be summarized as doing business, or attempting to do business, only with people who "wouldn't do that sort of thing." That is quite simple and obvious; the difficult part was identifying those who could be trusted. Some of the methods employed were equally simple and obvious and, to judge from the present collection, at least widespread and possibly universal. You could trust your close relatives not to defraud you and not to withhold commercial information that might cause you to blunder into ill-advised transactions. You could also trust members of the extended family, at least in cases where the family extension had been achieved by carefully negotiated, commercially advantageous marriages, as it fairly commonly was.[23]

You could normally trust people with whom you shared a religious affiliation. Insofar as this differed from family connections, it may have been a more reliable yardstick of trust because many religious beliefs incorporate that which is often absent from legal codes, namely specific assumptions about business ethics, with ostracism (or possibly hellfire) as the penalty for transgression.[24] Perhaps less reliable was the assumption that you could trust your fellow nationals in an expatriate merchant community, but it was certainly believed, acted upon and backed up by church communities for the settlers. Liverpool, for example, had churches for Greeks, Germans, Scandinavians, Welsh, Scots and several more. Some of these communities concentrated in particular trades as well as districts: the Welsh, for example, were noted for beginning in the building trades and, as they built up some capital, moving into (sometimes very extensive) property ownership, chiefly in the smaller types of domestic properties but also in occasional conspicuous cases into large warehousing businesses.[25] This large-scale building activity required bricks, slates,

---

[22]The arch example is again a fictitious one, namely Thackeray's "Old Colonel" in *The Newcomes*.

[23]Two sons and one daughter of Thomas Earle (1754-1822), a prominent Liverpool merchant, married into the Langton family. Graeme J. Milne has explored issues of trust in two works: *Trade and Traders in Mid-Victorian Liverpool* (Liverpool, 2000); and "Knowledge, Communications and the Information Order in Nineteenth-Century Liverpool," *International Journal of Maritime History*, XIV, No. 1 (2002), 209-224.

[24]Quakers and Unitarians were generally considered good risks.

[25]The Welsh were a standing joke for their serial schisms: at the turn of the twentieth century there were nineteen or twenty Welsh chapels in Liverpool. John R. Jones, *The Welsh Builder on Merseyside: Annals and Lives* (Liverpool, 1946), profiles

tiles, stones and mortar, much of which came from North Wales through the agency of Welsh merchants, shipowners or brokers.

The thing that emerges in all of this book's essays, which are in some ways quite diverse, is that these and other connections mattered and that the networks which resulted achieved a definite reduction in the risks inherent in any mercantile transaction. There was, however, a much wider application for them than judging somebody's honesty: the tricky matter of estimating "soundness." Some business failures were caused not by dishonesty or mere sharp practice on one side of a bargain but by rashness or stupidity on the other. Here, family, religious or national connections might not necessarily help and could indeed dull the judgement by encouraging the optimistic view that one's brother could never possibly have got himself into difficulties in the Overend Gurney collapse. This dulling of judgement is the root cause which brings us back to Thackeray's "Old Colonel."[26]

The reader might detect the existence of a potential moral dilemma here: success in a venture might well require a high level of secrecy which could conflict with a duty towards one's family or partners. This question was raised as long ago as 1771 in the entry for "Moral Philosophy" in the first edition of the *Encyclopaedia Britannica* where the contributor stated that it is not necessary in business to tell the *whole* truth but that what *is* said must be absolutely true.

There *were* ways of judging soundness, but they were largely subjective and anecdotal. They involved knowing a good deal of the track record of individuals or partnerships, and the principal method of dissemination was through personal contact – in other words, by networking. The credibility of the informant was a crucial ingredient, meaning that the relationship of trust extended to every person whose advice was sought. This in many ways was only slightly removed from gossip in which believing the wrong informant could result in speedy ruin. The disseminator of false gossip (whether maliciously or through misinformation) was capable of such harm that he might almost be added to the list of mercantile hazards above and his detection considered another function of networking.

It is clear that the system did not always work. Despite almost constant improvements in methods of communicating business intelligence, people continued to make erroneous decisions about buying and selling anything from Latin American gold to Greek currants only to discover when it was too late that the gold was non-existent and the bottom had dropped out of the currant market. If nobody had more need of his "character book" than a bank man-

---

a considerable number of these Welsh people. David Hughes (1820-1904) may stand as an example of those who both succeeded and diversified.

[26]It also suggests real-life examples like the Lafone Brothers, given in Milne, "Knowledge."

ager, how effective were the character books of those banks which failed in 1847-1848 through allowing large loans to what proved to be unsound people?[27] These crises of confidence happened approximately once a decade, and experience of the last one seemed to bring little in the way of recognition of symptoms as the next approached.

Neither "networking" nor anything else could ever be a complete solution to business risks; if it could, the merchants would have worked themselves out of a job.[28] It was their efforts at risk reduction for which their customers paid. While the following essays recognize business knowledge, contacts and reputation as major parts of the capital assets of a merchant or partnership, they also show us that the old school of business history in which the biographical treatment of great and successful men was prominent, while an incomplete approach was not necessarily entirely inadequate.[29] Certainly, it was not wrong to the point that any newcomer could walk out on "change" armed only with a few good contacts and a character book and make a fortune. There was a lot more to it than that. But much of what we know about the quiet skills of the networker has only emerged in the last fifteen years.[30] It has

---

[27]The Royal Bank of Liverpool had a paid-up capital of £600,000 and saw fit to advance £500,000 to the firm of Barton, Irlam and Higginson, East and West India Merchants. When they went down in October 1847, so did the Royal Bank. D. Morier Evans, *The Commercial Crisis, 1847-1848: Being Facts and Figures Illustrative of the Events of That Important Period Considered in Relation to the Three Epochs of the Railway Mania, the Food and Money Panic and the French Revolution* (London, 1849; reprint, New York, 1969), 94. Milne, "Knowledge," provides the example of the North and South Wales Bank advising a customer that a shipping firm was sound: it went down in the 1855 panic, taking the customer with it. The bank in question had itself to cease payment in 1847 for similar reasons to the Royal Bank of Liverpool.

[28]It may be argued that this has now happened in some fields, with retail customers willing to purchase quite costly items "sight unseen" on the internet.

[29]On the contrary, such works as Sheila Marriner and Francis E. Hyde, *The Senior, John Samuel Swire 1825-98: Management in Far Eastern Shipping Trades* (Liverpool, 1967); and Peter N. Davies, *Henry Tyrer: A Liverpool Shipping Agent and His Enterprise 1879-1979* (London, 1979) suggested new lines for further enquiry.

[30]One of the works which made people think more about networks and information transfer was Gordon H. Boyce, *Information, Mediation and Institutional Development: The Rise of Large-Scale Enterprise in British Shipping, 1870-1919* (Manchester, 1995). The bibliography is only marginally longer than the list of unpublished sources and contemporary published material. In his paper "Transferring Capabilities across Sectoral Frontiers: Shipowners Entering the Airline Business, 1920-1970," *International Journal of Maritime History*, XIII, No. 1 (2001), 1-38, Boyce pointed out that these mostly unhappy matches occurred because both parties sought to exploit the network of overseas contacts built up by the shipping/commercial side of the venture.

obviously impressed many people as an important and neglected area, for a recent "forum" of seven papers on the theme of "Information and Maritime History," amounting to nearly 100 pages, revealed a fast-growing corpus of secondary literature.[31]

The usefulness of network analysis for analyzing the role of entrepreneurs and the configuration of commercial transactions has been widely recognized by economic and business historians; it has also been widely used in evaluating overseas migration patterns.[32] Although the role of networks has been discussed extensively in economic and business theory, it is only in recent years that historical research on the contribution of networks to trade development from the early modern period to the twentieth century has contributed to a reassessment of commercial practices. It is increasingly acknowledged that the expansion of world trade was facilitated by the incorporation of distant places and regions within existing commercial networks, but there are still too few case studies to enable historians to assess the overall significance of networks in promoting commercial links and increasing international trade. At a local level, few attempts have been made to analyze the linkages between merchants, brokers, agents and other members of the business community, particularly in terms of its cultural, familial, political, religious and social construction.[33]

Networks have always operated within a specific social, economic and historical context, often with a well-defined, but malleable, spatial and hierarchical structure.[34] The contributors to this volume address a number of key issues relating to the development, operational framework and commercial significance of trading networks from the early seventeenth century to the early twentieth. They focus on a total of thirteen port cities (Amsterdam, Antwerp, Bristol, Calabar, Charleston, Corfu, Liverpool, Ostend, Piraeus, Stockholm, Syros, Odessa and Trondheim) to highlight the significance of port-city con-

---

[31]*International Journal of Maritime History*, XIV, No. 1 (2002), 153-246. See also Margrit Schulte Beerbuhl and Jörg Vögele (eds.), *Spinning the Commercial Web: International Trade, Merchants and Commercial Cities, c. 1640-1939* (Frankfurt, 2004).

[32]Mary B. Rose, *Firms, Networks and Business Values: The British and American Cotton Industries since 1750* (Cambridge 2000); and Gillian Cookson, "Family, Firms and Business Networks: Textile Engineering in Yorkshire, 1780-1830," *Business History*, XXXIX, No. 1 (1997), 1-20.

[33]Robin Pearson and David Richardson, "Business Networking in the Industrial Revolution," *Economic History Review*, LIV, No. 4 (2001), 659.

[34]For a further discussion of the spatial structure of networks, see Peter Haggett and Richard J. Chorley, *Network Analysis in Geography* (London, 1969).

nections and the importance of family ties and networks in facilitating trade and commerce. A number of common themes emerge from these studies.

First, ports can often be regarded as "network cities." As Ida Bull demonstrates in the case of Trondheim in the seventeenth and eighteenth centuries, they functioned not only as nodal points for inland regional networks but also as vital links to trading centres overseas. The transhipment of raw materials and manufactured goods was Ostend's key function, according to Jan Parmentier, which in turn required the development of a range of inter-connected trading networks. Urban merchants, whether in Calabar, Charleston or Stockholm, had strong links with hinterland production, in the latter case ultimately controlling important sections of the Swedish iron industry, as Chris Evans and Göran Rydén reveal. At the same time, the production and marketing of Swedish bar iron involved an international web of commercial exchanges which bound together merchant communities in a number of disparate ports, whether in Europe, Africa or North America.

Second, the development of trading networks was often dependent upon the in-migration and settlement of overseas merchants, as well as their successful integration into existing port-city communities. During the second half of the seventeenth century, the multiplicity of trading networks which underpinned Amsterdam's international position depended to a large degree on the existence of shared business values and strategies between in-migrant and native-born merchants, as Cátia Antunes indicates; the Portuguese Jews became partly assimilated for the purposes of domestic trade within the Dutch Republic but retained a distinct Jewish identity for fostering commercial ventures further afield. Sari Mäenpää's study of cotton merchants in late nineteenth-century Liverpool also reveals that over twenty percent had been born overseas; their international links, particularly with Germany and Switzerland, contributed to the port city's pre-eminence as a leading centre of the international cotton trade.

Third, a critical factor in determining the viability of extended trading networks was the extent to which in-migrant merchants were successfully assimilated within the social hierarchy of individual ports, irrespective of underlying religious, ethnic or cultural differences. In both Piraeus and Syros, as Sakis Gekas reveals, the in-migration of settlers from other Greek islands was extremely important for economic growth during the period 1835-1870, particularly in terms of human capital, while forty percent of the Jewish inhabitants of Corfu in 1864 were merchants, highlighting the religious diversity of the mercantile group as a whole. The marriage strategies pursued by in-migrant merchants or by representatives of the established business community often determined the configuration of new networks, whether in seventeenth-century Trondheim (Bull) or eighteenth-century Ostend (Parmentier), while upward social mobility for in-migrant merchants in Amsterdam (Antunes) generally necessitated a "stepping out" from traditional religious or social networks. In all these cases, the evidence confirms the extent to which marriage between in-migrant merchants and native-born women was an important means of constructing social capital and cementing family links which in turn helped to reinforce the viability of business networks. The case of Odessa (Oliver Schulz) is more extreme in that it not only became Greek-dominated but also came to play a part in defining "Greekness." This is a lofty claim but one which the essay seems amply to justify.

Fourth, the presence of in-migrant merchants was often associated with a greater level of trade specialization and diversification, whether in eighteenth-century Ostend or nineteenth-century Corfu. As Jan Parmentier indicates, many in-migrants relied on an extended network of trustworthy family ties which provided a more secure basis for specialized trading activities. In Corfu, as in other Greek ports, the gradual assimilation of overseas merchants directly fostered commercial specialization, as Gekas demonstrates, with a clear distinction between the *negozianti* and *mercanti*. Indeed, according to Hilde Greefs, there was increasing evidence in nineteenth-century Antwerp of the emergence of separate spheres of activity between in-migrant merchants and native-born members of the local business community. Whereas the former gradually assumed control of different branches of overseas trade, the latter tended to concentrate on local sectors of production, perhaps as a function of easier access to local banking circles.

Fifth, a number of contributions highlight the extent to which the structure of urban governance helped to structure the operative framework of merchant activity and the function of business networks. In Corfu, for example, the establishment of commercial institutions, including the Exchange and Chamber of Commerce, was directly linked to changes in the form of urban governance, particularly during the period of British rule between 1815 and 1864, which affected in turn the agency role of merchants and the formulation of collective business strategies (Gekas). In Liverpool the proliferation of trade associations in the second half of the nineteenth century played a similar role, although the role of the Cotton Exchange in articulating collective strategies among prominent cotton brokers was reinforced by extensive social networking in a range of local clubs and societies, as Mäenpää's contribution demonstrates. Indeed, the overall conduct of trade and business, whether in Calabar, Charleston or Stockholm, was invariably influenced by the existing institutional framework (Evans and Rydén), while changes in the form and structure of state control, as in the cases of Ostend (Parmentier) and Corfu (Gekas), had wider implications for the development and maintenance of trading networks.

Finally, several of the essays, especially the one by Schulz, demonstrate the need for more extensive research on the demographic development of individual port cities, in particular on the changing structure and scale of in-migration and its significance for the growth of distinct ethnic communities with both individual and collective links with external markets. A key feature of the demographic development of port cities from the early modern period onwards was a disproportionate dependence on in-migration. Because of their regional, national and international seaborne transport connections, port cities attracted human capital and natural resources from relatively distant locations, with a significant proportion of overseas, or non-national, in-migrants. As a result, port cities were often characterized by a broader ethnic mix than other types of urban centres. Genoa housed migrants from all over the Mediterranean, and Trieste accommodated different Armenian, Greek, Jewish and Serbian "nations."[35] Many of the leading merchants and shipowners in individual ports were in-migrants, and the existence of discrete ethnic communities provided important opportunities for the development of trading activities. Yet, as the article on Patras demonstrates, reconstructing the pattern of in-migration is often complex and problematic, primarily because of deficiencies in the archival record, but it is only on the basis of further research in this area that the interconnectedness between trade, migration and the role of urban networks will ultimately be revealed. Schultz illustrates a rather different state of affairs in Odessa where not just in-migrant enclaves but whole local societies could be formed through a trading diaspora. Some of the same people turn up not much later trading in Britain.

The essays which follow exhibit the variety of content and approach that might be expected in business practices which range over the whole of Europe and beyond over a period of several centuries. There are successes and failures, heroes and villains, and in that respect our networkers in the port cities were merely reflecting the population at large. But that diversity is only superficial: what characterized all the different merchants and mercantile communities treated here was actually a surprising degree of unanimity in approach to some of the key issues of risk reduction in trade. Some problems required collective action, while others necessitated an individual approach; most of the latter are themselves merely different manifestations of the most important single question that faced the merchant: "Whom can I trust?" This volume seeks out some of the answers merchants found to both individual and collective problems and shows that there are stronger and more definite common strands extending through both time and space than has been generally recognized.

---

[35]Giuseppi Felloni, "The Population Dynamics and Economic Development of Genoa, 1750-1939," in Richard Lawton and Robert Lee (eds.), *Population and Society in Western European Port Cities, c. 1650-1939* (Liverpool, 2002), 74-90; and Marina Cattaruzza, "Population Dynamics and Economic Change in Trieste and Its Hinterland, 1850-1914," in *ibid.*, 176-211.

Portuguese Jews in Amsterdam:
An Insight on Entrepreneurial Behaviour in the Dutch Republic

Cátia Antunes

In the last ten or fifteen years an increasing number of studies have appeared on entrepreneurs and entrepreneurship in the early modern period. Dutch economic and social history has followed this trend, and a good range of micro- and macro-level research has been published in both Dutch and in English.[1] Indeed, the Dutch contribution to the analysis of businessmen and the business environment in the United Provinces during the Republic has been quite broad. Scholars have dedicated most of their efforts to investigating business activities, investment preferences, production priorities and the socio-economic networks of entrepreneurs between the end of the sixteenth and the beginning of the nineteenth century. Dutch historiography has shown a clear preference for research on the traditional Dutch entrepreneur, men involved in the establishment, development and growth of the Dutch economy during the early modern era. Research in general has favoured native Dutch businessmen, immigrant groups (such as merchants and artisans from the Southern Netherlands or the French Huguenots) and Dutch entrepreneurship abroad.

Thus far, Dutch and international studies on early modern entrepreneurship in the Republic have failed to integrate fully one very important immigrant group – the Sephardic Jews of Portuguese origin.[2] Existing studies of

---

[1] Peter W. Klein and Jan W. Veluwenkamp, "The Role of the Entrepreneur in the Economic Expansion of the Dutch Republic," in Karel Davids and Leo Noordegraaf (eds.), *The Dutch Republic in the Golden Age* (Amsterdam, 1993), 27-54; Paul Klep and Eddy van Cauwenberghe (eds.), *Entrepreneurship and the Transformation of the Economy (10th-20th Centuries): Essays in Honour of Herman van der Wee* (Leuven, 1994); Clé Lesger and Leo Noordegraaf (eds.), *Entrepreneurs and Entrepreneurship in Early Modern Times: Merchants and Industrialists in the Orbit of the Dutch Staple Market* (The Hague, 1995); and Karel A. Davids, Joanna M.F. Fritschy and Loes A. van der Walk (eds.), *Kapitaal, ondernemerschap en beleid: Studies over economie en politiek in Nederland, Europa en Azië van 1500 tot heden* (Amsterdam, 1996).

[2] Some of the few exceptions to this rule are Jonathan I. Israel, "The Economic Contribution of Dutch Sephardi Jewry to Holland's Golden Age, 1595-1713," *Tijdschrift voor Geschiedenis*, XCVI (1983), 505-535; and Odette Vlessing, "The Por-

this particular group have focused either on its religious nature or its particularities. No effort has been made to establish the extent to which the Portuguese Jewish entrepreneur in the United Provinces actually shared business values and strategies with his Dutch counterparts.

The Portuguese Jewish community of Amsterdam was the result of a long-standing migration initiated when Spain expelled the Jews in 1492. Most of the Jewish families who fled the Spanish kingdoms crossed the border into Portugal to begin new lives. Others left for various cities in the Mediterranean and North Africa.[3] Many of the Portuguese and Spanish Jews actually remained in Portugal, although they had been forcefully converted to Christianity by the end of the century on the initiative of the king of Portugal and were henceforth named "New Christians." It was only with the coming of the Portuguese Inquisition during the sixteenth century that many were forced to leave the kingdom and settle elsewhere in Europe.

The diaspora of Iberian Jewry led them to different destinations, both within and beyond Europe. The new possessions of the Iberian kingdoms in the Atlantic islands, the west coast of Africa, central and southern America and Asia presented the perfect opportunity for a new start, far removed physically from the centres of religious and political decision making but still in a known cultural environment. These destinations enabled most of the migrants to recreate their personal stories and to engage in new lives away from the limits imposed by issues relating to the "purity of blood."

If some of the New Christians left for the empire, others joined the already prosperous communities in the Mediterranean or the new settlements in northern European cities. During the late sixteenth century, communities grew in Rouen, Antwerp and Hamburg, where the New Christians participated in the re-export of colonial products originally sent from America or Asia to Seville or Lisbon.[4] Many of the Portuguese communities in northern Europe ended up serving formally or informally as agents of the kingdom of Portugal

---

tuguese-Jewish Mercantile Community in Seventeenth-Century Amsterdam," in Lesger and Noordegraaf (eds.), *Entrepreneurs and Entrepreneurship*. These particular articles, however, do not pertain specifically to the role of the "Portuguese nation" of Amsterdam as entrepreneurs but rather provide a general assessment of the economic position of the group as a whole.

[3]Haim Beinart, "La Diaspora Sefardi en Europa y especialmente en la cuencia del Mediterraneo," *Judios y Cristianos en la Cuenca Mediterránea: Hispania Sacra*, XL (1988), 911-931; Avigdor Levy, *The Sephardim in the Ottoman Empire* (Princeton, 1992); and Jonathan I. Israel, *Diasporas within the Diaspora: Jews, Crypto-Jews, and the World Maritime Empires (1540-1740)* (Leiden, 2002), 67-96, 151-184 and 291-311.

[4]Hans Pohl, *Die Portugiesen in Antwerpen, 1567-1648: zur Geschichte einer Minderheit* (Wiesbaden, 1977).

and its empire, as did the Nunes da Costa family.[5] Many of the New Christians who settled in northern Europe belonged to the commercial and maritime elite in that they shared some familiarity with travelling and adapting to strange social and business environments. This ability to blend into foreign societies and entrepreneurial surroundings required expertise and communication skills which were important for the social and economic survival of the group.

When Antwerp fell in 1585 after a long siege which threatened to ruin most of its commercial elite, Protestants and Portuguese Jewish merchants fled the city and took refuge among Protestant and Jewish communities throughout northern Europe. The majority of these wealthy refugees ended up in London, Hamburg and the towns of the Northern Netherlands. The economic growth of the Northern Netherlands, and particularly of its maritime towns and cities, attracted many of Antwerp's refugees who ultimately decided to settle in Amsterdam after short stays at other commercial centres. Dutch historians are divided on the extent to which these Antwerp refugees contributed to the growth of the Dutch economy as a whole and to the city of Amsterdam in particular. Clé Lesger has argued that their presence in Amsterdam endowed the city with capital, commercial expertise and broad world networks which were decisive factors in the city's rise to become the largest commercial and financial centre in the seventeenth century.[6] By contrast, Oscar Gelderblom has claimed that the sample of Antwerp merchants he studied seemed to have had little capital when they arrived in Amsterdam. He argued further that most of their capital was earned in Amsterdam and that the reason for the flow of in-migrants was that the city was already developing rapidly, a fact which made it attractive to ambitious men.[7]

I agree with Gelderblom's assessment of Amsterdam's situation when the Antwerp refugees arrived. Indeed, Amsterdam was already growing economically, mostly due to its participation in the Baltic trade, leaving many of the other traditional Dutch ports behind.[8] But Lesger's argument that the refugees' contribution was essential for Amsterdam's "Golden Age" and the gen-

---

[5]Israel, *Diasporas within a Diaspora*, 313-354; and Cátia Antunes, *Globalization in the Early Modern Period: The Economic Relationship between Amsterdam and Lisbon, 1640-1705* (Amsterdam, 2004), 130-162.

[6]Clé Lesger, *Handel in Amsterdam ten tijde van de Opstand: kooplieden, commerciële expansie en verandering in de ruimtelijke economie van de Nederlanden ca. 1550-ca. 1630* (Hilversum, 2001).

[7]Oscar Gelderblom, *Zuid-Nederlandse kooplieden en de opkomst van de Amsterdamse stapelmarkt (1578-1630)* (Hilversum, 2000).

[8]Milja van Tielhof, *De Hollandse graanhandel, 1470-1570: Koren op de Amsterdamse molen* (Leiden, 1995).

eral expansion of the Dutch Republic as a major commercial and naval power cannot be dismissed. In fact, I agree with Lesger's argument that the power of the networks brought by Protestant and Jewish merchants globally provided Amsterdam with contacts, capital and knowledge of an expanding world. Similar arguments have been expounded by Jonathan Israel and Maurits Ebben in their works on the Portuguese Jewish and New Christian networks operating in the Dutch and Habsburg empires.[9]

The Portuguese Jewish community of Amsterdam, although composed of some of the immigrant families from the last quarter of the sixteenth century who had escaped the fall of Antwerp, also grew as a result of a new wave of immigration which originated in Iberia after the Union of the Crowns in 1580.[10] The rise of Amsterdam, together with the effects of the Inquisition throughout Iberia, generated a new exodus. Portuguese Jews also fled from Brazil, where the Inquisition had become quite active by the end of the sixteenth century.[11]

Given the rapid increase in the number of Portuguese Jews in Amsterdam during the first half of the seventeenth century, the goal of this essay is to examine their economic activities and to establish the extent to which their business practices and strategies differed from the general early modern entrepreneurial tradition. To achieve this objective, the study will focus on the economic relationship established between Amsterdam and Lisbon from 1640 to 1705. The analysis will be based on existing Dutch and international literature on early modern entrepreneurship and on materials in the notarial archives of Amsterdam.

Early Modern Entrepreneurs

It is difficult to provide a precise definition of an entrepreneur in the early modern period. One simple way of doing so is to say that an entrepreneur in

---

[9]Maurits A. Ebben, *Zilver, brood en kogels voor de koning: Kredietverlening door Portugese bankiers aan de Spaanse kroon, 1621-1665* (Leiden, 1996); and Jonathan I. Israel, *European Jewry in the Age of Mercantilism, 1550-1750* (London, 1998).

[10]In 1580, Philip II took the Portuguese Crown and with it the Portuguese kingdom and empire. The throne was left heirless after the death of King Sebastião, and Philip II was the best candidate because his mother was the sister of the late King Manuel. Portugal remained an independent kingdom. Philip II chose to call the annexation of the neighbouring kingdom a simple "union."

[11]*Primeira visitação do Santo Ofício às partes do Brasil pelo Licenciado Heitor Furtado de Mendonça: Denunciações da Bahia 1591-1593* (São Paulo, 1925); and *Primeira visitação do Santo Ofício às partes do Brasil: Denunciações e confissões de Pernambuco, 1593-1595* (Recife, 1984).

this period was a businessman who earned his living by investing in a range of economic activities, including manufacturing, trade and banking. Contrary to the contemporary definition of an entrepreneur, an early modern businessman was a merchant, a pre-industrialist or, in some cases, both. His business was mainly organized around his family and contacts at a time when social relationships were as important for a successful businessman as capital, information, expertise or luck. In an early modern context, relations revolved around an extended family, which included several generations, as well as the relationships that different members of the family had established with people outside the nuclear group. The ties both within and without the nuclear family were sealed by social ceremonies. Marriages and religious rites were excellent opportunities to unite different members of the same family or to tie the nuclear group to an outside family. Social and economic capital were clearly two sides of the same coin.[12]

These general characteristics of early modern entrepreneurs become more evident when we look at specific religious minorities. Entrepreneurs who belonged to religious minorities had their status defined both by belonging to a family and to a specific religious group. In such cases, kinship and religion bound people together within a common framework of shared values about everyday life and business practices.[13] Such a combination of kinship and religion had both positive and negative effects. On the positive side, individual members could access significant socio-economic capital both from the extended family and from the wider religious group. The role of the individual in the family could also be sanctioned by the group as a whole, which meant that the individual's character as an entrepreneur could be endorsed not only by blood relatives but also by those who belonged to the same congregation. On the negative side, a primary reliance on religious morals and an excessive dependence on a small group of allies imposed potential limitations on business. If a person became a social outcast due to a rejection of socio-religious norms or financial default (bankruptcy), the entire economic standing of the family

---

[12]For a broad definition of early modern entrepreneurs and entrepreneurship, see Luuc Kooijmans, "Risk and Reputation: On the Mentality of Merchants in the Early Modern Period," in Lesger and Noordegraaf (eds.), *Entrepreneurs and Entrepreneurship*, 25-34; and Peter Mathias, "Strategies for Reducing Risk by Entrepreneurs in the Early Modern Period," in *ibid.*, 5-23. Other historians refuse to try to conceptualize the idea of the early modern entrepreneur; for this group, such an entrepreneur does not exist. See Clé Lesger and Leo Noordegraaf, "Inleiding," in Lesger and Noordegraaf (eds.), *Ondernemers en bestuurders: Economie en politiek in de Noordelijke Nederlanden in de late middeleeuwen en vroegmoderne tijd* (Amsterdam, 1999), 17.

[13]Mathias, "Strategies," 15.

could be endangered.[14] Although some of the religious and economic outcasts managed to remain afloat and become successful businessmen, most fell prey to social pressure and suffered public bankruptcy. Cases of bankruptcy were common during the early modern period, but economic failure among individuals from religious minorities had a wider impact in the community and often provided ammunition for social stereotyping and labelling.[15]

The questions now are to what extent did entrepreneurs of a specific denomination use their religious status to further their business, and to what extent did kinship and religion threaten the individual choices of entrepreneurs? To answer these questions I have chosen to analyze the Portuguese Jewish community in Amsterdam during the seventeenth century. Since it is impossible to assess the situation of this community as a whole, I have decided to use as an example of kinship/religious entrepreneurship the Portuguese Jews living in Amsterdam during the seventeenth century who were involved in economic intercourse between Amsterdam and Lisbon.

The Portuguese Jews of Amsterdam, 1640-1705

By the end of the sixteenth century, some of the Jewish families who had left Iberia for northern Europe had moved to Amsterdam, which after the fall of Antwerp was in the process of becoming the most important port in Europe. The arrival of foreign merchants was not a new phenomenon for Amsterdam; others had previously been attracted by the city's advantages. Amsterdam benefited from an extensive hinterland which provided not only labour but also an important market. Moreover, the authorities permitted a great degree of religious tolerance, and the staple market was both established and known to be conducive to furthering business careers.[16]

Tjalling van der Kooij has argued that there were three types of entrepreneurs connected with the Dutch staple market. It was a specialized business

---

[14]For further information about the relationship between entrepreneurs, entrepreneurship and religion, see Mary Sprunger, "Entrepreneurs and Ethics: Mennonite Merchants in Seventeenth-Century Amsterdam," in Lesger and Noordegraaf (eds.), *Entrepreneurs and Entrepreneurship*, 213-221. For an example of the dramatic consequences for a family at odds with the religious group, see Lydia Hagoort, "The Del Sottos, a Portuguese Jewish Family in Amsterdam in the Seventeenth Century," *Studia Rosenthaliana*, XXXI, No. 1 (1997), 31-57.

[15]For example, in the Christian tradition Jewish communities and families were seen as repositories of large capital resources available to loan. Their lending practices left some Jewish businessmen open to criticism from the host society. Since the Middle Ages, this criticism sometimes became the basis for anti-Semitic discourse.

[16]Gelderblom, *Zuid-Nederlandse kooplieden*; and Lesger, *Handel in Amsterdam*.

activity in which entrepreneurs connected with the import, storage and export of products were clearly separate groups.[17] But the extent of entrepreneurial specialization has been questioned by several historians. Peter Klein, often considered the father of Dutch business history, recognized a certain degree of specialization in the function of the staple market but suggested that this was far less developed than van der Kooij had asserted. According to Klein, there were other specialized activities besides import, export and storage.[18]

Klein was less dogmatic in his overall assessment of the degree of entrepreneurial specialization than was van der Kooij, and he effectively demystified the importance of business activities during the "Golden Age" by demonstrating that the economic sectors in which Dutch entrepreneurs operated were limited, particularly in the case of trade, fishing and shipbuilding. By contrast, the truly revolutionary nature of Dutch entrepreneurial behaviour originated in the development of financial and banking activities.[19] Moreover, the idea of specialization has lost support in the last twenty years; Jan-Willem Veluwenkamp, in particular, has disputed the existence of any significant degree of specialization. By and large, entrepreneurs tended to invest in one or two activities, but that did not stop them from using their skills to invest in other opportunities, even if these did not fit their specialized profiles. According to Veluwenkamp, such an approach was the only way to foster monopolies and to achieve market control, often using the hidden hand of the state.[20] But was this also the case with the Portuguese Jews in Amsterdam?

The Portuguese Jews in Amsterdam maintained contact with various Jewish communities in Europe and overseas, as well as with their places of origin in Iberia, where their contacts with the New Christians provided access to the riches and wealth of the Iberian empires. As a result, they played an important role in the economic relationship between Amsterdam and various Iberian ports, especially Lisbon. Following Veluwenkamp's concept of business diversification from a single activity, we will now examine four examples of how Portuguese Jewish businessmen adapted to entrepreneurial diversifica-

---

[17]Tjalling P. van der Kooij, *Hollands stapelmarkt en haar verval* (Amsterdam, 1931), 16-26.

[18]Peter W. Klein, *De Trippen in de 17e eeuw: Een studie over het ondernemersgedrag op de Holandse stapelmarkt* (Assen, 1965), 6-7.

[19]Peter W. Klein, "Entrepreneurial Behaviour and the Economic Rise and Decline of the Netherlands in the 17th and 18th Century," *Annales Cisalpines d'Histoire Sociale*, I (1970), 7-19.

[20]For an example, see Jan-Willem Veluwenkamp, *Ondernemersgedrag op de Hollandse stapelmarkt in de tijd van de Republiek: De Amsterdamse handelsfirma Jan Isaac de Neufville & Comp., 1730-1764* (Leiden, 1981).

tion in their most prominent activity, trade. The analysis will focus on their preferred trade routes, the nature of the products they exchanged, the use they made of accumulated capital and the nature of their business networks.

A Multiplicity of Routes

Trade between Amsterdam and Lisbon was conducted via a number of different routes, each of which was determined by the products to be exchanged and the socio-economic links they promoted. There were three types of routes linking these two cities: a direct route (Amsterdam-Lisbon-Amsterdam), a Portuguese/European route (Amsterdam-Portuguese ports-Lisbon-European ports-Amsterdam) and a linked intercontinental route (Amsterdam-Portuguese ports-Lisbon-European ports-intercontinental ports-Amsterdam).

Both the direct and Portuguese routes were popular among men like Baltazar Alvares Nogueira (alias Albert Dircksz), a well-established member of the Portuguese Jewish community in Amsterdam who traded regularly on both. He used his Portuguese name to trade directly with Portugal, but for his European connections he used his Dutch name.[21] Nogueira maintained regular contacts with Lisbon, Porto and the Azores.[22] The latter destination was mainly used in partnerships with other Amsterdam Jews, such as Joseph Mendes da Costa, Antonio Luis, Jacques de Prado, Baltazar Pires Henriques, Diogo Mendes, Manuel Rodrigues Lucena and Manuel Gomes da Silva. Under the pseudonym Albert Dircksz, Nogueira expanded his business beyond the direct Amsterdam-Lisbon route. He had connections with Porto and Aveiro through trading partnerships shared with Antonio Luis, Joseph Mendes da Costa, Francisco Lopes Henriques and Jacob van den Bergh.[23] He also extended his interests to Spain, especially to cities like Cádiz, San Lucar de Barrameda and Bilbao. For

---

[21]In the early modern period it was common to find Jewish merchants with two or more names. One of the names was the birth name; the other the Jewish name they adopted when arriving at towns and cities that allowed the open practice of Judaism. Others used local names to facilitate their integration into business circles. Jewish businessmen used their aliases to circumvent the prohibitions imposed by foreign governments on Jewish business and entrepreneurship.

[22]Amsterdam City Archives (GAA), Notarial Archives (NA), 1535, 32, 14 July 1651; 2112, 337, 27 November 1651; and 974, 132, 25 March 1654.

[23]*Ibid.*, NA, 1434, 38, 9 June 1650; 1535, 32, 14 July 1651; 1536, 200 and 279, 4 September 1653 and 22 April 1654; and 1537, 43, 240 and 285, 21 May 1654 and 8 July 1655.

these destinations, he often engaged in partnerships with Francisco Vaz, Isidro de Gurre and his brother, Joseph.[24]

Nogueira (alias Dircksz) appears in most instances to have used both names selectively, although the actual choice almost always depended on the ship's destination. But he seems to have been comfortable with using both names to establish contacts with Lisbon. As Nogueira he was involved in a partnership with Gonçalo de Azevedo (alias Manuel Rodrigues de Sea) in a freight contract with Claes Loembertsz, the master of *St. Jan Baptista*. The skipper was to sail to the Azores and then to Lisbon for a total price of 5200 *guilders*. A clause in the contract clearly ordered him to sail to Lisbon on the return journey, although the partners gave him the flexibility to load a return freight at Setubal if the harbour in Lisbon was too crowded. In that case, the freight was to be worth 2400 *cruzados*.[25]

Using the name Dircksz, Nogueira also extended his contacts to London, Madeira and beyond Europe to Brazil. By order of Antonio Rodrigues de Morais – his business partner in Rouen – Dircksz signed a freight contract with Sijmen Sijmensz. The skipper of *St. Paulo*, Sijmensz was to load fish in London and transport it to Lisbon, where he was to stay no longer than twelve days, after which the ship had to return to Amsterdam via Le Havre. The total freight was agreed at 3600 *guilders*.[26] Another contract describes an agreement between Dircksz, Jacques de Prado and Antonio Luis to hire David Thomas to take *De Coningh David* on a long journey across the Atlantic. The ship was to leave Amsterdam and head for Aveiro, where a Portuguese captain and his crew were to replace Thomas and the Dutch crew. The next destinations were Madeira and Bahia; after eight weeks in Bahia, the vessel was due to return via Lisbon to Amsterdam. The total price to be paid for this journey was 9200 *guilders*; in addition, the master was entitled to a bonus of 150 *guilders* if no incidents occurred during the trip.[27]

The second group of Portuguese Jews active in the Amsterdam-Lisbon-Amsterdam trade were involved in two further networks. In contrast to the Dutch merchants, the Jewish businessmen also had contacts with Portuguese ports other than Lisbon and with European networks. Moreover, again

---

[24]*Ibid.*, NA, 1534, 158 and 162, 12 and 23 December 1650; 1535, 63, 2 August 1651; and 1536, 211, 15 October 1653.

[25]*Ibid.*, NA, 1534, 136, 10 October 1650. During the second half of the seventeenth century, one Portuguese *cruzado* was roughly worth two Dutch *guilders*, depending on inflation and currency fluctuations.

[26]*Ibid.*, NA, 1534, 161, 22 December 1650.

[27]*Ibid.*, NA, 1536, 36, 30 September 1652.

in contrast with the Dutchmen, none invested exclusively in the Lisbon or European trades. A good example of such an entrepreneur was Lopo Ramires.

Lopo Ramires' first contact with Lisbon came when he accepted orders from Tristão de Mendonça Furtado, the Portuguese ambassador in The Hague who acted in the king's name, to ship weapons, grain and several pieces of luxury textiles to Lisbon. Subsequently, his business activities in Lisbon increased significantly, mainly involving grain and military supplies.[28] Although Ramires was involved in the grain trade, his business was often more closely connected with the Mediterranean than with the northern networks. His contacts spread throughout Morocco, Tunisia and Italy, and his personal contacts were not limited to the Jewish communities but extended to local merchants or Dutch representatives in the southern ports. In addition, he had close ties to the secretary of the Dutch embassy in Paris, Aert de Meijer, to whom he sent grain more than once.[29]

Some Portuguese Jews in Amsterdam invested in bilateral Amsterdam-Lisbon trade but also extended their dealings to intercontinental, European and Portuguese markets in a similar manner to Dutch merchants involved in global trade. Manuel Fernandes Miranda is a good example of this group. He had broad interests in the Amsterdam-Lisbon trade, as he often financed individual enterprises or joint ventures to Lisbon. This was clearly the reason for his relationship with Miguel Osorio de Almeida and Luis Rodrigues de Matos – merchants in Amsterdam – and Jorge Gomes do Alemo, a merchant in Lisbon. Apart from financing the Lisbon trade, Miranda had wide-ranging contacts with prominent members of the Portuguese Jewish community in Amsterdam, such as Jeronimo Nunes da Costa, as well as ordinary Dutch merchants, such as Ferdinand van Collen and Hendrik van Baerle. Van Collen and van Baerle were stockholders in the Dutch West India Company (WIC) and used their partnerships with Miranda to transport slaves from the West African coast to Surinam.[30]

By contrast, Francisco Vaz Isidro can be cited as an example of the Portuguese Jewish merchants of Amsterdam who had a three-dimensional interest in the Lisbon, European and intercontinental trades. Isidro was often used as a middleman between merchants of the Jewish community in Amsterdam and their business contacts in Lisbon. His name was associated with

---

[28]*Ibid.*, NA, 961, 1156, 14 December 1644; 1530, 199, 1 October 1646; and 2188B, 942-943, 2 October 1649.

[29]*Ibid.*, NA, 1527, 136, 19 September 1642; 2188A, 608-611, 25 June 1649; 899, s/p, 673-675 and 693-695, 15 and 24 November and 8 December 1649; and 2189, 493-494, 29 June 1650.

[30]*Ibid.*, NA, 3681, 347, 13 November 1673; and 4774, s/p, 8 December 1696 and 3 December 1697.

righteousness and honesty.[31] On a European level, he had contacts in Paris with Luis Alvares and Jean Verbeecq – both involved in the jewellery business – Abraham Joseph de Avila in Constantinople and Abraham and Jacob Levi Lousada in Leghorn. Isidro was connected to all these merchants through trading partnerships or because he had financed their joint ventures.[32] Apart from his European investments, he had vast interests in the WIC in Brazil, from where he seems to have withdrawn handsome amounts of sugar and tobacco. He was also a joint shareholder in the Dutch East Indian Company (VOC) with Isaac Gomes Silveira, Duarte Rodrigues Mendes and Moises Rodrigues Carion.[33]

The participation of different merchants in one or more trading routes linking Amsterdam and Lisbon provides an insight into the significance and influence of their contacts on a spatial level. On the basis of the above examples it is possible to divide the Portuguese Jewish merchants from Amsterdam into three groups: the global businessmen, whose networks reached out to different continents; the European businessmen, whose networks were mainly focused on the opportunities offered by European ports; and the local merchants, who mostly acted as middlemen between local ports and their hinterlands, and the European and global routes.[34] This element of geographic diversity in terms of trade and business transactions allowed Portuguese Jewish merchants in Amsterdam to spread their entrepreneurial risks across various routes, thereby safeguarding their initial investments, since an involvement in multiple routes effectively served to even out the inherent dangers connected with early modern trade, such as wars, embargoes or political turmoil.

Product Diversification

Global, European and local Portuguese Jewish merchants used the geographic diversity provided by the different trading routes to spread their risks. The same strategy was used in relation to the products exchanged by these merchants. Instead of specializing in a specific commodity, early modern Jewish entrepreneurs opted to deal in a wide variety of products.

Baltazar Alvares Nogueira, for example, used a combination of fish, olive oil, sugar and bay leaves in an attempt to optimize the different trading routes and the range of available products within a strategy designed to enable

---

[31]*Ibid.*, NA, 961, s/p, 9 September 1644.

[32]*Ibid.*, NA, 2902, 817, 28 August 1670; and 3698, 293, 26 February 1686.

[33]*Ibid.*, 1059, 77v, 18 April 1641; 4075, 125 and 199, 25 August 1672 and 26 September 1672.

[34]Antunes, *Globalization in the Early Modern Period.*

him to achieve the highest possible efficiency by avoiding the risk inherent in over-specialization in a single product. [35] But higher rates of profit as a result of a reduction in risk and increased trading efficiency had to be offset against a lower level of control over production outlets and consumption markets which was implicit in trading in a range of different products. In the case of Lopo Ramires, his close contacts with the Portuguese ambassador in The Hague, Dutch representatives in several Mediterranean ports and the secretary of the Dutch embassy in Paris gave him ample opportunities to trade in weapons, military supplies, grain and luxury textiles. [36] This ability to combine trade in bulk and luxury products was common among the "global" businessmen, since their main economic interests relied on the interconnections they were simultaneously able to foster between various trading routes and diverse products.

The capacity shown by Portuguese Jewish entrepreneurs to invest and exchange both bulk and luxury goods reflected the true nature and advantage of Amsterdam during the seventeenth century. In exploiting this capacity, the "Portuguese nation" followed the entrepreneurial pattern set by Dutch merchant houses like the Trips and the Neufvilles. [37] The city had begun to enjoy a "Golden Age" primarily because of the ability of its entrepreneurial class to trade simultaneously in bulk goods (mostly European) and luxury items from Asia and the New World. The Portuguese Jews, with their extensive connections in Iberia and its empires, were able to extend this general pattern even further.

It can therefore be argued that neither bulk nor luxury trades made Amsterdam great nor its entrepreneurial groups wealthy, contrary to the views of Israel, van Tielhof and Lesger. According to Israel and most of his followers, Amsterdam's unique position for fostering economic growth was a result of its capacity to connect colonial production outlets and consumption markets, either directly or indirectly (using its redistribution function in relation to the Iberian ports). [38] Van Tielhof and Lesger, on the other hand, downgrade the importance of the luxury trades by arguing that the basis for the explosive growth of Amsterdam was for the long-standing importance of the bulk trades and the connection with the Hanseatic cities and Baltic ports: it was not so

---

[35]GAA, NA, 1535, 32, 14 July 1651; 2112, 337, 27 November 1651; and 974, 132, 25 March 1654.

[36]*Ibid.*, NA, 961, 1156, 14 December 1644; 1530, 199, 1 October 1646; and 2188B, 942-943, 2 October 1649.

[37]Klein, *De Trippen in de 17e eeuw;* and Veluwenkamp, *Ondernemersgedrag op de Hollandse stapelmarkt.*

[38]Israel, "Economic Contribution of Dutch Sephardi Jewry;" and Israel, *European Jewry in the Age of Mercantilism.*

much a phenomenon of the early modern period as the culmination of a trend which had been apparent since the Middle Ages.[39]

Yet it is the work of Jan de Vries and Ad van der Woude on the genesis of modernity and the Dutch "economic miracle" which provides confirmation that Amsterdam's advantage as a business centre actually was the result of the healthy functioning of the staple market (for both luxury and bulk commodities) supported by an efficient capitalist structure, including banking and finance.[40] The exploitation of such a combination is the key characteristic to emerge from an analysis of the examples presented above.

Range of Trading Capital

The diversification of both trade routes and products by the Portuguese Jewish merchants in Amsterdam was also evident in the way they financed their business ventures. There were three types of capital instruments used by Amsterdam merchants in general and by Jewish merchants in particular: short- and long-term credit and insurance.

Short-term credit was a fairly common form of capital transaction among businessmen involved in trade and was often reflected in the sources by temporary consignments of goods to masters or representatives of the main trading party. This was the case, for example, when skippers or the firm's representatives were instructed to exchange the products in question to the best of their abilities. In such a situation, neither the payment for the products nor the expected profit for the businessman was fixed in advance. A second form of short-term credit was the permission given in advance by the merchant for the delayed payment of a certain consignment. These delayed payments comprised the majority of capital transactions relating to trade, since this was the safest and least risky way to secure a profit. The fact that this was a fairly common practice suggests that most of the commercial transactions controlled by businessmen from Amsterdam, and possibly throughout early modern Europe, were conducted in this way.

Short-term credit was undoubtedly useful when dealing with relatively inexpensive cargoes or with masters and representatives known for their honesty and trustworthiness. But not all business partners were equally honourable, and credit was an instrument not completely dependent on trade. As a result, several forms of long-term credit gradually developed. A good example was the bill of exchange, which grew from a form of currency exchange dur-

---

[39]Clé Lesger, *Hoorn als stedelijk knooppunt: stedensystemen tijdens de late middeleeuwen en vroegmoderne tijd* (Hilversum, 1990); and van Tielhof, *De Hollandse graanhandel*.

[40]Jan de Vries and Ad van der Woude, *The First Modern Economy: Success, Failure and Perseverance of the Dutch Economy, 1500-1815* (Cambridge, 1997).

ing the Middle Ages into a means of providing long-term credit in the early modern era. In essence, bills of exchange represented a loan to an individual whose purchasing power was safeguarded by the value of the bill. Bills were then endorsed and exchanged throughout the world for long periods until they were returned to the main European financial centres to be cashed, with the debt paid to the original lender.[41]

To a certain extent, bills of exchange can be regarded as the equivalent of modern cheques, and their relative anonymity facilitated the growth of personal and individual forms of credit. But they did not replace the traditional personal loan, which was a common form of capital transaction well before the early modern period. Indeed, family, personal and religious connections remained the primary source of personal loans, although in most cases it was not expected that they would be held for long periods of time. For example, on 30 June 1621 Lopo Ramires gave a power of attorney to Eduardo and Aloisio Nunes da Costa, well-known merchants in Florence. They were required by Ramires to travel to Pisa and demand from Abraham Cohen de Lucena the payment of a personal loan which Ramires had provided years before; according to Ramires, the date for the repayment of the loan had passed a couple of months earlier.[42] The power of attorney did not mention the amount of the loan, the interest payable or the original judicial framework of the contract. Yet given the tone and urgency of the request, it is reasonable to wonder how long Ramires had been unable to use his capital and for how long he had been expecting repayment. Lucena was, of course, one of his Jewish connections in Pisa who had used his family connections with the Nunes da Costas to secure payment of the debt.

If both short- and long-term credit were important sources of capital for trade and suitable investment opportunities for accumulated capital, they were complemented by a range of insurance practices which were used to reduce the risks associated with commerce and as viable options for businessmen who wished to invest their capital in a financial endeavour. The choice available for early modern insurers in Amsterdam was either to secure the cargo, the ship or both. Depending on the general political situation at the time and the geo-strategic position of the trade route, businessmen were able to provide a fairly efficient service for the protection of products, ships and crews. For example, on 9 January 1631 Lopo Ramires announced that he had insured the sugar and all other goods loaded on the ship *L'Ange Raphael* for a voyage from Lisbon to Hamburg under the command of Jean Marcus. The goods were sent by Luis Freitas, a Portuguese Jewish merchant in Antwerp, and destined

---

[41]I have argued elsewhere about the development and practical uses of bills of exchange in general, with practical examples from the Amsterdam market; see Antunes, *Globalization in the Early Modern Period*, chapter 5.

[42]GAA, NA, 645, 1260, 30 June 1621.

for Paul Berenberg or his representative in Hamburg. As the party responsible for the insurance, Ramires confirmed to Freitas that his goods had been safeguarded in case of disruptions on the trade route.[43]

As with the multiplicity of trading routes and the complementary nature of trade goods, both the Portuguese Jewish businessmen of Amsterdam and other well-positioned entrepreneurs in the city were able to exploit a wide range of possibilities in terms of capital transactions for commercial activities. In fact, the available evidence shows a clear tendency towards an increased diversification of options for financing any single activity. In a general sense, therefore, the availability of all these trading options and capital possibilities tended to encourage early modern entrepreneurs to avoid undue specialization in their daily business activities.

Social Networks

Diversity was clearly a key characteristic of the routes, products and capital investments linked to the trading activities of Portuguese Jewish entrepreneurs in early modern Amsterdam. The social networks within which Portuguese Jewish businessmen operated were also characterized by a similar variety. Baltazar Alvares Nogueira, for example, relied on a group of Portuguese Jews to share his business, as was the case with Joseph Mendes da Costa, Antonio Luis, Jacques de Prado, Baltazar Pires Henriques, Diogo Mendes, Manuel Rodrigues Lucena, Manuel Gomes da Silva, Antonio Luis, Francisco Lopes Henriques, Francisco Vaz Isidro de Gurre, his brother Joseph, Gonçalo de Azevelo and Antonio Rodrigues de Morais. At the same time, he was also involved in joint ventures with Jacob van den Bergh.

In the case of Lopo Ramires, his dealings with diplomatic personnel extended to the Portuguese ambassador in The Hague, as well as several Dutch representatives in southern European ports and the secretary of the Dutch embassy in Paris. These cross-cultural contacts enabled Ramires to promote business interactions between representatives of different political interests and to take advantage of his role as a middleman. The network of Manuel Fernandes Miranda was probably the most diverse, since his contacts eventually included important Portuguese Jewish entrepreneurs, such as Miguel Osorio de Almeida, Luis Rodrigues de Matos, Jorge Gomes do Alemo and Jeronimo Nunes da Costa, as well as well-known Dutch merchants like Ferdinand van Collen and Hendrik van Baerle.

These few examples indicate that Dutch and Portuguese merchants in Amsterdam often operated in discrete manners, both economically and so-

---

[43]*Ibid.*, NA, 941, 15-16, 9 January 1631.

cially, using their own religious, ethnic and family networks.[44] Some individuals in both groups, however, went beyond their "natural" partnerships to utilize what Yoram Ben-Porath has called "the F-connection" (families, friends and firms).[45] They often entered into long-term joint ventures that crossed the boundaries of their traditional networks. For those who behaved in this way, there was a whole new world to explore.[46] Despite their different religious backgrounds and the contemporary political context, Dutch and Portuguese Jewish businessmen were able to create, maintain and improve intra-group relationships to further their economic goals. The partnerships established with Portuguese Jews gave the Dutch a distinct competitive advantage in Iberia and its empires, while the "Portuguese nation" was generally welcomed in Dutch ports and colonial territories as an important source of capital and expertise for trade in the Atlantic and Asia. In addition, Dutch ports, especially Amsterdam, effectively protected the socio-economic and cultural identity of this group.

It is important to understand that this degree of cross-cultural networking had to be balanced and required a more-or-less equal status for the different partners in each network. In practice, that was not always the case, but the available evidence seems to suggest that there was no hierarchical structure within these networks. This is not to say that there was no distinct hierarchy between different networks, but it was definitely not the case as far as individuals operating within a specific network were concerned. This confirms Mark Casson's theoretical position that:

> a network comprises a web of long-term co-operative relationships between firms. It is distinctive because the relationship between the firms is not authoritarian like an employment relationship, and it differs from a spot market relationship because it involves a long-term commitment. It is intermediate between firm and market because, like the employment relationship, it is long-term, whilst like the spot market relationship, it involved firms of equal status.[47]

---

[44]Klein, *De Trippen in de 17e eeuw*; Daniel M. Swetschinski, *Reluctant Cosmopolitans: The Portuguese Jews of Seventeenth-Century Amsterdam* (London, 2000), chapter 3; and Antunes, *Globalization in the Early Modern Period*, 108-129.

[45]Yoram Ben-Porath, "The F-Connection: Families, Friends, and Firms and the Organization of Exchange," *Population and Development Review*, VI, No. 1 (1980), 1-30.

[46]Antunes, *Globalization in the Early Modern Period*, 106-128.

[47]Mark Granovetter, "The Strength of Weak Ties," *American Journal of Sociology*, LXXVIII, No. 6 (1973), 1360-1380; and Mark Casson, "Economic Analysis

Conclusion

The assessment of a sample of Jewish merchants involved in the trade between Amsterdam and Lisbon shows that their trading activities did not conform to van der Kooij's definition of Dutch entrepreneurial specialization. On the contrary, the evidence reinforces Veluwenkamp's assertion that Dutch entrepreneurial behaviour was diverse and often characterized by a fair amount of free choice. Moreover, the Portuguese Jewish merchants in Amsterdam had fully absorbed the key entrepreneurial characteristics of their Dutch counterparts, and their mode of business operation reflected well-established attitudes. The "Portuguese nation," as much as its Dutch counterpart, used all the business possibilities presented by trade to diversify its interests and to spread its entrepreneurial risks. By doing so, Portuguese Jewish merchants were active in local, European and intercontinental trade routes, using a mixture of bulk and luxury goods and supporting these endeavours with a whole range of short- and long-term credit, as well as a relatively efficient set of insurance practices.

If Dutch historiography has hinted that business multiplicity was a reality in the Republic, it has said nothing about social diversity in the business networks. The examples presented in this study show that Portuguese Jewish entrepreneurs were willing and able to step out of their religious and social networks to improve their economic position. While it is impossible to estimate the proportion of the group that dared to go beyond established social boundaries to advance business interests, group counterparts, religion and kinship were not always the most important considerations when choosing business partners, especially in the group involved in European and intercontinental trade. Their position as dealers in quality and diversity meant that they had enough financial support to pursue their goals and were therefore able to bypass social links and replace or add new economic connections.

of Social Networks," in *Actas del X Simposio de Historia Economica: Análisis de Redes en la Historia Económica* (Bellaterra, 2005), 3 (cd-rom).

Contrasting Merchant Communities in the Early Eighteenth Century: Stockholm, Calabar and Charleston

Chris Evans and Göran Rydén

This essay examines the nature of merchant communities and the trades they conducted in three eighteenth-century ports: one in the Baltic, one on the Bight of Biafra and one in British North America. These were three apparently disparate ports, but in the early eighteenth century they were brought together in a trading network centred on a fourth – Bristol. The empirical foundation for what follows is the amply documented activity of a Bristol merchant named Graffin Prankard. Prankard (d. 1756) was part of a Quaker trading network in the English West Country. He settled in Bristol in the first decade of the eighteenth century and soon distinguished himself in the city's Atlantic trade. At the height of his powers in the 1730s he was Bristol's leading iron merchant. International commerce was a volatile environment, however, and Prankard became insolvent in 1740. He was bailed out by his son-in-law, Caleb Dickinson, a wealthy Somerset landowner. For that reason, many of Prankard's accounts and letter books, which might otherwise have gone the way of most business records of the period, have been preserved in the estate archive of the Dickinson family.

In the 1720s and the 1730s Prankard began to put together an innovative web of commercial exchanges that brought together the Baltic and Atlantic worlds. Swedish bar iron was imported from Stockholm and then exported to West Africa and South Carolina, either in bar form or embodied in manufactured goods that had been wrought in Bristol's hinterland. We will use the cat's cradle of commodity exchanges that Prankard orchestrated to illuminate mercantile enterprise in each of the ports concerned. Three particular aspects of port life will be highlighted: the role of the state in regulating trade, the importance of ethnic affinity within the merchant class and the relationship of urban merchants to production in the hinterlands of their respective ports.

Stockholm

Stockholm was by far the largest of the port cities under consideration. With 70,000 inhabitants in the mid-eighteenth century, it stood alone at the head of Sweden's urban hierarchy, with Karlskrona, the southern naval base, a distant

33

second.[1] Set at the eastern end of Mälaren, the vast lake system that defined the ancient kingdom of the Svear, Stockholm was Sweden's premier port. It was also an industrial city whose southern island, Södermalm, boasted the biggest concentration of textile production in Sweden, and whose harbour was ringed by maritime industries. Moreover, Stockholm was an administrative centre and a national capital. It was the seat of royal government, home to palaces and the various governmental *collegia*.[2]

The heart of the city was Stadsholmen, the Old Town of today. The eastern shore of this island was given over to a long quay (*Skeppsbron*), against which the saltwater of the Baltic lapped. This was the point of departure for over sixty percent of Sweden's iron and tar, the two major export commodities. Likewise, most of the grain imported from the southern Baltic came ashore on these wharves. The quay was lined with the tall, imposing houses of the great merchants: the Plomgrens, Hebbes, Bedoires, Grills, Samuel Worster and others.

The trade that was conducted from *Skeppsbron* was tightly regulated by the Swedish state. The territorial ambitions of Sweden's rulers in the seventeenth and eighteenth centuries were at odds with the country's meagre agriculture and sparse population. Sweden could only assert itself as a major European power if its latent mineral wealth and forest resources were exploited effectively. Swedish iron had been sent south via Stockholm and Danzig since the Middle Ages, but a significant growth in Sweden's industrial output required a substantial injection of foreign capital. This came in the 1620s from a group of Dutch merchants who were alert to the advantages that preferential access to Swedish copper and iron could give them. The Dutchmen were awarded wide-ranging privileges by the state, allowing them to establish a network of processing plants. The greatly increased revenues that accrued to the state allowed Gustavus Adolphus to make his sensational entry into the Thirty Years' War. It was this twin industrial-military initiative that ushered in Sweden's "Age of Greatness" (*Stormakstiden*).

Stockholm played a central role in all of this. The passage of iron, the fastest growing export commodity of *Stormakstiden*, onto the European market was entrusted to a class of international merchants based in Stockholm and Gothenberg. The export of iron, as of other commodities, could only take place via the twenty-four "staple towns" (*stapelstäder*). Those towns through which bar iron passed were authorized – indeed, compelled – to have a *Jernvåg* ("iron weigh") at which the bars were weighed and their quality moni-

---

[1]For information on Swedish urbanization, see Sven Lilja, *Tjuvehål och Stolta Städer. Urbaniseringens Kronologi och Geografi i Sverige (med Finland) ca 1570-tal till 1810-tal* (Stockholm, 2000).

[2]For an overview of the city in the early modern period, see Lars Nilsson (ed.), *Staden på vattnet. Del I: 1252-1850* (Stockholm, 2002).

tored. In central Bergslagen iron was routed through inland ports, such as Västerås or Arboga on the shores of Mälaren, and thence to Stockholm.

The Stockholm merchant community was highly cosmopolitan, reflecting the paucity of indigenous capital. The Dutch presence was enduring. Many Dutch families that had settled in Sweden in the mid-seventeenth century were still active a century later. They were joined by Scots, ubiquitous in the seventeenth-century Baltic world and, from the 1670s, by the English. Indeed, by 1700 the English were clearly dominant. In the 1730s, when bar iron accounted for over two-thirds of Sweden's exports, the leading exporters bore names of Dutch (Grill), English (Worster) or Irish (Jennings) origin.

In theory, the merchant community was hedged with restrictions. The Swedish state had ordained a new social division of labour for the iron industry in the hope of boosting the quality of the product and optimizing the use of charcoal reserves in its manufacture. Iron making had traditionally been the province of peasant-miners (*bergsmän*) in Bergslagen, the mining district that extended north and west of Mälaren. From the early seventeenth century onwards, however, the *bergsmän* were restricted to the smelting of ore. The making of malleable bar iron – the high value-added part of the manufacturing process – was allotted to a class of more capitalized professional forge masters (*brukspatroner*) operating in clearly defined production centres spatially separate from the smelting districts. The *brukspatroner* were forbidden to export their output themselves; access to international markets was the prerogative of licensed traders in the staple ports, above all in Stockholm. By means of this specialization, the officers of the *Bergskollegium* (the State Board of Mines) hoped to prevent the over-harvesting of fuel resources in Bergslagen, and, not least, to ensure that the maximum tax revenues were levied on exports.

The hoped-for division of labour broke down, however. The *brukspatroner*, although notables in their home districts, tended to be short of capital and so relied on financial advances from their customers. For production to take place, credit had to be advanced by the merchant class in Stockholm. This, in turn, was obtained from iron merchants in Britain, which by 1700 had supplanted the Dutch Republic as the most important destination for Swedish bar iron. This placed the *brukspatroner* in a position of some weakness. No sooner had they redeemed their debts through the delivery of iron at the *Jernvåg* in Stockholm than they were obliged to apply for fresh credit. Often, through mishap or mismanagement, ironmasters were unable to redeem their debts fully, thereby setting in train a cycle of ever-deepening indebtedness to the merchant class. Over time, many *brukspatroner* were reduced to debt bondage, and for some the only means of liquidating their debt was to assign their ironworks (*bruk*) to their merchant creditors. It was in this way that many of the most prestigious *bruk* in Sweden became the property of Stockholm's merchant princes, in defiance of the Swedish state. Francis Jennings (1692-1754), the Belfast-born trader who settled in Stockholm in 1719, was one of the beneficiaries of this process. By the time of his death he was not merely the port's most important iron exporter but also the proprietor of several major *bruk* in the county of Uppland.[3]

Calabar

In the 1720s and 1730s Francis Jennings' leading customer in Britain was the Bristol merchant Graffin Prankard. Together, Prankard and Jennings had established Bristol as an important centre for the trade in Swedish bar iron, which had hitherto found its most lucrative markets in eastern Britain. The arrival of Swedish iron on the Bristol quayside coincided with the port's unholy apotheosis as Britain's leading slave port. Hence, a good part of what was sold by Prankard was destined for the Guinea trade as "voyage iron." The commercial sequence was as follows. Prankard advanced credit to Jennings in Stockholm, who in turn advanced credit to the ironworks at Gammelbo, deep in Bergslagen. The forge men at Gammelbo would then begin drawing out bars to the specific measurements requested by the African traders. There was a seasonal rhythm to this. The Gammelbo forge men would spend the winter, when communications with the outside world were slow and the difficulties in transporting iron at their most extreme, making generic bars. For these, a market of some sort would always exist, and they could be safely stockpiled. Demand for voyage iron, on the other hand, was conditional upon developments in a volatile branch of the Atlantic economy, so the Swedes awaited instructions from Bristol. When these arrived in the spring, the Gammelbo men turned to voyage iron and usually made nothing else until early autumn. The instructions on which they acted were precise. For 1732, Prankard's customers wanted bars that "run neare about 92 to ye ton," or about twenty-five pounds apiece; each or them was to be "10 foott 6 Inch or 10 foott 8 long."[4]

In the 1730s much of the voyage iron that passed through Prankard's hands was shipped to the Bight of Biafra, the new frontier of the Atlantic slave trade. At the start of the eighteenth century the Bight was of small consequence for English slavers, for the Royal African Company had its headquarters at Cape Coast Castle on the Gold Coast, hundreds of miles to the west. But in the 1730s the trading towns of the River Niger and the Cross River delta assumed major importance as Bristol merchants strengthened their links with Bonny and Calabar. Slave shipments from the Bight rose from 34,100 in 1731-1740 to

---

[3]Chris Evans and Göran Rydén, *Baltic Iron in the Atlantic World in the Eighteenth Century* (Leiden, 2007), 31-37.

[4]Somerset Archives (SA), DD/DN 424, Graffin Prankard to Francis Jennings, 1 December 1731.

nearly 152,100 in 1761-1770.[5] Calabar, an important node in the trading networks that snaked up and down the region's rivers and estuarial creeks, became more intimately involved in the wider Atlantic economy.[6]

The coastal areas, with their sandy spits and saltwater swamps, did not support an intensive agriculture. The Efik people of the coast obtained yams and other staple foods by trading salt and dried fish with the Ibos of the interior. By supplying European goods they were also able to obtain slaves. Calabar's trade with the interior was controlled by a small group of African merchant dynasties, known to their English counterparts by Anglicized versions of their local titles. It was they who comprised the ruling elites of the different "wards" into which Calabar was divided: the Robin family, for example, was active in Old Town, while the Duke clan was the dominant force in New (or Duke) Town. These powerful lineages developed a polyglot cosmopolitanism to ease their integration into the Atlantic economy. "The Black Traders of Bonny and Calabar" were said to be "very expert at reckoning and talking the different Languages of their own Country and those of the Europeans."[7] English, or a pidgin version thereof, became the language of commerce. Some Efik traders affected a European mode of dress: they "Drisht [like] whit men," as one of them put it.[8] Others built two-story, wooden houses in the European style, employing visiting ships' carpenters for the purpose. Egbo Young of Duke Town called his mansion "Liverpool Hall" in honour of his trading partners from the Mersey. So strongly was Calabar's elite imbued with the spirit of circum-Atlantic enterprise that by the second half of the eighteenth century it was not uncommon for the sons of the most eminent families to be sent to England for their education. Robin John Otto Ephraim, the son of "King George" of Old Town, was one such, sent to Liverpool in 1767.[9] He

---

[5]David Eltis, *et al.* (eds.), *The Transatlantic Slave Trade: A Database on CD-ROM* (Cambridge, 1999).

[6]See A.J.H. Latham, *Old Calabar, 1600-1891: The Impact of the International Economy upon a Traditional Society* (Oxford, 1973); David Northrup, *Trade without Rulers: Pre-Colonial Economic Development in South-Eastern Nigeria* (Oxford, 1978); and Lorena S. Walsh, *From Calabar to Carter's Grove: The History of a Virginia Slave Community* (Charlottesville, VA, 2001), 67-76.

[7]*Report of the Lords of the Committee of the Privy Council* (1789), quoted in Elizabeth Donnan (ed.), *Documents Illustrative of the Slave Trade to America* (4 vols., New York, 1965), II, 598.

[8]"The Diary of Antera Duke," in Cyril Daryll Forde (ed.), *Efik Traders of Old Calabar* (London, 1956), 84.

[9]Paul E. Lovejoy and David Richardson, "Trust, Pawnship, and Atlantic History: The Institutional Foundations of the Old Calabar Slave Trade," *American Histori-*

retained a vivid impression of his time there. Years afterward he added a post-script to a letter to Ambrose Lace, the Liverpool slave merchant: "Remember me to your Wife and your son Joshua [and to] Ambrose[,] William and Polly."[10]

The arrival of European ships was a matter for celebration among the Efik trader chiefs. Guns would be fired in salute as slaving vessels nosed around Seven Fathom Point to drop anchor in the turbid, mangrove-fringed waters of the Cross River. Slave trading usually began in the late summer or early autumn. Spring was the yam-planting season, when the movement of slaves was suspended, but once the harvest had been brought in shipments could begin in earnest, not least because yams were now available as proven-der for the human cargo during the Middle Passage.[11] To set the trading cycle in motion, European articles were advanced to the merchant dynasts of Cala-bar. As a guarantee that the credit placed at their disposal would be repaid, the merchants would hand over "pawns" to the slave captains, usually personal slaves but sometimes family members. These human pledges would be kept on board ship until slaves equivalent to the value of the goods advanced were sup-plied. If the Calabar merchant failed to fulfil his obligations, as sometimes happened, his unfortunate pawns would be shipped to the Caribbean.

The European manufactures would be entrusted to lesser merchants in marketing centres in the interior. They would buy up captives at the monthly fairs at Bende or Uburu and send them downriver.

> Twenty or Thirty Canoes, sometimes more and sometimes less, come down at a Time. In each Canoe may be Twenty or Thirty Slaves. The Arms of some of them are tied behind their Backs with Twigs, Canes, Grass Rope, or other Liga-ments of the Country; and if they happen to be stronger than common, they are pinioned above the Knee also. In this situation they are thrown into the Bottom of the Canoe, where they lie in great Pain, and often almost covered with

---

cal Review, CIV, No. 2 (1999), 342. See also Randy J. Sparks, *The Two Princes of Calabar: An Eighteenth-Century Atlantic Odyssey* (Cambridge, MA, 2004).

[10]Quoted in Gomer Williams, *History of the Liverpool Privateers* (London, 1897), 549.

[11]For the seasonality of slaving in the Bight, see Stephen D. Behrendt, "Mar-kets, Transaction Cycles, and Profits: Merchant Decision Making in the British Slave Trade," *William and Mary Quarterly*, 3rd ser., LVIII, No. 1 (2001), 184-185.

Water. On their landing they are oiled, fed, and made up for Sale.[12]

Slaves were sold in small parcels, sometimes individually. The 566 captives taken on board the Liverpool vessel *Dobson* between July 1769 and January 1770 arose from no fewer than 326 transactions. One supplier, Antera Duke, furnished *Dobson* with thirty-seven slaves over a six-month period. Duke's first sale, on 31 July 1769, was of two males for whom he received eight iron bars, fifteen copper rods, four kegs of gunpowder, two basins, two trade guns, four pounds of beads and an assortment of fabrics.[13]

This basket of goods is worthy of note, for the goods traded for slaves on the Cross River differed from those used on the Gold Coast or in Senegambia. Each sector of the African coast had its distinctive pattern of demand, as one English commentator explained. "Brass-mounted Cutlasses are peculiar to the Windward Coast," he wrote, "as are brass Pans from Rio Sesthos to Apollonia." At Whydah cowry shells were most sought after, but at Calabar it was "Copper and Iron Bars."[14] These broad claims are borne out by the experience of the Bristol and Liverpool slave ships that sailed south during or immediately after the Seven Years' War. Bar iron accounted for just 1.82 percent of the cargoes shipped to the Windward Coast, but 11.7 percent of the cargoes for Calabar and 18.8 percent of those sent a little further east along the Bight of Biafra to the Cameroons.[15] This thirst for metals did not arise from an absence of iron along the Bight. Quite the contrary – there was a flourishing tradition of iron making in Africa. "The basic smelting process diffused from the Middle East to West Africa (as it had to northwest Europe) during the last half-millenium before Christian era."[16] The savannah zone that extended between

---

[12]*Report of the Lords of the Committee of the Privy Council* (1789), quoted in Donnan (ed.), *Documents Illustrative of the Slave Trade*, II, 598.

[13]P.E.H. Hair, "Antera Duke of Old Calabar – A Little More about an African Entrepreneur," *History in Africa*, XVII (1990), 361.

[14]John Atkins, *A Voyage to Guinea, Brasil, and the West-Indies* (1735), quoted in Donnan (ed.), *Documents Illustrative of the Slave Trade*, II, 274.

[15]Data for the Windward Coast (five observations 1760-1771), Calabar (six observations, 1757-1770) and the Cameroons (eight observations, 1758-1769) are taken from David Richardson, "West African Consumption Patterns and Their Influence on the Eighteenth-Century," in Henry A. Gemery and Jan S. Hogendorn (eds.), *The Uncommon Market: Essays in the Economic History of the Atlantic Slave Trade* (New York, 1979), table 12.2.

[16]Philip D. Curtin, *Economic Change in Precolonial Africa: Senegambia in the Era of the Slave Trade* (Madison, WI, 1975), 208.

latitudes 10° and 15° North was rich in ore and dry woodland. From here iron was brought south to the forest belt. Iron was therefore a very familiar commodity in Calabar's hinterland, where it was worked up by the Awka, itinerant smiths who were a conspicuous feature of Ibo society.[17] In fact, iron tokens were used as a currency. It was a demand for additional iron, not a lack of metallurgical knowledge in African society, which drew European imports. It was this that brought the Ibo people into a relationship with forest communities in midland Sweden.[18] The *barracoons* of Calabar also brought Ibo captives into a forcible relationship with the plantation economies of the New World. In the 1730s a crisis of over-production in the sugar trade slowed the flow of slaves to the Caribbean, but a boom in rice cultivation in the Lower South drew dozens of slave vessels to Charleston, South Carolina.

Charleston

The ship that Graffin Prankard despatched to Charleston from Bristol in 1735 carried seventy casks containing more than two million nails of various sorts. Nearly 500 bars of Swedish iron had also been lowered into its hold, together with bars of German steel and faggots of English steel. Whip saws, saw files, ploughshare moulds, hoes and gunpowder completed the cargo.[19] This was an extraordinarily utilitarian consignment. There was nothing modish or ornamental: no ceramic wares, no fine furniture, no glassware, no millinery and no fabrics; none, in fact, of the consumer goods that were routinely despatched to the Chesapeake or the Delaware. The goods listed on *Baltick Merchant*'s manifest marked Charleston as a place apart.

Charleston in the early 1730s was a town of some 4500 inhabitants. Situated on a spur of land at the confluence of the Cooper and Ashley rivers, it was the commercial centre of South Carolina. It was British North America's fifth largest city, some way behind Boston (13,000 inhabitants), Philadelphia (11,500) and New York (8600), but neck-and-neck with Newport, Rhode Island. The picture that the colony's propagandists painted of Charleston was one of order, godliness and prosperity: "There are between 5 and 600 Houses in Charles Town, the most of which are very costly; besides 5 handsome

---

[17]Lars Sundström, *The Exchange Economy of Pre-Colonial Tropical Africa* (London, 1974), 188.

[18]But note that it has been suggested that climatic change and desertification, by raising fuel costs, increased the price of indigenously made iron, opening the way for European imports. See Candice L. Goucher, "Iron is Iron 'til It Rust: Trade and Ecology in the Decline of West African Iron-Smelting," *Journal of African History*, XXII, No. 3 (1981), 179-189.

[19]SA, DD/DN 448.

Churches, viz. one for those of the Church of *England*, one for the Presbyterians, one for the Anabaptists, one for the Quakers, and one for the *French*."[20] "The Inhabitants," another booster trumpeted, "by their wise Management and Industry, have much improv'd the Country, which is in as thriving Circumstances at this Time, as any Colony on the Continent of *English America*."[21] Wealth there was, but it had been born of violence and ruthless expropriation, not order.

The period following the foundation of South Carolina in 1670 were years of carnage. The earliest English settlers had come to the area from Barbados. Conscious of the spread of a sugar monoculture in the West Indies and the demand that it generated for labour, the English were soon encouraging the Native Americans with whom they traded to raid neighbouring communities for slaves. This triggered a long series of Indian wars that furnished a steady supply of captives for the plantations of the Caribbean and resulted in a massive depletion of the indigenous population.[22] Intertwined with these bloody developments was a growing trade in deerskins, supplied by Native American hunters and eagerly awaited by European leather workers. The process reached its savage apogee in the Yamasee War of 1715-1716 that left thousands of acres denuded of human inhabitants.[23]

As the coastal lowcountry was emptied of its native residents, it was re-populated with a new ethnic group and dedicated to the production of a new commodity for international markets. The commodity was rice, cultivated by African slaves. The province that had once been an exporter of unfree labour now bought slaves on a massive scale. Experiments in the growing of rice had begun in the 1690s, and by the 1710s the crop was a critical element in South Carolina's economy.[24] Its cultivation was highly labour intensive. Tidal

---

[20]"A Description of the Province of South Carolina, Drawn Up at Charles-Town in Sept. 1731," *Gentleman's Magazine*, XX (August 1732), 896.

[21]John Lawson, *A New Voyage to Carolina* (London, 1709), 2.

[22]Alan Gallay, *The Indian Slave Trade: The Rise of the English Empire in the American South, 1670-1717* (New Haven, 2003).

[23]Daniel K. Richter, "Native Peoples of North America and the Eighteenth-Century British Empire," in P.J. Marshall (ed.), *The Oxford History of the British Empire. Vol. II: The Eighteenth Century* (Oxford, 1998), 352 and 360.

[24]Peter H. Wood, *Black Majority: Negroes in Colonial South Carolina from 1670 through the Stono Rebellion* (New York, 1975); Daniel C. Littlefield, *Rice and Slaves: Ethnicity and the Slave Trade in Colonial South Carolina* (Baton Rouge, 1981); Judith A. Carney, *Black Rice: The African Origins of Rice Cultivation in the Americas* (Cambridge, MA, 2001); and S. Max Edelson, *Plantation Enterprise in Colonial South Carolina* (Cambridge, MA, 2006).

marshes and inland swamps had to be converted into rice fields through the construction of embankments, dikes, canals and sluices. The spread of this infrastructure along the tidal floodplains of the Atlantic coast could only be accomplished through an injection of African labour.[25] At first, Africans were obtained through Caribbean slave marts, but by 1714 a direct trade with the Guinea coast was underway. Imports remained modest until the mid-1720s, but then an upward surge began, culminating in 1738 when 3658 slaves were disembarked in the Carolinas in a single year.[26]

Rice brought about an "Africanization" of South Carolina.[27] Blacks had formed a minor part of the province's non-indigenous population in its early days, just 200 individuals out of 1200 in 1680. Yet by 1700, as rice exports began to climb, blacks comprised forty-three percent of South Carolina's inhabitants. By 1720 the figure was seventy percent. Carolina, as a Swiss migrant remarked in 1737, "looks more like a negro country than a country settled by white people."[28] In the rice-growing lowcountry, the dominant language was a pidgin that drew on the linguistic heritage of West Africa as much as it did on English. The Europeans clustered in and around Charleston. In part, this was a legacy from the Indian wars, one dictated by a basic need for security during the many periods of mayhem. It was also a response to the conditions of rice cultivation. Planters were fearful of the numbers and the

---

[25]White servants were in short supply and could not be persuaded to submit to the gruelling labour in sufficient numbers. Additionally, Africans had a greater immunity to the malarial disorders endemic in the lowcountry. See Wood, *Black Majority*, chapters 2 and 3. It should also be stressed that many Africans were experienced farmers of rice, which was a staple food in West Africa. The crop was not grown in northern Europe. See Carney, *Black Rice, passim*. But for scepticism about the decisiveness of African influence, see David Eltis, Philip Morgan and David Richardson, "Agency and Diaspora in Atlantic History: Reassessing the African Contribution to Rice Cultivation in the Americas," *American Historical Review*, CXII, No. 5 (2007), 1329-1358.

[26]David Richardson, "The British Slave Trade to Colonial South Carolina," *Slavery and Abolition*, XII, No. 3 (1991), 125-172; Kenneth Morgan, "Slave Sales in Colonial Charleston," *English Historical Review*, CXIII, No. 3 (1998), 905-927; and Eltis, *et al.* (eds.), *Transatlantic Slave Trade*. The influx of slaves gained extra momentum from 1731 when rice was removed from the list of enumerated articles that had to be routed through a British port before re-export to European markets. Carolinian rice could now be sent direct to Iberian and Mediterranean consumers.

[27]For an exploration of this, see Leland Ferguson, *Uncommon Ground: Archaeology and Early African America* (Washington, DC, 1992). See also Philip D. Morgan, *Slave Counterpoint: Black Culture in the Eighteenth-Century Chesapeake and Lowcountry* (Chapel Hill, NC, 1998).

[28]Quoted in Wood, *Black Majority*, 132.

disturbingly alien culture of their chattel labourers. Such fears were amply borne out by the disclosure of planned slave insurrections: "a very wicked and barbarous plott" was uncovered in 1720, for example, "of the Negroes rising with a designe to destroy all the white people in the country."[29] The nature of the rice trade also explains why it was that Charleston became the marketing centre for the Lower South as a whole. Rice was a crop that was marketed in a wide variety of European markets – unlike tobacco, which was funnelled through just a few British ports. Carolina's planters therefore found it too taxing to deal with a large number of commission agents in Europe, preferring to cooperate with specialist agents in a single centre. Rice's low value relative to its shipment cost exacerbated the trend toward centralization in Charleston. It called for specialist shippers who could exploit a detailed knowledge of freight rates. For the producers of more valuable crops, such as tobacco, freight costs were of less importance, and planters were prepared to handle the shipping arrangements themselves in their different localities around the Chesapeake.[30]

The growing dependence of the colony upon rice exports and the dependence of rice exports upon slave imports determined South Carolina's articulation with the wider Atlantic economy. Rice had to be carried to European markets, yet there was a restricted local market for European manufactured goods. The white farmer-settlers who spread up the Delaware and Hudson valleys, thereby populating the hinterlands of Philadelphia and New York, had no counterparts on the banks of the Cooper or Santee rivers.[31] The appetite for European consumer goods was therefore far lower among Carolinians. African slaves, after all, exercised little in the way of consumer choice. It is significant in this respect that Charleston was slow to develop an autonomous merchant class of the sort found in more rounded entrepôts like Philadelphia or Boston. Before 1750 its merchant houses were essentially offshoots of London- or Bristol-based partnerships that were concerned with rice exports and little else.[32]

---

[29]Quoted in D.D. Wax, "'The Great Risque We Run:' The Aftermath of the Slave Rebellion at Stono, South Carolina, 1739-1745," *Journal of Negro History*, LXVII, No. 2 (1982), 137.

[30]R.C. Nash, "The Organization of Trade and Finance in the Atlantic Economy: Britain and South Carolina, 1670-1775," in Jack P. Greene, Rosemary Brana-Shute and Randy J. Sparks (eds.), *Money, Trade and Power: The Evolution of South Carolina's Plantation Society* (Columbia, SC, 2001), 77-78.

[31]T.H. Breen, "An Empire of Goods: The Anglicization of Colonial America, 1690-1776," *Journal of British Studies*, XXV, No. 4 (1986), 467-499; and Nuala Zahedieh, "London and the Colonial Consumer in the Late Seventeenth Century," *Economic History Review*, New ser., XLVII, No. 2 (1994), 239-261.

[32]Jacob M. Price, "Economic Function and the Growth of American Port Towns in the Eighteenth Century," *Perspectives in American History*, VIII (1974), 123-

The relative weakness of the merchant class was a reflection of the political power of the planters, entrenched in the colony's assembly. The planters were able to pursue their sectional interests very successfully. Nowhere was this more evident than in the assembly's willingness to issue large volumes of paper currency. The steady expansion of local currency led to its progressive depreciation against sterling, which was very much to the advantage of planters whose debts were thereby diminished in real terms. Charleston's merchants, on the other hand, compelled to accept payment in a deteriorating currency, were severely disadvantaged.

Carolina was not a market that merchants could disregard, however. Quite apart from anything else, its population grew from 5704 in 1700 to 45,000 in 1740. The Indian trade flourished, despite the devastations of the Yamasee War, not least because bovine epidemics in Europe cut the supply of cowhides and drove up the demand for deerskins. Above all, the extension of rice cultivation along the coast and into inland swamps called for a wholesale reshaping of the landscape. This, in turn, rested upon an infusion of European-made *matériel*: axes, hoes, spades, ploughshares, ox chains and the like. It was this requirement that attracted the attention of metalware manufacturers in Britain.

John Crowley, Britain's largest hardware manufacturer, was exporting sizeable quantities of iron goods to South Carolina in the 1720s. This was understandable. At his factories in the North East of England an array of goods designed expressly for plantation agriculture was turned out. The inventory made after Crowley's death in 1727 revealed that both "Barbados" and "Virginia" hoes were manufactured at Swalwell, each in eight different gauges.[33] That Charleston provided a ready market for these sorts of products is evident

---

188, reprinted in Price, *The Atlantic Frontier of the Thirteen Colonies and States: Essays in Eighteenth-Century Commercial and Social History* (Aldershot, 1996), 162-163, stresses the under-development of Charleston's merchant class. R.C. Nash, "Urbanization in the Colonial South: Charleston, South Carolina, as a Case Study," *Journal of Urban History*, XIX, No. 1 (1992), 3-29; and Peter A. Coclanis, "The Hydra Head of Merchant Capital: Markets and Merchants in Early South Carolina," in David R. Chesnutt and Clyde N. Wilson (eds.), *The Meaning of South Carolina History: Essays in Honor of George C. Rogers, Jr.* (Columbia, SC, 1991), 1-18, emphasize the wealth and diversity of the port's merchant class.

[33]Suffolk Record Office (SRO), HAI/GD/5/15, "Goods in Robt. Armstrongs Hands." The Crowleys also specialized in producing the hatchets that were an important commodity in South Carolina's Indian trade; see Torsten Berg and Peter Berg (eds.), *R.R. Angerstein's Illustrated Travel Diary, 1753-1755: Industry in England and Wales from a Swedish Perspective* (London, 2001), 264.

from the scale of the debts incurred by the town's merchants. Several of them owed John Crowley sums in excess of £1000 at the time of his death.[34]

John Crowley's ships would sail for Carolina with a cargo of ironware, occasionally swinging south to Madeira to pick up some pipes of the local wine. On their return they would carry rice, deerskins and timber products. Graffin Prankard pursued the same course. *Parham*, launched in 1722, sailed for Charleston every winter. Its cargo would include metalware, such as hoes and chains, Swedish bar iron, English steel and nails, by the hundred thousand. The return cargo was of course rice, augmented by dyestuffs such as indigo and logwood. This was a flourishing trade, for Prankard soon built a new, far larger ship to join the 100-ton *Parham*. The 226-ton *Baltick Merchant*, registered at Bristol in 1732, was capable of carrying over 1300 barrels of rice.

There was no paradox in a ship named *Baltick Merchant* engaging in transatlantic trade, for Graffin Prankard was seeking to capitalize on a potential symmetry between Baltic commerce and the passage of goods to and from Charleston. There was a complementarity between Swedish iron and Carolinian rice that allowed Prankard to employ his shipping in a year-round circuit. In May, just as Prankard's ships were entering the Baltic, thousands of Africans were spreading out across the rice fields of Carolina to plant the new crop. During the summer, as *Baltick Merchant* made its way back across the North Sea, African field hands were occupied with irrigating, hoeing and weeding. The rice harvest, which began in late August and lasted until October, coincided with the fitting-out of Prankard's ships for the transatlantic phase of their circuit. During November and December, as *Baltick Merchant* struggled across a stormy Atlantic, slaves were engaged in laboriously "pounding out" the rice in order to separate the husk from the grain. At the year's end, when *Baltick Merchant* tied up at Charleston, hundreds of barrels of rice were ready to be stowed on board. This rice would be delivered to Hamburg or Amsterdam in April or May. Then *Baltick Merchant* would pass eastward through the Sound once more, ready for another load of Swedish bar iron.

This pattern of trade throve through the 1730s. But the headlong development of South Carolina's rice economy was about to undergo a sharp deceleration. The outbreak of war between Britain and Spain in 1739 brought a general disruption to Atlantic traffic, while the slave rebellion at Stono, near Charleston, delivered an abrupt check to Carolinian trade in particular. The Stono uprising was, in fact, facilitated by Anglo-Spanish antagonism. The armed slaves who gathered at Stono on 9 September 1739 had heard of an edict issued by the Spanish governor of Florida promising freedom to refugee

---

[34]SRO, HAI/GD/5/2, "Credit Ledger A."

English slaves.[35] Those who marched south, killing many of the Europeans they encountered *en route*, were intent on reaching the Spanish stronghold at St. Augustine. The rebels were surrounded by militia forces before the day was out and subjected to merciless reprisals, but the brevity of the rebellion could not disguise its seriousness. Nearly two dozen whites had died in an enterprise that spoke of concerted planning among its participants. The colony's rulers were seized by panic.

South Carolina's General Assembly devoted the winter of 1739-1740 to upgrading the repressive mechanisms needed to counter future outbreaks. The legislators met in an atmosphere of dread. The 1730s was a time of mounting slave resistance in the Caribbean islands with which Carolina had so marked a typological affinity. The British authorities in Jamaica were engaged in a bitter war of suppression against the "Maroons," the runaway slaves who defied their erstwhile masters from mountain fastnesses in the interior of the island, while a major revolt was only just thwarted in Antigua in 1736. Rebellious outbreaks sprouted across the Caribbean whether the islands were claimed by the English, Spanish, French, Dutch or Danes.[36] Amid such tensions, South Carolina's rulers were inescapably drawn to the question of the colony's racial imbalance. Steps were needed, it was decided, to curb the continuing inflow of African labour. Unless this was done, blacks would reach such a numerical preponderance that the Europeans would lose the coercive critical mass upon which their security rested. Moreover, it was felt necessary to reduce the ratio of African-born slaves in the unfree population. Africans, it was thought, were intransigently wedded to memories of their former freedom, whereas American-born blacks, knowing nothing but servitude, were more biddable. Accordingly, the Negro Duty Bill, enacted in April 1740, placed a prohibitively high tax on the importation of slaves.[37] The effect was instantaneous. Slave sales collapsed: 22,215 slaves had been landed in the Carolinas in

---

[35]The rebels, it was suggested at the time, originated in Angola where "Thousands of the Negroes profess the Roman Catholic Religion" and where Portuguese, which was "as near Spanish as Scotch is to English," was widely spoken. "An Account of the Negroe Insurrection in South Carolina" (c. 1740), quoted in John K. Thornton, "African Dimensions of the Stono Rebellion," *American Historical Review*, XCVI, No. 4 (1991), 1102 – although Thornton argues that the kingdom of the Kongo was a more likely point of origin. See also Edward A. Pearson, "'A Countryside Full of Flames:' A Reconsideration of the Stono Rebellion and Slave Rebelliousness in the Early Eighteenth-Century South Carolina Lowcountry," *Slavery and Abolition*, XVII, No. 2 (1996), 22-50.

[36]See Richard B. Sheridan, "The Formation of Caribbean Plantation Society, 1689-1748," in Marshall (ed.), *British Empire*, 406.

[37]Wax, "'Great Risque We Run;'" and Wood, *Black Majority*, 323-326.

the 1730s, but just 2841 were disembarked in the 1740s.[38] Once again the subordination of Charleston's merchant-importers to the planters of the lowcountry – the latter being able at least to maintain production with their existing stock of slaves – was made plain.

Conclusion

The merchant communities we have considered were diverse. That of Stockholm, the largest and richest, was the most ethnically varied. Stockholm was an old city, founded in 1252, and had been a major port since the Middle Ages. It had been home to a variety of mercantile diasporas over the centuries – German, Dutch, Scottish and English – and foreign merchants continued to be disproportionately prominent in the city in the eighteenth century. Charleston, founded only in 1670, housed a rather less motley merchant community. The English and Huguenots dominated. Calabar, which did not feature on European charts before the mid-seventeenth century, was the most ethnically uniform. Efik traders controlled the town, but the Efik community was politically fractured by divisions between different merchant lineages.

Each merchant community had to contend with a different form of state power. The Swedish state was robust and centralized. The state had featured prominently in the industrial development of the country, and its agencies operated with a strong sense of mercantilist purpose. Stockholm's merchants had a clearly defined place in a wider social division of labour. That place was a privileged one: they held monopoly rights over foreign trade. Authority in Calabar was more diffuse, splintered between the rival wards of the town. Yet it was to a large extent coterminous with the merchant community, for each of the merchant lineages exercised political power of its own. Charleston's merchants were confronted by the most unstable conditions. Carolina's frontiers were indistinct, and Charleston's hinterland was racked by endemic violence. Political power was disputed between an increasingly powerful planter class and the absentee proprietors of the colony.

In each location a different institutional framework prevailed, affecting in different ways the conduct of business. The difficulties were greatest at Calabar, where the cultural distance between indigenous merchants and their European trading partners was considerable. Trust was established between the two by a process of acculturation: Calabar's merchants adopted European mores and bearing, while English slave captains made obeisance to local sensibilities. Political authority in the Cross River delta was somewhat amorphous. The more centralized royal jurisdictions that were to be found further west along the African coast, with relatively developed structures of government and standing armies, were absent. Hence, at bottom, it was the institution of

---

[38]Eltis, *et al.* (eds.), *Transatlantic Slave Trade.*

"pawnship," the offering up of human pledges, that underwrote the extension of credit to slave merchants operating in Calabar's hinterland.

In Stockholm, although many members of the merchant community were foreigners, they shared a basic understanding of legality and property rights with those with whom they traded. More important, the Swedish state was present to enforce its code of commercial law. The relationship between Stockholm's merchants and their suppliers in the hinterland was not an equal one, however. Upcountry *brukspatroner* were often reduced to dependence on the so-called "quayside nobility" of the capital. Indeed, sometimes they were obliged to relinquish their estates to their merchant-creditors. The hinterland was subservient to the port.

In South Carolina the opposite was true. The lowcountry rice planters prevailed over Charleston's merchants. The grandeur that Charleston acquired in the eighteenth century disguised this reality somewhat. Almost all planters of importance chose to live in Charleston for part of the year, for the reasons explained above. That gave the port a splendour that was absent in its damp and fetid hinterland. "An European at his first arrival," exclaimed a visitor to the city, "must be greatly surprised when he sees the elegance of their houses, their sumptuous furniture, as well as the magnificence of their tables; can he imagine himself in a country, the establishment of which is so recent?"[39] Yet the source of wealth and power in South Carolina lay in its rice fields, not in Charleston. That gave authority to the planter-gentry. And that authority, expressed through the colonial assembly, enabled them to manipulate the system of transatlantic credit in their favour. The local state, for all the colonial regulation to which it was theoretically subject, was vulnerable to the machinations of the planter class. The Swedish state, with its aloof absolutist ethos, could not be bent to the will of the provincial ironmasters, still less the peasant-miners of Bergslagen.

---

[39]J. Hector St. John de Crèvecouer, *Letters from an American Farmer* (London, 1782; reprint, Mineola, NY, 2005), 215.

Integration of Immigrant Merchants in Trondheim in the Seventeenth and Eighteenth Centuries

Ida Bull

Anno 1766, 5. of May did I travel from Flensburg with ship-master H.H. Wulf to Drontheim, where we, thank God, *Anno* 1766, 11 of June at ten o'clock in the morning arrived. At the same day I also in the name of the God of Trinity went into my service, in which the highest happiness and health graciously will be given to me.[1]

Introduction

Herman Hoë, who wrote the above note in his diary, was one of many immigrants to move into the mercantile trade in Trondheim in the seventeenth and eighteenth centuries. He arrived as a fifteen-year-old boy to take an apprenticeship with an older merchant, Otto Beyer, who born in Flensburg in 1711 and was a relative of Herman's mother. In his youth Otto had been sent to Trondheim to learn the trade, as had young Herman.[2] The immigration of merchants to the city, which began in the seventeenth century, was already an established practice in the eighteenth. Many more young boys followed older countrymen and established themselves in Trondheim. The city became an important port, connected to the larger European economic network around the North Sea and the Baltic. Emigrants from London, Hamburg, Amsterdam and above all Flensburg settled in Trondheim and soon monopolized the region's growing exports of fish, timber and copper. Moreover, they came to comprise the main part of the city's political elite.

This essay will deal with some aspects of their integration into a new community. Their position was based not only on the resources they brought but also on the strategies they used to construct new networks and to secure their position at the apex of society. I will concentrate on the economic, social

---

[1]Author's translation. Regional State Archives of Trondheim (RSAT), Private Archive 280, Hoë 16.4.

[2]Chr. Thaulow, *Personalhistorie for Trondhjems by og omegn i et tidsrum af circa 1½ aarhundrede* (Trondheim, 1919), 258.

and political strategies they followed. They had to use economic strategies to construct local, regional and international networks. They also employed social tactics, making friends with useful people and marrying into important families. Politically, they took on influential administrative and elected positions.

The research is based mainly on sources relating to four immigrant trading families, each of which was in business for at least two generations, and together they covered the period from about 1660 to 1900. I have followed them up to the 1830s. The first member of each family I will examine came from Flensburg, but through intermarriage they were related to others from Hamburg, England and elsewhere. For the oldest of these families, the Angells, only scattered archival sources have survived, most concerning the disposal of the property of the family's last merchant, an unmarried member of the third generation who died in 1767.[3] For the Horneman family there is some correspondence and accounting material from the first generation but more from the second-generation merchant, who died in 1764.[4] From the Hoë and Lorck families, both of which started their activities in Trondheim in the 1760s and 1770s, there are large archives covering their private and business activities.[5] These four families formed part of the business elite in Trondheim, and their connections stretched throughout the region and into Europe and the larger world.[6]

The City and Its Merchants

Even if Trondheim was the third largest city in Norway, it was still a small place. In 1600 the population was only about 2500, but it grew rapidly thereafter, reaching about 5000 in 1700 and nearly 9000 by 1801.[7] In 1600 there was little social stratification, and most inhabitants were common people who lived

---

[3]Ida Bull, *Thomas Angell: Kjøpmannen som ble hjembyens velgjører* (Trondheim, 1992). The material on the Angells comes mainly from Thomas Angells Stiftelser, Trondheim, apart from official documents in the RSAT.

[4]RSAT, Private Archive 236, Horneman; Ida Bull, *Katalog over privatarkiv i Statsarkivet i Trondheim, Vol. 5* (Trondheim, 1989); and Knut Sprauten, "Hans Horneman og næringslivet i det trondhjemske" (unpublished mss.). I would like to thank Mr. Sprauten for allowing me to consult his manuscript.

[5]RSAT, Private Archive 280, Hoë, and Private Archive, Lorck; and Ida Bull, *Katalog over privatarkiv i Statsarkivet i Trondheim, Vol. 6* (Trondheim, 1998).

[6]Ida Bull, *De Trondhjemske handelshusene på 1700-tallet: Slekt, hushold og forretning* (Trondheim, 1998).

[7]Steinar Supphellen, *Trondheims historie 997-1997, Vol. 2* (Oslo, 1997), 101, 339 and 350.

modestly. During the seventeenth century, however, the population became more diversified, and a capitalist class began to develop. From the early 1600s some international merchants settled in the town. Many of these came from Holland, the leading trading nation at the time, but there were also English, German and Danish traders, and from the middle of the seventeenth century a number started to arrive from Flensburg, a city in the duchy of Schleswig. The Danish immigrant merchants were mostly from the southern part of Jutland. Schleswig bordered on Jutland and belonged, in part, to the Danish king. During the seventeenth, eighteenth and early nineteenth centuries many Flensburgers came to Trondheim, and a number entered into mercantile activities. Some ended their careers as heads of important merchant houses, while others enjoyed more modest success. According to a description in 1708, the city then had sixty-three merchants, twenty-five of whom were from Flensburg, and some were members of the second or third generations in Trondheim. The nineteen described as "capital" merchants were all immigrants or sons of immigrants.[8] From 1708 until the end of the eighteenth century, sixty Flensburgers registered as burghers in Trondheim, fifty of them as merchants, making them the largest immigrant group among the burghers. Most engaged in foreign trade and were among the leading group in the city.[9] In the census of 1801, among the nearly 9000 inhabitants, about seventy-five were characterized as merchants (*kiøbmand*) and another eighty-five as small-scale dealers (*kremmer* or *høker*).[10] The merchants were allowed to trade internationally and could also work as wholesalers and retailers, while the *kremmere* and *høkere* were allowed to trade only within the city and domestically.

Merchants with an International Background

Before the seventeenth century, little international trade originated in Trondheim. Bergen was Norway's leading commercial city and handled Trondheim's exports. That changed during the seventeenth century as the merchants who came from abroad built up a direct international trade from Trondheim. Their presence in the city and region was not entirely new, for merchants from Holland, England and Germany had previously sailed along the Norwegian coast as far as Finnmark, trading and buying fish from the peasants. Indeed, until the mid-seventeenth century foreigners could trade this way quite freely, but thereafter official policy shifted to give privileges to Norwegian merchants and to centralize trade in the cities. Flensburgers had been active in this earlier

---

[8]Bernt Moe (ed.), *Tidskrift for personalhistorie* (Christiania, 1846).

[9]Bjørn Sogner, *Trondheim bys historie, Vol. 2* (Trondheim, 1962), 452.

[10]Http://www.digitalarkivet.no/cgi-win/webcens.exe?slag=visbase&filnamn =f11601&spraak=n&metanr=394.

trade. Some scholars have suggested that the war between Sweden and Denmark-Norway, which ravaged the Flensburg area, made it difficult for them to equip their ships for trade. By war's end, Norwegian traders based in Trondheim had taken over this commerce, and Flensburg merchants bought what they needed through them.[11] Others have maintained that Danish protectionist policy, which favoured Danish and Norwegian merchants, and northern Norway merchants from Bergen and Trondheim, was the main reason for this shift.[12] Sources in Flensburg suggest that the problems Flensburg merchants encountered in northern Norway in the 1640s, 1650s and 1660s were so severe that they simply abandoned direct trade.[13]

Regardless of why the Flensburgers gave up the older itinerant trade, we know that in the first half of the seventeenth century some began to settle in Trondheim, where they specialized in foreign commerce as middlemen between local fishermen, fish traders and sawmill owners, on the one hand, and merchants in Holland and England on the other.[14] We know the family backgrounds of some of these men and can trace their roots in long-distance trade in the region to earlier generations. One of these was Henrik Horneman, born in Flensburg in 1644, who married a merchant's widow in Trondheim in 1669. His grandfather is known to have traded with northern Norway in the early 1600s. How Henrik Horneman first came to Trondheim is unknown, but it is likely that he had been sailing on one of the many Flensburg ships trading with the town. The immigrant merchants kept in contact with their place of origin, as did the Englishman Thomas Hammond, for example, whom we can first trace in Trondheim in the 1650s. He was then travelling as a merchant, but in 1659 he married in Trondheim and settled there, continuing to trade with his brother in London as a partner.

---

[11]Sogner, *Trondheim bys historie*, 220; Gerhard Kraack, *Die Flensburger Geburtsbriefe: Auswanderung aus Flensburg 1550-1750* (Flensburg, 1977), 11; and Theodor Link, *Flensburgs Überseehandel von 1755 bis 1807* (Neumünster, 1959), 22 ff.

[12]Link, *Flensburgs Überseehandel*, uses this as his main explanation. See also Olaus Schmidt, "Den slesvigske indflytning til Trondhjem paa 1600- og 1700-tallet," *Norsk Slektshistorisk Tidsskrift*, III (1932), 1-27; and Erick Hoffmann, *Flensburg. Geschichte einer Grenzstadt* (Flensburg, 1966), 127.

[13]Flensburg Stadtarchiv (FSA), Altes Archiv, A 305, I, Handel på Finnmark, 23 February 1641, 3 March and 2 April 1652 and 27 January 1655; Brev fra kommersekollegiet til borgermester og råd i Flensburg, 20 December 1684; Brev fra Moth i danske kanselli, 26 May 1688; A 34, Ratsgerichtprot. No. 18 (1679-1686), fol. 337b, 30 December 1684; and No. 19 (1687-1692), fol. 86b, 1 June 1688.

[14]Sogner, *Trondheim bys historie*, 24 and 57.

What kinds of resources did these immigrants bring with them when they settled in Trondheim? Most had cultural capital from being brought up in a family environment with experience in international trade. In addition, they had social capital from their family and friendship connections in their home town and possibly from an apprenticeship with merchants who were part of an international mercantile network.[15] When Herman Hoë was sent to Trondheim as an apprentice, his cultural and social background was well known to his employer. Several other apprentices were in the same way brought from their city of origin. The first immigrants probably had a history of family connections or had been trading and travelling for some years before settling in Trondheim; they thus had an opportunity to establish acquaintances or even to arrange a marriage.[16] A concrete example should illustrate this point. The Altona merchant Johan Hinrich Mathiessen sent a letter to his business partner, Herman Hoë, for delivery to Otto Sommer, a pharmacist in Trondheim. In the letter he explained that his son, after several journeys to Trondheim, wanted to settle there and marry Sommer's daughter.[17]

Some of the immigrants brought financial capital as well. When Lorentz Angell settled in Trondheim about 1650, he arrived with his brother and sister on his own ship.[18] He must already – through inheritance, trade or the accumulation of credit – have amassed sufficient resources to purchase a vessel and to launch his trade. Herman Hoë mentioned that after completing his apprenticeship he started his business with some inherited capital.[19] Some of the merchants had quite large amounts of initial capital, as did the brothers Henrik and Broder Lysholm, who settled as merchants in Trondheim in 1751 and 1761, respectively, and soon became part of the city's elite.[20] For most, how-

---

[15]The concepts of economic, social and cultural capital, as used by the French sociologist Pierre Bourdieu, are useful in describing how this integration worked. See Pierre Bourdieu, "Sur le povoir symbolique," *Annales*, No. 3 (1977), 405-411; and Bourdieu, *La distinction: Critique sociale du jugement* (Paris, 1979).

[16]For some of the early immigrants, the first certain reference to their stay in Trondheim was their marriage. For example, Lorentz Mortensen Angell married Margrethe Hansdatter Puls in 1653, and Henrik Horneman married the widow Anna Nilsdatter Tønder in 1669. Thomas Hammond is known to have sailed to Trondheim before he married Elisabeth Sommerschield in 1659.

[17]RSAT, Private Archive 280, Hoë 16.4.

[18]Bull, *Thomas Angell*, 28.

[19]RSAT, Private Archive 280, Hoë, 16.1, January 1773.

[20]Kraack, *Die Flensburger Geburtsbriefe*, 38; and FSA, A 235, II/754, 27 February 1748.

ever, it is difficult to establish what economic resources they brought. Yet contemporaries felt that with the right kind of cultural and social capital it was
possible to succeed in trade even without initial economic resources.[21]

The Merchants' Position in Trondheim

The position of individual merchants was based in part on the resources they
brought with them. This included their international networks, as many had
strong family trading traditions in trade, often involving Norway, and were
eager to maintain their connections abroad. But to be successful they also
needed to integrate into the local elite socially, and intermarriage was an important way to do this. Another method was to become involved in city administration and political activities. This was logical, since much of their success depended upon their position as intermediaries between the hinterland, the
city and international markets. The connections they developed enabled them
to recruit inhabitants of the region into the export industries as workers in the
forests, sawmills and mines, as well as in shipping and fishing. As intermediaries between city and hinterland, the merchants managed, with the support of
the growing state, to a large degree to monopolize foreign connections and
divide commerce between themselves and other traders who were only allowed
to trade inside the country.[22] This prominence gave them visibility, and it was
only natural that they should be seen as the kinds of people who ought to be
entrusted with political power. This clout in turn aided them in developing
their businesses.

Economic Strategies

A merchant involved in international trade had to build networks. The centre
of his trade was the household, where the merchant not only lived but also
often conducted his business.[23] Most merchants in Trondheim had their houses
along the river, which served as the city's harbour. Their warehouses lay in
close proximity to their dwellings and other buildings. The operation of the
household depended on all its members, which implies that the married couple

---

[21]RSAT, Private Archive 280, Hoë 16.4, 16 July 1771.

[22]Ida Bull, "Handelskapitalismens tid 1650-1850," in Bull, *et al.* (eds.),
Trøndelags historie, Vol. 2 (Trondheim, 2005).

[23]Ida Bull, "Merchant Households and Their Networks in Eighteenth-Century
Trondheim," *Continuity and Change,* XVII, No. 2 (2002), 213.

was the core of the business in a sort of joint household economy.[24] Indeed, under Norwegian law the husband and wife owned their property in common. Although the husband had the right to dispose of their common property (as well as anything the wife might have brought to the marriage as a dowry), he could not do so without his wife's consent.[25] For some of the early immigrants, entering an already existing household by marrying a widow gave them a head start in their new environment. One example was Henrik Horneman, who first appeared in local sources in 1669 when he married Anna Nilsdatter Tønder, the widow of Ole Fastesen Schancke, a merchant and member of the magistracy. Anna Tønder had been Ole Schancke's third wife, and after his death she was left with a considerable fortune which enabled Horneman quickly to become one of Trondheim's most important merchants.[26] Thus, establishing a household was not only a social but also an economic strategy. A "good" marriage enabled an aspiring merchant to acquire additional economic resources in the form of a dowry, inheritance or even credit. Moreover, besides his own family network he could enter the economic network of his wife's family. A wife would also mean an extra pair of hands and additional knowledge.[27]

To secure a position in the upper ranks of the city's economy it was also important to have a house and warehouse along or near the river. Marrying a widow, as Henrik Horneman did, was one way to do this. Marrying a daughter from an important family could also bring other benefits. For example, Lorentz Mortensen Angell received property on the death of his father-in-

---

[24]The concept "household economy" or "family economy" was introduced in the 1970s by Hans Medick in connection with the debate on proto-industry, and about the same time by Louise Tilly and Joan Scott as part of their studies of women's work. See Hans Medick, "The Proto-Industrial Family Economy: The Structural Function of Household and Family during the Transition from Peasant Society to Industrial Capitalism," *Social History*, III, No. 1 (1976), 291-315; and Joan Scott and Louise Tilly, *Women, Work and Family* (New York. 1978; 2nd ed., New York, 1989). How the household was integrated into capitalist enterprise was further analyzed by Leonore Davidoff and Catherine Hall, *Family Fortunes: Men and Women of the English Middle Class 1780-1850* (London, 1987).

[25]*King Christian V's Norwegian Law (1687)*, book 5, chaps. 1-10.

[26]Henry Berg, *Trondheim før Cicignon: gater og gårder før reguleringen 1681* (Trondheim, 1951), 274.

[27]Catherine Hall, *White, Male and Middle Class: Explorations in Feminism and History* (Cambridge, 1992), 180.

law who, as an immigrant himself, seems to have come into this by marrying an heiress of some means.[28]

Later immigrants often were introduced into the circle of traders as apprentices. It seems that the migration of young men most often was arranged by their family rather than by the boys themselves. The migration was a sort of exchange within a network that tied individuals in Trondheim and Flensburg to each other. Trondheim was not the only place to which Flensburgers sent their sons, but after the first ones had settled there it was easier for others to follow. An example, albeit hardly typical, was Hans Lorenzen, who was born in 1662. When he was fifteen years old his mother decided to send him to Trondheim to apprentice with Henrik Horneman. For him the journey was fateful; the ship was captured, and he landed in prison before taking an apprenticeship in Amsterdam.[29] Herman Hoë had at least two apprentices from Flensburg, arranged through family and neighbours, and he also arranged apprenticeships for boys from Flensburg with fellow merchants in Trondheim.[30] After completing his apprenticeship, a young boy could stay in Trondheim, return to his city of origin or move elsewhere. Hilmar von Lutten, who was member of the city council in Flensburg when he died in 1722, had been an apprentice in Trondheim between 1667 and 1674.[31] Christian Andersen Lorck for some years had a son of a second cousin from Flensburg as an apprentice. The young man later returned to Flensburg, bringing with him some commissions for Lorck.[32] Such men with experience in both cities would obviously strengthen the knowledge of the other place and might influence others to go there. When parents in Flensburg considered sending their sons to Trondheim, having relatives, former neighbours or friends in the town made the decision easier. Moreover, when merchants in Trondheim decided to have apprentices from Flensburg, one reason was to strengthen the existing network. A Danish civil servant travelling in the Trondheim area commented that the merchants preferred newcomers from Flensburg because they usually had more of the "spirit" that made a good merchant. He might also have added that the established mer-

---

[28]Berg, *Trondheim før Cicignon*, 272.

[29]O.H. Moller, "Lebensbeschreibung des Hans Lorenzen," in *Das Flensburger Schiffergelag in Vergangenheit und Gegenwart: Kleine Reihe der Gesellschaft für Flensburger Stadtgeschichte, Vol. 3* (Flensburg, 1979), 70.

[30]Bull, *De Trondhjemske handelshusene*, 102.

[31]Kraack, *Die Flensburger Geburtsbriefe*, 13.

[32]RSAT, Private Archive Lorck, innenlandsk kopibok, 1811-1812; and Bull, *De Trondjemske handelshusene*, 117.

chant more than likely knew the new arrival's parents and that this would make the transition much easier.[33]

Establishing a good relationship with their employer was a good economic strategy. Herman Hoë's family wrote several letters urging him to behave in a way that would please the employer and his wife so that they might help him to start his own business after completing his apprenticeship.[34] Indeed, several apprentices were helped in this way by former employers.[35] Loans might be one method. Herman Hoë's debt to his employer was mentioned in 1777, after he had started his own business, and when his estate was assessed at what for him was a difficult time in 1791, his former employer's widow had a considerable amount of money invested in the warehouses he had bought from her. Herman's brother, Christian, also received start-up loans from his employers, the Meincke family. We can not know how far this help would have brought him, since he died after only a few years in trade. Herman took over his brother's loans, and he got them on good terms due to his brother's good relationship with Meincke.[36]

The most important economic assistance the apprentices received from their employers took the form of recommendations and letters of introduction to their economic networks. Herman Hoë asked his employer to recommend him for credit from a merchant house in Amsterdam, believing that many people there and in other countries would trust him if they knew that he had been in Beyer's service. Beyer wrote letters of introduction to several of his business connections, which enabled Hoë to start his own network. He was even allowed to start building up his own business before leaving Beyer's employ. That meant that he had food, shelter and a salary when he started to trade.[37] Similarly, Christian Lorck received letters of introduction which he brought on an introductory tour to Copenhagen, Hamburg and Amsterdam.[38]

References from employers, however, did not guarantee success. Of the many letters that Herman Hoë wrote to merchants in various cities, only a few led to anything. Given the commercial importance of the Dutch Republic, the most important connections for a new merchant were in Amsterdam. The house of Nedermeyer and Voogd declined to advance credit to Hoë despite

---

[33]Christen Pram, *Kopibøker fra reiser i Norge 1804-06* (Oslo, 1964), 51.

[34]RSAT, Private Archive 280, Hoë 16.4.

[35]Sogner, *Trondheim bys historie*, 483 and 489 makes this an important point.

[36]RSAT, Private Archive 280, Hoë 16.1 and 16.3.

[37]*Ibid.*, Hoë 16.1.

[38]*Ibid.*, Private Archive Lorck, copybook, 1778-1784.

Beyer's recommendation. Another of Beyer's connections, the firm of Laasbye, was willing to start a connection on credit, albeit on conditions that Hoë considered impossible to accept. For his part, Laasbye believed that the terms were reasonable and were offered only because of Beyer's recommendation. Hoë was obviously offended, and the connection did not last. A connection in Amsterdam was necessary, though, and the same day that he terminated the Laasbye connection Hoë wrote to the house of Linsen and Weening, asking for credit on the same terms as those extended to Beyer. The answer again was negative, but Hoë had to accept a trading connection even without credit. The fish and copper he sent Linsen and Weening in 1773 was the beginning of a long-term relationship.[39] Hoë had fewer problems starting a relationship in Altona, but unless Beyer was willing to guarantee to underwrite his losses, his connection there would not advance anything more than short-term credit.

Even if starting a new connection on favourable terms was not easy, support from an employer was a great help. Lorck, for example, managed to secure credit with the help of letters of reference. On his introductory tour he arranged a large credit from the Suhrs in Copenhagen upon which he could draw to purchase goods to bring home for sale.[40] Even if the employer was the main source of letters of reference, a larger network in Trondheim could be useful. Both Hoë and Lorck sometimes referred to other merchants in Trondheim with whom they were familiar. Support from employers, relatives and friends was important at the outset. Sometimes this support might be in the form of capital, inheritances, loans or guarantees, but at other times it was merely a statement indicating that the new merchant belonged to the "right circles" at home and ought to be admitted to those circles abroad where this social and cultural capital could be transformed into money and credit.

To start a business from Trondheim it was important not only to establish a local position and international connections but also to build a regional network that was able to produce goods for export. Otto Beyer came to Trondheim from Flensburg as a young apprentice, which enabled him to establish a network of friends and contacts before he started as an independent merchant. His marriage in 1739 connected him to a district and a trade of importance for his export business. His wife, Else Lind, was the sister of a man on the Møre coast who for many years brought fish to Trondheim.[41] Herman Hoë did not marry early, but when he did, his wife connected him to a family in Helgeland, which made him better able to enlarge his fish trade. By the time of the marriage, he had already been receiving fish deliveries from his future father-in-law for some time. Connections who could deliver quality goods

---

[39]*Ibid.*, Private Archive 280, Hoë 1.6, 11.1 and 13.1.

[40]*Ibid.*, Private Archive Lorck, copybook, 1778-1784.

[41]Aashild Berg, *Smøla bygdebok*, *Vol.* 2 (Trondheim, 1983), 222 ff.

were important. In his early years as a merchant, Hoë was eager to make a good impression on his foreign commission agents by sending them excellent goods. In his letters to agents in the fishing districts, he took care to explain that the herring he would buy had to be fat, of a standard size, shiny and well salted. In his letters to commission agents abroad he expressed regret if the quality did not always meet expectations.[42]

To reduce risk, trading with family members could be useful. Hoë imported corn from his uncle in the Flensburg area and traded with a childhood friend there for some years. Lorck also traded with family members in Flensburg. Family and kin comprised an important network because they were reliable, more committed than others and could be counted on to provide information. This was one of the reasons for sending young boys as apprentices abroad. Besides learning the trade, they would enlarge and strengthen the family network. That was obvious in the case of Henrik Horneman and his eldest son, Ole, who was sent to Amsterdam to learn the trade. While in the Dutch Republic he married a merchant's daughter, and the two opened a trading business. Henrik Horneman and several of Trondheim's merchants used Ole, and later his widow, as their commission agent in Amsterdam.[43] The immigrants' abilities to construct economic networks locally, internationally and regionally, and to integrate these networks, were important elements in the success of their economic strategies.

Social Strategies

When they immigrated to Trondheim, a few of the merchants brought money. But more important was their experience in international trade and their contacts in an international network. Those who came to the city as a result of the network of the long-distance trade were already in a position to integrate into the circle of people who belonged to this network, however small it may have been. To shape these contacts into an integrated circle, marriage was important. When Thomas Hammond moved from London to Trondheim, it was motivated by his marriage to Elisabeth Sommerschield, the daughter of another immigrant merchant, Henry Sommerschield or "Henry Englishman." The father-in-law made his fortune from trade in timber and herring, while the son-in-law continued the timber trade using his brother in London as the recipient. Lorentz Mortensen Angell was another example of an immigrant who married into the local elite. Indeed, he married not once but three times. His first marriage in 1653 was to Margrethe Puls, the daughter of an established immigrant merchant from Hamburg. With this marriage Lorentz entered the leading circle

---

[42]RSAT, Private Archive 280, Hoë 11.1, 1773.

[43]Sprauten, "Hans Horneman;" and Bull, *Thomas Angell*, 53.

of the city. The marriage also brought him a considerable inheritance. His second marriage was to a woman with a strong family background in the northern Norwegian fisheries. His third marriage was to a woman who was not wealthy herself but was the widow of a man who had been trading in copper. Lorentz's three marriages strengthened his connections with the city's merchant elite, the fishing interests in northern Norway and the mining interests in Trøndelag. Many other examples of marriages establishing important relationships could be cited.

The Trondheim merchants were well aware of the importance of a good marriage. For immigrants, the knowledge and connections to family and friends were extremely important. Through marriage they could construct their social capital in a way that would help them to convert it into financial success. A description of Trondheim in 1702 divided the most important merchants into three kinship circles. Around Albert Angell (a second-generation immigrant), Henrik Horneman (a first-generation immigrant) and Jens Hansen Collin (a Dane who came to Trondheim as a civil servant and then entered business) were clustered their sons, sons-in-law and brothers-in-law; together, they comprised the upper strata of the Trondheim bourgeoisie.[44] Later, these circles integrated further through intermarriage between the families.

Political Strategies

The merchants were part not only of the economic and social but also of the political elite. The English immigrant Henrik Sommerschield was more than merely a merchant. He is known to have operated in 1605-1611 from London, where he imported timber from Norway. In the years immediately following he sailed often to Trondheim, finally settling there some time in the early 1620s. He soon became part of the administrative elite as well, was entrusted with some tasks for the Cathedral in 1625 and became a member of the city council in the period 1631-1648.[45] He was not the only immigrant merchant to achieve such positions. When the Danish-Norwegian king in 1660 usurped absolute power, the city administrations were tied more closely to the crown. Henrik Sommerschield, as an early immigrant, was elected to the city council by the burghers, but after 1660 the king alone had the power to appoint the council. While members of the council increasingly were bureaucrats who specialized in administration, some of the members were still recruited from the city, primarily from the circle of the long-distance merchants comprised of first- or second-generation immigrants. When the merchants Hans Hagerup

---

[44]Sogner, *Trondheim bys historie*, 279.

[45]Bull, *Thomas Angell*, 45; and Svein Tore Dahl, *Embetsmenn i Midt-Norge i tiden 1536-1660* (Trondheim, 1999), 18 and 39.

(married to the daughter of the immigrant Thomas Hammond) and Hans Horneman (son of an immigrant) were appointed to the council in 1731, it was even suggested that there *should* be merchants on the council.[46] Among other things, they could be useful sources of credit for the city.

At the same time this bureaucratization developed, a consultative organ was founded that was elected from among the town's burghers (*de eligerte menn*). This body was legitimated in the Norwegian law of Christian V in 1687, which stated that the city accounts should be investigated by the council and the "best burghers," who should sign and agree to the register of taxes.[47] This board developed as a more powerful organ towards the end of the eighteenth century. Immigrant merchants were among those elected to this board and to several special commissions. The immigrants and the long-distance merchants were obviously involved in governing the city. But how far did their involvement go? And was it a result of a conscious strategy?

The politics and economic regulations enacted by the city authorities and the state were obviously of great importance to the merchants. The state in the seventeenth and especially the eighteenth century followed policies that favoured trade and manufacturing. This was a result of the bourgeoisie's growing influence and their stronger involvement in bureaucracy. [48] It is clear that the immigrants were part of this.

Several of the new immigrants became church wardens. In the Cathedral, Johan Manzin, who was born in Flensburg, was a church warden in the period 1733-1748.[49] Otto Beyer occupied the same post between 1748 and 1760. Among his ancestors in Flensburg were several members of the city council, as was his father. Mathias Friis was a church warden in 1761-1772, and Ditlev Gadebusch followed in 1772-1810.[50] Apart from being a church warden for many years, Gadebusch was also elected director of the bourgeois social club, *Borgerklubben,* in 1790. All these men were merchants born in Flensburg. Immigrant merchants also played a role in the other church in

---

[46]RSAT, Magistrates Archives Db22; and Bull, *De Trondhjemske handelshusene*, 284.

[47]Ida Bull and Synnøve Rian, *Katalog over Trondheim magistratsarkiv* (Trondheim, 1998), 97.

[48]Ståle Dyrvik, *et al.*, *Norsk økonomisk historie 1500-1970, Vol. 1* (Bergen, 1979), 84 ff.

[49]Sogner, *Trondheim bys historie*, 225.

[50]Mathias Friis was in 1786 described as a man who by diligence had achieved considerable means. His belief in God was said to be so great that he never insured any ship, even though sometimes this led to large losses; Thaulow, *Personalhistorie*, 336.

Trondheim, Our Lady. Hans Puls came from Hamburg, likely before 1650. He soon got a position in the church, where he was mentioned in 1657 as one of the men deciding who to appoint as the vicar and in 1659 as church warden. His son-in-law, Lorentz Mortensen Angell, inherited the latter position. Christen Rasmussen Flensburg was a church warden from 1665 to 1679.[51] Henrik Horneman had the position until his death in 1717, when his son Hans followed in his footsteps.[52]

Some of the immigrant merchants were also appointed members of the city council. Henrik Sommerschield was a member of the council as well as mayor and a member of the court of protection. The merchant Marcus Jacobsen Angell served on the council between 1670 and 1676, as did Lorentz Mortensen Angell from 1671 until 1685. Both were also among the four captains of the civic guards. Lorentz Angell was one of the burghers who set up the tax register. Søren Bygball, a member of the council in the period 1693-1708, was born in Jutland and was one of the richest merchants in Trondheim. He was the second husband of Sara Hammond, who had first been married to the president of the council, Albert Angell.[53] Later, however, fewer immigrant merchants were members of the council. Hans Horneman, a second-generation immigrant, and Hans Hagerup, who married the daughter of an immigrant, were exceptions. After Horneman's death in 1764, no active merchants entered the city council until Hans Knudtzon, an immigrant from Bredstedt in Schleswig, who was vice-mayor and mayor in the period 1789-1806.[54] Otherwise, the members of the council at this time were mostly bureaucrats with juridical education.

While the city council evolved as a more specialized bureaucratic organ in the late eighteenth century, the elected burgher representatives on the parallel board became more influential. Their influence especially concerned economic matters, and they were asked for advice on most such issues. To be elected only required the possession of burgher rights, but in practice only merchants were elected, and most often they were the ones engaged in international trade. Both Herman Hoë and Christian Andersen Lorck were members of this board. A register of elected men and those responsible for the tax register in the period 1779-1787 included eighteen names, and international merchants, often of foreign origin, dominated. Six of the eighteen were born in Flensburg, four in the German region surrounding Flensburg, one in Ham-

---

[51]Berg, *Trondheim før Cicignon*, 270.

[52]Supphellen, *Trondheims historie*, 306.

[53]Dahl, *Embetsmenn i Midt-Norge*, 33 and 40; and Bull, *Thomas Angell*, 31.

[54]Henrik Mathiesen, *Magistratspersoner i Trondhjem 1377-1922* (Trondheim, 1945).

burg, one in Denmark, one in Jemtland (the Swedish region east of Trondheim), one in Levanger (a small town north of Trondheim), three in Trondheim itself (albeit one with ancestors from the Flensburg region), and one was of unknown origin. All but the last were merchants who possessed the right to trade internationally. The last was also a merchant, but he only had the right to trade inside the country.[55]

Membership in the city council or to other appointed or elected official positions conferred a degree of power over the city's economy and the circumstances under which merchants operated. These men could influence what kind of tasks the city undertook and how much they should pay in taxes. Positions on the council also gave access to the regional commissioner (*stiftamtmann*), the king's highest civil servant in the region, and enabled them to influence decisions at a higher level. A second-generation immigrant, Albert Angell, and a first-generation migrant, Søren Bygball (married to Angell's widow), functioned as deputies in the regional commissioner's absence. These positions could also involve economic reward. Members of the city council were given salaries, and the elected men could be given salaried commissions, such as being a warden for one of the charitable institutions. Those positions also provided access to deliveries of goods to the institutions, as for instance when a new workhouse was built in 1788. Material for the buildings and linen and cotton for the inmates' work were supplied by the merchants.[56] In addition to what the positions could confer in power, influence and income, they also imparted a certain prestige.

While official positions provided benefits they also entailed some discomfort. The workload for members of the city council was usually two or three days per week. Albert Angell complained that his official commitments consumed so much time that he was forced to neglect his own business. Others thought the opposite, claiming that Angell was too absorbed in private business to handle his official duties properly.[57] Although some merchants had positions on the council after Angell, they did not dominate. To accept election to the board of elected men was a duty for burghers, but it did not involve a heavy workload unless the task was combined with other assignments. Tax collectors and registrars of taxes had time-consuming jobs, and the burghers were supposed to perform such tasks in turn to develop a joint responsibility. Some of the assignments involved substantial economic responsibility, such as tax collectors and the wardens of charitable societies. It was not without cause that such assignments were often called civic "burdens." Actually, the posts of tax

---

[55]RSAT, Trondhjems stift og amt, Fe 18; and Bull, *De Trondjemske handelshusene*, 285.

[56]RSAT, Trondhjems arbeidsanstalt, møteprotokoll og journal, 1788-1808.

[57]Bull, *Thomas Angell*, 60.

collector or warden of a charitable society were so unpleasant that they were eventually transformed into salaried positions. The former was supposed to be taken in turn, but in 1740 Hans Brun stated that for ten years he had been hired by the appointed tax collectors to do the job. He was then given the position as a permanent post.[58]

Not everyone freely offered to take on such burdens. Indeed, quite a few tried to avoid these tasks, and being an immigrant was one of the reasons offered to avoid election. In 1728, for example, Henrik Meincke applied to be excused because as a man of foreign origin he did not have sufficient knowledge of his fellow citizens' habits or Norwegian law. As an immigrant, he argued, he was qualified only to take care of his own business, which would suffer if he accepted an official assignment. The city council did not accept his rationale, believing that if Meincke were exempted many more would demand the same thing, and there would not be enough men to fill the necessary positions. Meincke had settled in the city five years earlier, married a wealthy widow and became one of the most successful merchants. He was young and healthy, and could, like most people in Flensburg, speak and write good Danish. The regional commissioner supported the city council, and Meincke had to register as a burgher and take on those posts to which he was appointed.[59] Herman Hoë and Hans Knudtzon in 1776 tried the same gambit, using similar arguments. They were willing to pay a fee to be exempted, but neither application was accepted. Both had official assignments in the following years, and Knudtzon even became mayor.[60] It was not impossible to avoid the civic burdens, though. A younger Henrik Meincke in 1774 was given royal permission to be excused from all civic burdens if he paid 1000 *daler* to the city for the privilege. His grounds were the same as the others, as well as poor health. This time the regional commissioner supported his position.[61] The main reason that his application waqs approved was that the price was high enough. While Hoë had offered only 200 *daler*, Meincke's 1000 *daler* would mean a considerable supplement to the city treasury.

To influence national politics and economics, a position in the local community was an important point of departure. As long as there was an absolute monarchy, political influence had to go through the king's civil servants,

---

[58]Bull and Rian, *Katalog*, 64.

[59]RSAT, Trondhjems magistratsarkiv FE 9, Trondheim stift og amt B35, copybook 1728, 27 November1728; and Norway, National Archives, Supplikker 1728, II, 520.

[60]RSAT, Trondheim stift og amt FZ 14; Trondheim magistratsarkiv FE 9; and Private Archive 280, Hoë 42.2.

[61]RSAT, Trondhjems magistratsarkiv CA 2.

friends and confidants. An entire system of patron-client relationships and influence systems evolved. The immigrants have not been studied closely in this respect, but there is no reason to believe that they tried such approaches any less eagerly than the next generation. The second-generation immigrant Hans Horneman cultivated a particularly large circle of friends within the civil service, both locally and in the central administration. He used his connections shrewdly to further his own interests. His connections made him useful as a broker between the local community and the central administration, and his services in such matters were used by his friends and neighbours.[62] The merchants used all their networks to advance their own and their friends' interests.

As politics became more democratic, the same group of men remained active. Hans Knudtzon, who was sent from his home in Schleswig as a young man in 1767 to learn the trade in the house of Broder Brodersen Lysholm (also from Schleswig), was one of the most important merchants and shipowners, as well as an influential politician around 1800. Locally, he advanced to become mayor; nationally, he was elected to the first parliament (*Stortinget*) in the autumn of 1814. From parliament he was chosen to take part in a delegation to Stockholm in December 1814 to inform the Swedish king that he was also elected to be the Norwegian monarch. Knudtzon was also involved in establishing the first national bank.[63] But by that time mercantile immigration to Trondheim was no longer important. Descendants of earlier immigrants were still among the city's elite, although in the years to come they mixed with people of diverse origins, often from the Norwegian countryside. The distinctiveness of this group was slowly but surely being eroded.

Conclusion

What was the position of the immigrant merchants in Trondheim? Can we see conflicts with the native population? When people of foreign origin started to enter international trade from Trondheim in the early to mid-seventeenth century, they did not so much compete with other merchants as continue an activity that had previously been performed by travelling merchants and ship masters. They quickly and smoothly found their niches in the city and entered its elite, from where they strengthened their position through marriage. Their rapid integration into the elite, which implies that any bad feelings against them were soon dissipated, are not easily visible in the records.

---

[62]Knut Sprauten, "Hans Horneman: Med embetsverket i lomma," in *Trondheim på 1700-tallet: Årbok Trøndelag folkemuseum – Sverresborg* (Trondheim, 1993). Albert Angell, another second-generation immigrant, obviously had the same kind of connections, even if the source material is poorer in his case.

[63]Ida Bull, "Hans Carl Knudtzon," *Norsk biografisk leksikon, Vol. 5* (Oslo, 2002).

Before the merchants of foreign origin started to settle in Trondheim, there was only a small and weak group of native traders. When more immigrants followed the pioneers, they were often relatives, or at least came from the same city and had the same social and cultural baggage. There could of course be conflicts between the merchants, but these were not especially frequent between new immigrants and more settled traders, except when the newcomers tried to evade their civic burdens by claiming ignorance of local conditions. They were expected to take up their position in the bourgeoisie.

There are signs that the lower social strata took a different view. For instance, in times of food shortages, merchants could become the target of popular insurrection. One such event occurred in 1796, when people in the city unloaded corn from a ship in the harbour. The cargo belonged to some wholesalers in the city, including Christian Andersen Lorck. This riot, however, was about issues of class and wealth. In the same way, there are comments in broadsheet ballads which show hostility towards the rich and "fine" people. But there is no reason to see this as indicative of a general hostility towards immigrants: rather, it was about the class into which the immigrant merchants had integrated with remarkable speed and effectiveness.

In the Eye of the Storm:
The Influence of Maritime and Trade
Networks on the Development of Ostend and
Vice Versa during the Eighteenth Century

Jan Parmentier

Introduction

In the Austrian Netherlands Ostend was the sole mercantile port city with an international character. Situated in the southern part of the North Sea and surrounded by major ports (including London, Dunkirk and Rotterdam) belonging to the main maritime nations of the eighteenth century, Ostend had become quite attractive to merchants and entrepreneurs who wanted to develop or expand their business networks on the Continent or in the British Isles.

During the last three decades of the eighteenth century these networks reached as far as North America, the West Indies and East Asia. Surprisingly, however, the trade opportunities and buoyant business environment hardly affected the demographic evolution of the town throughout the first half of the eighteenth century. The population of Ostend fluctuated in this period between 5000 and 6000 inhabitants. In 1698 the town had 5728 citizens, but this number dropped markedly during the War of the Spanish Succession to 5000. After 1770 the population increased and doubled during the early 1780s.[1] This phenomenon can be explained by the fact that Ostend functioned mainly as a transhipment port and a distribution centre. Besides a few maritime enterprises like shipyards, ropewalks and sawmills, hardly any proto-industries were established in or around the town. Moreover, the optimal waterway connections with Bruges, Ghent and Dunkirk, which existed from the mid-seventeenth century, made it unnecessary for entrepreneurs from Flanders and the north of France to move their companies to the coast. To stimulate traffic between the port and the inland towns, the Bruges-Ostend Canal was opened in 1623 and was further improved in 1666-1669 to allow small seagoing vessels to sail as far as Bruges. In 1672-1676 a massive sluice was constructed on the canal in Slijkens, five miles south of Ostend, to improve this connection. From 1641

---

[1]J. Mertens, "Het haardgeld te Oostende in 1533, haar inwoners en hun sociale stratificatie," *Ostendiana*, II (1975), 40; and Daniël Farasyn, *1769-1794: De 18de eeuwse bloeiperiode van Oostende* (Oostende, 1998), 187.

onwards, Ostend profited from the opening of a new canal between Bruges and Dunkirk, which was mainly navigated by barges.[2]

As a result, Ostend did not experience rapid demographic expansion in the eighteenth century similar to port towns, such as Rotterdam, Cork or Dunkirk, which were less dependent economically on other urban centres.[3] On the other hand, the population explosion of the 1780s was due to massive immigration during the Fourth Anglo-Dutch War when the Austrian Netherlands was neutral.[4] The economic boom also attracted a number of young people, which stimulated population growth. By 1789 it had 14,851 residents, its maximum in the eighteenth century. During the following years, when economic life in Flanders was disrupted by the French occupation, the number of inhabitants dropped again to only 10,222 in December 1798.[5]

Competition between the various ports scattered along the southern shore of the North Sea was also noticeable in Ostend, especially in the case of Dunkirk. During the Eighty Years' War (1568-1648) Dunkirk emerged as a privateering centre, but it also developed rapidly-growing mercantile activities. Between 1600 and 1650 the Dunkirk merchant community comprised about 150 firms with a primary emphasis on international maritime trade. Merchant families based in Antwerp, Ghent, Bruges and Ostend represented about half of this group, and the textile trade with the Iberian Peninsula, Dover and the Thames Estuary provided their main source of income.[6] Dunkirk only came

---

[2]André Vandewalle, "Op zoek naar nieuwe uitwegen," in Valentin Vermeersch (ed.), *Brugge en de zee: Van Bryggia tot Zeebrugge* (Antwerpen, 1982), 76-81; and Jan Parmentier, "Een vermaeck'lijck treck-schuytje: Een spiegel van de trekvaart in de Nederlanden tijdens de 17de en 18de eeuw," in *Een trekschuit voor koningen: De barge tussen Gent en Brugge* (Gent, 1993), 38-39.

[3]David Dickson, *Old World Colony: Cork and South Munster, 1630-1830* (Cork, 2005), 303-311; Joannes P. Sigmond, *Nederlandse zeehavens tussen 1500 en 1800* (Amsterdam, 1989), 112-123; and Alain Cabantous, *La Mer et les Hommes: Pêcheurs et matelots dunkerquois de Louis XIV à la Révolution* (Dunkerque, 1980), 41-45.

[4]Jan Parmentier, "Profit and Neutrality: The Case of Ostend, 1781-1783," in David J. Starkey, E.S. van Eyck van Heslinga and J.A. de Moor (eds.), *Pirates and Privateers: New Perspectives on the War on Trade in the Eighteenth and Nineteenth Centuries* (Exeter, 1997), 207.

[5]Rijksarchief Brugge (RAB), Leiedep. no. 1569; and Universiteitsbibliotheek Gent (UBG), Fonds Hye-Hoys (FHH), no. 1908, Tableau de la Population d'Ostende (December 1798).

[6]Jan Parmentier, "Een maritiem-economische schets van de deltahavens, 1400-1800," in Maurits Ebben and Simon Groenveld (eds.), *De Scheldedelta als ver-*

under the control of the French crown in 1662, so many maritime and mercantile families had relatives on both sides of the border. Indeed, even in the eighteenth century it was considered Ostend's twin. Any noticeable increase in employment opportunities in one of these ports was accompanied by a temporary migration of mariners and merchants.[7] The close links between the two ports also offered businessmen in Flanders and northern France an opportunity to react at short notice to changing political and economic circumstances in both countries and to make use of whichever port provided the more advantageous facilities to transport and distribute commodities. Therefore, the network of merchants based in Ostend always sought to maintain an active link with Dunkirk.

On the other hand, after 1662 the port of Ostend, with a harbour that could handle middle-sized merchantmen, became the sole outlet to the sea for Flemish and Brabant merchants.[8] Nieuwpoort, the second port on the Flemish west coast, served only as a centre for fishing and privateering. Despite the fact that Ostend offered many advantages to enterprising merchants, shipping to and from this Flemish port was often problematic. The lack of a deep natural harbour on a shallow, sandy coast obliged the local magistrate and the States of Flanders, the provincial government, to invest substantial sums to prevent the silting of the channel. Moreover, several sandbanks constantly hindered access to the port.[9]

Finally, to understand the complete panorama of Ostend we have to bear in mind that throughout the eighteenth century it remained an important garrison town. The French often saw it as a gateway to Britain, while England traditionally considered it a stronghold on the Continent. This explains why Ostend frequently played a key role in maritime conflicts during the century.

At the dawn of the eighteenth century the involvement of the Ostend merchant community in international maritime trade was rather modest. Barely twenty or thirty merchant houses earned their living from such activities, and

---

binding en scheiding tussen Noord en Zuid, 1500-1800 (Maastricht, 2007), 24; and Eddy Stols, *De Spaanse Brabanders of de handelsbetrekkingen der Zuidelijke Nederlanden met de Iberische Wereld* (2 vols., Brussel, 1971), II, 63.

[7]Cabantous, *La Mer et les Hommes*, 64-81.

[8]After the Treaty of Munster (1648) the Dutch controlled all traffic on the River Scheldt with Antwerp and Ghent; Victor Enthoven, "The Closure of the Scheldt: Closure, What Closure? Trade and Shipping in the Scheldt Estuary, 1559-1609," in Poul Holm and John Edwards (eds.), *North Sea Ports and Harbours – Adaptations to Change* (Esbjerg, 1992), 11-36.

[9]Roland Baetens, "Het uitzicht van de infrastructuur van een kleine Noordzeehaven tijdens het Ancien Régime: het voorbeeld Oostende," *Mededelingen van de Marine Academie*, XXIII (1973-1975), 47-52.

they relied strongly on commission assignments. This picture changed suddenly with the introduction of direct East India trade in 1715. The number of firms operating at an international level doubled and remained more or less constant until the last quarter of the century. Furthermore, the international importance of Ostend was reinforced by the development of trade relations with London, neutral status during the Fourth Anglo-Dutch War and the revival of private trade with the East Indies. As a result, it became the hub for between 150 and 200 merchant houses, many of foreign origin with elaborate international networks, during the latter decades of the eighteenth century.[10] In this essay I intend to analyze the evolution of Ostend's trading networks at a time of constantly changing circumstances based upon a detailed examination of three local firms in the years 1700-1745, 1746-1763 and 1781-1787.

The Irish Connection

In the first decade of the eighteenth century, privateering was the main maritime business in the port of Ostend. The War of the Spanish Succession (1702-1713) provided ideal conditions for the local population involved in maritime affairs to scour the English Channel and the North Sea in search of heavily laden hostile merchantmen.[11] But as a result of this European conflict the port was devastated, and in 1706 an Anglo-Dutch bombardment ruined the town: according to an eyewitness the destruction was comparable with that of Troy.[12] The siege of Ostend led to a major reduction in maritime activity, as about one-third of local mariners migrated to Nieuwport and Dunkirk to reinforce the French privateers. Nevertheless, the profits derived from privateering served as a basis for the development of the East India trade after 1715 when the Austrian administration actively encouraged entrepreneurs from the Southern Netherlands to explore this new market.

The merchant house of the Irish immigrant Thomas Ray, with its link with the Irish diaspora, is a good example of this era. An additional "pull" factor for in-migrant Irish merchants was the presence of fellow countrymen – largely from the counties of Cork, Wexford and Waterford – both in Ostend

---

[10]The estimates of the number of Ostend merchant houses involved in international trade are based on my PhD research; see Jan Parmentier, "De maritieme handel en visserij in Oostende tijdens de achttiende eeuw: Een prosopografische analyse van de internationale Oostendse handelswereld, 1700-1794" (Unpublished PhD thesis, Universiteit Gent, 2001), 1056-1060.

[11]Reinoud Magosse, *Al die willen te kap'ren varen: de Oostendse kaapvaart tijdens de Spaanse Successieoorlog (1702-1713)* (Oostende, 1999), 209.

[12]Stadsarchief Antwerpen (SAA), Insolvente Boedelkamer (IB), no. 547, 15 July 1706.

and the neighbouring Flemish communities. From the middle decades of the seventeenth century, and especially after the outbreak of the 1641 rebellion, Irish merchants, shipowners and, in particular, privateers frequented Flemish ports, and during this period agents of the Confederation of Kilkenny, the body which governed Catholic Ireland during the 1640s, actively recruited experienced mariners in the Spanish Netherlands to man an Irish fleet of privateers. These men originated mainly from Dunkirk and Ostend but included some French, Spanish and even English skippers.[13] Wexford served as the home port for this international community of mariners, who frequently sold captured prizes in Dunkirk, Ostend and occasionally Nieuwpoort.[14] The capture of Wexford by Oliver Cromwell in 1649 deprived the privateers of a safe, well-situated haven and forced some to relocate to Waterford, Galway or the Channel Islands.[15] But the majority chose to settle in the Flemish ports, especially Dunkirk. The shallow waters of the Flemish banks and the Goodwin Sands gave them the opportunity to use small frigates with which the enemy's cumbersome men-of-war found it difficult to deal.[16] Others settled in Ostend, which soon boasted "an Irish quarter."[17] The majority of Irish migrants continued their mercantile and maritime activities during the late seventeenth and early eighteenth century on the Flemish coast or in Bruges. Prominent among them were members of the Carew family from Waterford and the Hamilton family from Killybegs, County Donegal. They moved to Ostend in the summer of 1658 when Cromwell's fleet blockaded Dunkirk, and a coalition of French and English troops besieged the town. Once in Ostend, both families played pioneering roles in the expansion of an international trade network and were dominant in local politics until the late 1680s. They paved the way for a sec-

---

[13]Jane H. Ohlmeyer, "'The Dunkirk of Ireland:' Wexford Privateers during the 1640s," *Journal of the Wexford Historical Society*, XII (1988-1989), 23-25; and Algemeen Rijksarchief Brussel (ARB), Admiraliteit no. 886, Registre de sentence de l'Admirauté de Dunkerque, 1649-1652.

[14]Great Britain, National Archives (TNA/PRO) State Papers (SP), Flanders 77/31, ff. 289-334; and ARB, Admiraliteit no. 886.

[15]Ohlmeyer, "Dunkirk of Ireland," 25-39; and Julian Walton, "The Merchant Communities of Waterford in the 16th and 17th Centuries," in Paul Butel and Louis M. Cullen (eds.), *Cities and Merchants: French and Irish Perspectives on Urban Development, 1500-1900* (Dublin, 1986), 183-192.

[16]ARB, Admiraliteit nos. 275, 276, 604 and 886; TNA/PRO, SP, Flanders 77/31, f. 331; and Roland Baetens, "The Organization and Effects of Flemish Privateering in the Seventeenth Century," *Acta Historiae Neerlandicae*, XI (1976), 48-76.

[17]"Het Ierse kwartier," or the area where the Irish lived in Ostend, was first mentioned in 1654; RAB, Staten van Goed Brugse Vrije, 2de reeks, no. 4836.

ond wave of Irish in-migrants with commercial aspirations and entrepreneurial qualities who arrived in Flanders in the early 1690s.[18]

Thomas Ray (O'Regan) originated from Youghal, a small Irish port and market town near Cork, which emerged during the last quarter of the seventeenth century as an export centre for butter to Flanders and northern France.[19] Ray started his career on the Flemish coast during the late seventeenth century. At first he concentrated on the traditional Irish export trades of butter and hides to the Southern Netherlands and northern France. Through his family connections in Youghal, Cork and Waterford, he managed to build up a prosperous merchant house. In Cork, for instance, he placed orders with his brother, Charles, and his uncle, Thomas Coppinger, who was recognized as an influential and substantial wholesaler. His major business partner in Youghal, besides his father, was another relative, Jasper Lucas, who was appointed "Mayor of the Staple" in 1695.[20] To distribute Irish products in northern France he could call on the services of Edward Gough, who was also linked to his family.[21] Prior to the Treaty of Utrecht (1713), Ray's Irish connection was clearly evident in his overseas trading activities. In the years 1704-1707 he frequently chartered Flemish convoy ships laden with woollens, linen and yarn as a result of orders from the Irish merchant colonies in Cádiz and Seville.[22] He combined these activities with lucrative investments in privateering. During the Anglo-Dutch regime in Ostend (1706-1713) he equipped two small snows with orders to scour the French-Flemish coast, particularly the shipping roads

---

[18]Jan Parmentier, "The Irish Connection: The Irish Merchant Community in Ostend and Bruges during the Late Seventeenth and Eighteenth Centuries," *Eighteenth-Century Ireland*, XX (2005), 32-38.

[19]David Dickson, "Butter Comes to Market: The Origins of Commercial Dairying in County Cork," in Patrick O'Flanagan and Cornelius G. Buttimer (eds.), *Cork History and Society: Interdisciplinary Essays on the History of an Irish County* (Dublin, 1993), 369.

[20]Cork Archives Institute (CAI), Council Book of the Corporation of Cork, 1690-1800, f. 17; and Youghal Corporation Minute Book, 1666-1725, f. 282.

[21]Edward Gough moved shortly after 1713 to Cádiz, where he managed the prosperous merchant house Gough and Browne; RAB, Notariaat Oostende, J.F. Pille, dep. 1940, no. 12, akte 263, 7 August 1705; and no. 15, akte 9, 4 February 1713; and Wilhelm Von Den Driesch, *Die ausländischen Kaufleute während des 18. Jahrhunderts in Spanien und ihre Beteiligung am Kolonialhandel* (Köln, 1972), 108, 127 and 181.

[22]His main business partners in Cádiz were Patrick White (from Dublin) and Richard Hore (from Waterford); Stadsarchief Brugge (SAB), no. 80, Convois and Prises, 1704-1707.

of Dunkirk and Nieuwpoort. His privateers proved quite successful and brought twenty prizes into Ostend and the English Channel ports.[23]

As citizens of the Austrian Empire after 1713, the merchants of Ostend were able to tap new opportunities for long-distance trade. As a result of the Treaty of Münster (1648), the Southern Netherlands had been excluded from the East India trade, but such a restriction was no longer enforced by the Imperial government in Vienna. Thomas Ray reacted quickly and obtained permission in 1715 to organize the first East India venture from Ostend. The voyage was financed by his national and international mercantile network and proved very profitable, thereby encouraging other entrepreneurs in both Ghent and Antwerp to exploit the new trading opportunities. Often using small companies co-financed by merchant houses in London, Amsterdam and France, they managed to organize more than thirty expeditions to Mocha, India and China in a short period.[24] As a result of his competence in the East India trade, in 1723 Thomas Ray was made one of the directors of the Generale Keyserlijcke Indische Compagnie (GIC), better known as the Ostend Company, which obtained a monopoly from the Austrian Emperor for trade with Asia. Because of this trading connection Ostend became and remained a staple market for Asian products throughout the eighteenth century. Ray clearly moved in the highest circles of Ostend's merchant community and in 1728 used his status to acquire the influential position of mayor (*burgomaster*), an office he retained for a decade.[25] His appointment opened the possibility of a significant expansion of Ostend's commercial infrastructure with the construction of warehouses and quays, and Ray proposed to invest 30,000 *guilders*, a small fortune at the time, to dredge the harbour channel. Although the silting of the port seriously hampered access by large East Indiamen, the government failed to follow Ray's initiative in tackling this problem.[26]

During the period of Austrian rule, the long-standing trade links between the Southern Netherlands and Spain were increasingly under threat, but early in 1713 Ray persuaded a handful skippers from Cork and Youghal to migrate to Ostend. These captains, accompanied by a group of Irish sailors, manned the "Irelandmen" and three frigates which Ray despatched to Cádiz

---

[23]ARB, Admiraliteit nos. 584 and 801-803, 1707-1708.

[24]Jan Parmentier, "The Private East India Ventures from Ostend: The Maritime and Commercial Aspects, 1715-1722," *International Journal of Maritime History*, V, No. 2 (1993), 75-102.

[25]Jan Parmentier, *Het gezicht van de Oostendse handelaar: Studie van de Oostendse kooplieden, reders en ondernemers actief in de internationale maritieme handel en visserij tijdens de 18de eeuw* (Oostende, 2004), 302.

[26]Baetens, "Het uitzicht," 51-53.

and San Sebastián with British passports. By this arrangement he was able to circumvent the loss by Flemish merchants of their protected status in Iberia. This "clandestine management," as the British consul in Ostend wrote, lasted until 1718.[27]

The rapidity of Thomas Ray's integration into the local community was remarkable. Only a few years after his settlement in Ostend he married Isabella de Duenas, the daughter of the *burgomaster* at the time. Estevan de Duenas was an influential figure in Ostend; he had acted for two decades as the clerk of the Admiralty, an institution which controlled privateering. In addition, he was the General Collector of the convoy fleet, which opened exciting opportunities for Ray's Iberian trade.[28] His reputation as an excellent businessman was also noticed in his home country. From 1710 Thomas Ray was considered the godfather of young Irish merchants who wanted to learn the trade and hoped to make their fortunes in Ostend. By offering opportunities in his merchant house, Ray helped to shape the careers of his nephew, John Ray (1710-1714), Patrick Sarsfield (1716-1717), John Gould (1718-1719), James Adam Coppinger (1722-1726), John Galwey (1726-1732) and Patricius Roche (1735-1749).[29]

At the end of his active career, a well-considered marriage policy proved a crucial factor in securing the continuity of his international merchant house. His master-stroke was to marry his daughter in 1744 to Cornelis Carpentier, whose father, Nicolaes, directed an elaborate mercantile network and shipping company. Nicolaes made his fortune shortly after this marriage as *pourvoieur général* of the British army on the Continent during the War of the Austrian Succession.[30] Although this major European conflict crippled Ostend's maritime trade, merchants like Ray, who possessed considerable financial assets, saw it was an ideal moment to speculate. Prior to the outbreak of war there was a shortage of grain in Liguria and Tuscany when English and Irish imports were paralyzed due to the successful action of Spanish privateers.[31] Ray reacted at once and within a few weeks managed to charter four

---

[27]TNA/PRO, SP, no. 77/67, 30 September 1717 and 24 August 1718.

[28]Parmentier, *Het gezicht*, 299-300; and Magosse, *Al die willen*, 32.

[29]Jan Parmentier, "The Ray Dynasty: Irish Mercantile Empire Builders in Ostend, 1690-1790," in Thomas O'Connor and Mary Ann Lyons (eds.), *Irish Communities in Early Modern Europe* (Dublin, 2006), 374-376.

[30]Nicolaes Carpentier held also the office of *burgomaster* in Ostend between 1740 and 1745; Parmentier, *Het gezicht*, 62-68.

[31]David J. Starkey, *British Privateering Enterprise in the Eighteenth Century* (Exeter, 1990), 119.

vessels in Norway and Holland to transport Flemish wheat to Genoa and Leghorn.[32] To organize this major operation he received assistance from the London merchant Jonathan Colley, who was recommended to him by John Fitzgerald.[33] Fitzgerald, who was of Irish origin, lived in the British capital but was one of the most important businessmen in the Irish mercantile network.[34] To spread the risk Ray persuaded two Dutch shipowners to invest in the project.[35] On the return voyages from Italy Ray's vessels loaded salt in Alicante, a well-calculated strategy because whenever war erupted throughout the seventeenth and eighteenth centuries the price of salt always increased rapidly. These examples of Ray's business activities demonstrate that maritime trade was not only possible but often quite lucrative during highly volatile periods, especially if an entrepreneur could rely on a solid mercantile and family network. Still, Ray's personal capacities were undoubtedly decisive in determining the extent to which the available opportunities were seized.

An Opportunistic All-round Commissioner

A less striking entrepreneur in Ostend who nevertheless built up an important merchant house in the middle of the eighteenth century under difficult conditions was Andreas Jacobus Flandrin. As a descendant of a mariner, with a successful record commanding several Ostend privateers and an Ostend East Indiaman, he began his mercantile career in 1725 as a junior supercargo on the GIC vessel *Keyzerinne* bound for Canton.[36] He capitalized on his Chinese ex-

---

[32]RAB, Notariaat Oostende, F. Rycx, dep. 1941, no. 35, akten 2, 8, 11, 14 and 16, 4, 13 and 24 January and 1 and 7 February 1744.

[33]Jonathan Colley also originated from Ireland; see Thomas Mortimer, *The Universal Director: or, The Nobleman and Gentleman's True Guide to the Masters and Professors of the Liberal and Polite Arts and Sciences, and of the Mechanical Arts, Manufactures...Established in London and Westminster, and Their Environs, etc.* (London, 1763), 20; and SAA, IB, no. 1736, 29 May 1744.

[34]Members of the Fitzgerald family, who lived initially in Waterford, were dispersed throughout England, France and Spain after the Williamite conquest of Ireland; Jacob M. Price, *France and the Chesapeake: A History of the French Tobacco Monopoly, 1674-1791, and of Its Relationship to the British and American Tobacco Trade* (2 vols., Ann Arbor, 1973), I, 557-562.

[35]The two were Justus van Maurik and David Crema from Amsterdam and Dordrecht, respectively; RAB, Notariaat Oostende, F. Rycx, dep. 1941, no. 35, akten 14 and 16, 1 and 7 February 1744.

[36]Karel Degryse and Jan Parmentier, "Kooplieden en kapiteins: Een prosografische studie van de supercargo's en scheepsofficieren van de Oostendse

perience to rise gradually, first in the service of the Ostend Company and later as second supercargo on two Swedish China expeditions and one to the Ganges delta.[37] Having accumulated sufficient wealth, he returned to Ostend in 1746 and shortly thereafter married Isabella Françoise Bernaert. It may well be that this was not a marriage based on love or affection but rather a well-prepared arrangement. His new father-in-law, Louis Bernaert, belonged to an influential circle of local merchants who had managed their affairs well during the prosperous days of the direct trade to the East Indies and controlled an elaborate business network which ranged from Archangel to Iberia and Mexico.[38] Marriage into such a family was always accompanied by a substantial dowry.

At the start of his business activity in Ostend, Flandrin specialized in East Indian products. His excellent contacts in Göteborg meant that he could count on a constant supply of tea, china and silk at reasonable prices.[39] His Swedish stocks were regularly replenished by placing orders at the East India auctions in Copenhagen, Lorient and Nantes. But in the mid-1750s the profits in the European tea market fell, so Flandrin started to diversify his affairs. The salt trade had attracted his attention since 1747. At first he purchased salt in association with Nathan Brame and his nephew, François Louis Carpentier, mainly in the traditional production centres near the estuary of the Loire (Seudres and Bourgneuf) and in Spain (Cádiz and Alicante). But after 1755, with the introduction of rock-salt mined in Cheshire, Flandrin chartered a few ships each year to transport salt from Liverpool to Ostend. He intensified this traffic spectacularly as soon as rumours spread of the possible outbreak of the Seven Years' War (1756-1763). To spread the risk of his speculative trade, he formed a small company with Nathan Brame and the Antwerp merchant William Hollier, both of whom were of English origin and had good business contacts in Liverpool.[40] Flandrin's trade in rock-salt flourished until his death in 1763, and he often combined it with the import of West Indian tobacco.

The fact that Flandrin earned most of his living as a commission merchant acting for a large number of firms in Flanders and Brabant opened the possibility of expanding his network to the Iberian Peninsula and Latin Amer-

---

handel op Oost-Indië en Guinea (1716-1732)," *Collectanea Maritima*, VI (1995), 177-178.

[37]Christian Koninckx, "Andreas Jacobus Flanderin: Een achttiende eeuwse middelgrote koopman," *Bijdragen tot de Geschiedenis*, LVI (1973), 243-280.

[38]Parmentier, *Het gezicht*, 40-43.

[39]Robert Parkinson was his main agent in Göteborg; *ibid.*, 173.

[40]Nathan Brame was born in Lowestoft and settled in Ostend permanently in 1739; UBG, FHH, nos. 2002-2004 and 2022; and Parmentier, *Het gezicht*, 53-54.

ica. An important factor in this decision was the presence in Cádiz of his cousin, Franciscus Verbeke. On several occasions Flandrin shipped small cargoes of Brabant and Silesian linen to Cádiz to be sold in Vera Cruz, Mexico, but this trade was seldom lucrative. As return cargoes, he received from his contacts in Cádiz salt, fruits and dyes, such as cochineal and indigo.[41] A few months prior to the outbreak of the Seven Years' War, two tempting opportunities for speculative trade emerged. Like many Ostend merchants with international networks, Flandrin took advantage of French crop failures to export a few shiploads of Flemish grain to Nantes.[42] In 1754-1755 the brandy trade became even more lucrative. Due to privateering in the English Channel, French wine and brandy firms were obliged to ship their products for London via Ostend and other ports in the Low Countries, which were then still neutral.

When we examine Flandrin's commercial correspondence and focus on an average business year in the middle of his mercantile career (November 1754-November 1755), it is apparent that his principal partners, contacts and customers were located in the Southern Netherlands, despite his involvement in an elaborate international network: twenty-eight percent of the letters written by Flandrin were addressed to Flemish and Brabant businessmen. As most of his family was resident in Ostend, only four of the recipients were relatives. In terms of the residential location of business contacts in Flanders, about thirty-five percent were based in Ghent, with Brussels and Bruges accounting for 18.5 and 14.8 percent, respectively. The remaining correspondents were scattered throughout the Austrian Netherlands, from Nieuwpoort on the coast to Namur and Liège on the banks of the Meuse. By contrast, over one-third of Flandrin's foreign correspondents were based in France, especially in Dunkirk (where he supplied several clients with tea re-exported from Scandinavia) and Nantes. This was followed by his correspondence with partners in Holland and Zeeland, although most of his Dutch contacts were shipowners. Flandrin also acted as commission agent for a handful of merchants in Rotterdam and Amsterdam. He sent letters relating to trade with the East Indies to three different business partners in Göteborg and one in Copenhagen, but his trading links with England were negligible at this stage, and trade with Cádiz was poor.[43]

Atlantic Tradesmen and Smugglers

---

[41]Verbeke Octavio Barbou was Flandrin's major partner in Cádiz. The Barbou family also managed an influential merchant house in Amsterdam; Parmentier, *Het gezicht*, 173; and UBG, FHH, no. 2111.

[42]Flandrin set up these shipments together with Guillielmo de Brouwer, an important shipowner in Bruges, and Charles de Tollenaere, a Flemish merchant who had already lived for some decades in Nantes. Both partners were also involved in the brandy trade; Parmentier, *Het gezicht*, 173-174; and UBG, FHH, no. 2002.

[43]UBG, FHH, no. 2002.

The third Ostend firm included in this analysis, Gregorie, Benquet et Cie, was a typical product of the Fourth Anglo-Dutch War. In this international conflict the neutral status of the port of Ostend was crucial. Moreover, on 11 June 1781 Emperor Joseph II proclaimed Ostend a free port. From that date on, Ostend, and to a lesser extent Bruges and Ghent, became attractive places for Dutch, French and English merchants intent on continuing their commerce.[44] The founder of the company, George Gregorie, was of Scottish origin but had built his career on the European continent. His father, David, had migrated about 1774 to Dunkirk from the Zeeland town of Veere to enlarge his involvement in contraband trade.[45] The Gregories mainly smuggled tea, tobacco and geneva to England, and within this context it was entirely logical for the firm to open a branch in Ostend in November 1781. From there it organized a "smuggling line" with Guernsey to ship wine, brandy and even champagne to customers in London. Even after the Treaty of Versailles in 1783, the contraband trade continued. The Gregories worked closely together with the merchant house of Rosenmeyer, Flore et Cie, based in Torshavn in the Faroe Islands, to transport Virginia tobacco and geneva from Schiedam to the Scottish coast.[46] In Ostend they found in François Benquet the ideal partner for all kinds of commercial transactions with maritime entrepreneurs in the belligerent nations. Benquet was originally from Bordeaux, but his contribution to the firm lay principally in his excellent contacts with the French West Indies and the Isle de France (Mauritius). The firm participated in the emergent West India trade from Ostend but did not organize separate ventures. Gregorie and his partner often acted as minor investors in trading undertaken by English and Irish shipowners who wanted to sail under a neutral flag. But they developed an even greater financial and commercial involvement in voyages to Curaçao, Demerara and Essequibo which were organized from Zeeland and Holland. Indeed, it is remarkable that more than half of these "Dutch" expeditions were actually initiated by British merchants living in the Dutch Republic.[47] At first sight, the family framework of this merchant house does not seem to have been

---

[44]Parmentier, "Profit," 206-226.

[45]Since 1541 a permanent colony of Scottish merchants was present in Veere; Tiny Polderman and Peter Blom, *Veere van vissersbuurt tot vestingstad* (Goes, 1996), 68-69.

[46]Parmentier, *Het gezicht*, 201; and ARB, Hof van Beroep, no. 2575.

[47]The most conspicuous English firms were in Rotterdam: Thomas Littledale and Cie, James Smith and Thomas Roche. In Middelburg, the Scottish entrepreneur James Turing was the main partner of Gregorie, Benquet et Cie; ARB, Hof van Beroep, nos. 2575-2576.

important, but the Ostend branch could always rely on the support of relatives in Dunkirk and Veere. John Gregorie of Veere, in particular, introduced them to several merchants in Zeeland involved in trade with the West Indies and Demerara. François Benquet also had two brothers who managed a merchant house in Cap François (Santo Domingo), a link which was vital for purchasing the necessary return cargoes in Martinique, Guadeloupe and Santo Domingo.[48]

Gregorie and Benquet probably earned most of their income during the war years through the transit trade in English products. Large shipments of coal from Newcastle and Sunderland were received in Ostend labelled as *charbon de Hainaut* and were subsequently transferred to Dunkirk, Morlaix and Bordeaux. Irish butter and beef were handled in the same manner and transported as Flemish cargoes to Porto and Cádiz. In Ostend all the English textiles and hardware received from the London merchant John Hopkins were certified as "made in Germany" before being sent to customers in Holland and France, while the Ostend firm was involved extensively in the maritime trade between London and Rotterdam.[49] After the lucrative wartime trading, the partnership continued to operate in Ostend but no longer engaged in trade with the West Indies. Gregorie and Benquet now focused on the Chesapeake and Philadelphia and, like other merchant houses in Ostend, made a considerable profit from the American tobacco boom in the Austrian Netherlands during the years 1784-1787. Gregorie also supplied many customers in Middelburg. Finally, the growth between 1787 and 1793 of private trade in Ostend with the East Indies posed a new challenge for the firm, but it mainly acted as a commission house that initiated a number of ventures in Bengal and organized the public sale of imports in Ostend.

Conclusion

A comparison of the three merchant houses active in Ostend at different periods during the eighteenth century reveals several similarities. Owing to the force of circumstances, Ray, Flandrin, Gregorie and Benquet settled in Ostend, and their decisions to start companies in the port were clearly influenced by local opportunities for trade. All three relied primarily on trustworthy family ties to launch their enterprises. Both Ray and Flandrin made strategic marriages to benefit their businesses, and George Gregorie probably tried to improve his economic position by extending his family circle. Although the necessary information is lacking in this case, kinship ties existed between the Gregories and Anthony Brown, who lived initially in Veere and during the late

---

[48]Parmentier, *Het gezicht*, 201.

[49]ARB, Hof van Beroep, nos. 2575-2576.

1770s in Essequibo.[50] On the business level, each of the three merchant houses originally specialized in one market or one type of product. Thomas Ray dealt mainly in Irish commodities; Flandrin in Chinese tea; and the Gregories in contraband. Due to changing trading conditions, especially as a result of war, all three were forced to re-orient their business activities, but they proved sufficiently flexible to adapt their trading patterns and to adjust their mercantile networks. Earnings from privateering and the Iberian commission trade provided Ray with the opportunity to invest in the East India trade. Andreas Jacobus Flandrin, with fewer financial possibilities, focused on shipping salt in conjunction with the international commission trade. Gregorie, Benquet et Cie concentrated on its shipping links with the West Indies, which enabled the firm to move into the North American tobacco trade after the Fourth Anglo-Dutch War.

By and large, though, it was the ability to diversify their trading activities which underpinned the strength of all three companies. Although such a strategy can be regarded as a defensive reaction designed to spread the risk, the success of these merchant houses can be attributed ultimately to the personal qualities of the individual merchant-entrepreneurs. This was evident in particular in the pioneering work of Ray in the East India trade and the eagerness of all three firms to invest in speculative business ventures, often created by exogenous political or economic factors, which affected the port of Ostend. While Ostend was in the "eye of the storm" during most of the eighteenth century, this also meant that it offered excellent trading possibilities to entrepreneurs with an ability to spot opportunities and to seize the initiative.

---

[50]Zeeuws Archief, Gemeentearchief Veere, Archief Anthony Brown, no. 17.

Exploiting International Webs of Relations: Immigrants and the Reopening of the Harbour of Antwerp on the Eve of the Nineteenth Century[1]

Hilde Greefs

The transition from the eighteenth to the nineteenth century is a fascinating period in Western European history. The French Revolution and the outward spread of industrialization from Great Britain were pivotal points in a broader social and economic development process. Key transitional moments, which often resulted in winners and losers as far as states, regions, cities and people were concerned, have always fascinated historians. It is increasingly clear, however, that the industrialization process also initiated structural changes in the international trading environment.[2] In this context, the position of Antwerp was rather unique. In 1795 the lock on the River Scheldt, which had been closed for two centuries to direct maritime transport, was removed as a manifestation of the French ideals of freedom.[3] As a consequence, Antwerp was

---

[1]I would like to thank Greta Devos, Catharina Lis and Hugo Soly for their suggestions on an earlier version of this article.

[2]Some historians have stressed the importance of trade for the process of industrialization. They consider the expansion of commerce as a power that made a new, integrated and more harmonious economy possible. See, for example, Richard P. Thomas and Donald N. McCloskey, "Overseas Trade and Empire, 1700-1860," in Roderick Floud and Donald N. McCloskey (eds.), *The Economic History of Britain since 1700. Volume 1: 1700-1860* (Cambridge, 1983), 87-102; and John A. Davis, "Industrialization in Britain and Europe before 1850: New Perspectives and Old Problems," in Peter Mathias and John A. Davis (eds.), *The First Industrial Revolutions* (Oxford, 1989), 56-58.

[3]As an international centre of trade, industry and finance, the port city of Antwerp stood in the centre of the world economy during the "golden" sixteenth-century. After the rebellion of the Northern Netherlands against the Spanish government, the fall of Antwerp in 1585 and the restoration of Spanish authority in the Southern Netherlands, the estuary of the Scheldt came under the control of the Northern Netherlands. This meant that seaworthy ships could no longer sail directly to Antwerp. Instead, their cargoes had to be loaded onto smaller vessels under the control of the government of the Northern Netherlands. Transaction costs rose dramatically, exacerbated by high import and export duties. Amsterdam thus became the new international

able to regain its position as the best situated harbour town in the Southern
Netherlands (which became the separate kingdom of Belgium in 1830). While
Antwerp's transformation from a small trading place highly dependent upon
(and controlled by) businessmen in the Northern Netherlands to a flourishing
international seaport and trading centre is well known, much less attention has
been given to the businessmen and traders who supported this evolution.[4] This
essay will analyze the businessmen who were keen to profit from Antwerp's
changing position and who successfully revived its international trade.

For centuries, different pressure groups in Antwerp had kept alive the
dream of reopening the River Scheldt so that the city could regain its former
importance as an international port and trading centre.[5] Hence, they were all
keen to profit, especially the business community, from the events of 1795, but
the key question is to determine which businessmen were able to turn the new
situation to their advantage. The expansion of commerce in Antwerp during
the nineteenth century was accompanied by a significant influx of merchants
both from within Belgium and from abroad, and some historians have sought
to establish a link between the reopening of the river and the sudden influx of
foreign businessmen.[6] Guillaume Beetemé and later specialists in the port history of nineteenth-century Antwerp have argued that immigrants played a key
role in the rapid growth of the local economy as a result of their experience in
international trade and their overseas business contacts.[7] But this hypothesis

---

trading centre at the expense of Antwerp. See Alfons K.L. Thijs, "The River Scheldt
Closed for Two Centuries, 1585-1790," in Gustaaf Asaert, *et al.* (eds.), *Antwerp: A
Port for All Seasons* (Antwerp, 1986), 165-273; and Bruno Blondé and Harald Deceu-
laer, "The Port of Antwerp and Its Hinterland: Port Traffic, Urban Economies and
Government Policies in the 17th and 18th Centuries," in Randi Ertesvåg, David J.
Starkey and Anne Tove Austbø (eds.), *Maritime Industries and Public Intervention*
(Stavanger, 2002), 21-44.

[4]For an overview of the economic development of Antwerp during the first
half of the nineteenth century, see Karel Veraghtert, "From Inland Port to International
Port, 1790-1914," in Asaert, *et al.* (eds.), *Antwerp*, 274-422; and Catharina Lis, *Social
Change and the Labouring Poor: Antwerp, 1770-1860* (New Haven, 1986), 27-31.

[5]Ilja van Damme, "Het vertrek van Mercurius: Historiografische en hypothe-
tische verkenningen van het economische wedervaren van Antwerpen in de tweede helft
van de zeventiende eeuw," *NEHA Jaarboek voor economische, bedrijfs- en techniek-
geschiedenis*, LCVI (2003), 6-39.

[6]Guillaume Beeteme, *Antwerpen, moederstad van handel en kunst* (3 vols., Antwerp, 1892-1893), II, 14.

[7]For further information, see the section on "Explaining the Dominance of
Immigrants in Maritime Trade" below.

has never been substantiated because of the continuing absence of any analysis of the economic behaviour of the immigrants or a detailed review of their trading activities.[8] The present contribution will focus specifically on these two key points.

This essay explores the question of who took advantage of the reopening of the port and seeks to explain the dominance of certain groups in maritime trade. The following topics will be discussed. First, the development of maritime trade in Antwerp during the first half of the nineteenth century will be examined along with its relative attractiveness as a port town. Second, the trading activities of the business elite will be analyzed using documents relating to port traffic and the arrival of ships in the harbour. Since it is impossible to obtain a complete picture of Antwerp's business world, the research has been confined to the business elite. Third, I will discuss the dominance of certain groups in foreign trade, arguing that in the specific context of Antwerp, access to overseas relation networks was a crucial factor for entrance in international trade. The analysis will highlight the importance of social networks for business behaviour using theoretical constructs which have been applied in economic and business history.[9] By examining different kinds of relations, individual economic behaviour will be placed within a social context, given that all activities, including economic actions, are "embedded in ongoing networks of personal relations rather than carried out by atomized actors."[10] An examination of the business behaviour of immigrants in Antwerp will provide an excellent example of this statement.

---

[8]Only Greta Devos has done significant research on German businessmen in Antwerp. See, for example, Greta Devos, "Die Deutschen und die wirtschaftliche Entwicklung vom Ende des 18. Jahrhunderts bis zum ersten Weltkrieg," in Gustaaf Asaert, *et al.* (eds.), *Antwerpen und Deutschland: Eine historische Darstellung beider Beziehungen vom Mittelalter zur Gegenwart* (Antwerpen, 1990), 49-73; and Devos, "Die Firma Königs-Günther & Co. Ein Beitrag zum Häute- und Wollhandel deutscher Kaufleute in Antwerpen im 19.-20. Jahrhundert," in Wilfried Feldenkirchen, Frauke Schönert-Röhlk and Gunther Schulz (eds.), *Wirtschaft – Gesellschaft – Unternehmen: Festschrift für Hans Pohl zum 60. Geburtstag* (2 vols., Stuttgart, 1995), II, 862-875.

[9]See, for example, recent overviews such as Jonathan Brown and Mary B. Rose (eds.), *Entrepreneurship, Networks and Modern Business* (Manchester, 1993); the various essays on "Réseaux marchands," *Annales, Histoire, Sciences sociales*, LVIII, No. 3 (2003), 569-674; and Margrit Schulte-Beerbühl and Jörg Vögele, *Spinning the Commercial Web: International Trade, Merchants, and Commercial Cities, c. 1640-1939* (Frankfurt, 2004). See also the section below on "The Importance of Building and Maintenance Business Relations."

[10]Mark Granovetter, "The Social Construction of Economic Institutions," in Amitai Etzione and Paul R. Lawrence (eds.), *Socio-Economics: Towards a New Synthesis* (Armonk, NY, 1991), 76.

Antwerp's Attractiveness in a Changing International Trade Environment

At the beginning of the nineteenth century fundamental changes occurred not only in industry but also in international trade. The rise of London in the eighteenth century signalled a shift in commercial activity as the increasing predominance of transatlantic trade was accompanied by a shift in the centre of gravity of global commerce from a north-south axis (between the Baltic and the Mediterranean and onwards to Asia) to an east-west orientation (from the Continent to Britain and beyond to the Americas).[11] These long-term developments affected the competitiveness of individual ports and were reinforced by the Anglo-French War (1793-1814), which reaffirmed British economic dominance.[12] Moreover, these shifts had important consequences for Western European ports. According to the French historian Louis Bergeron, after 1815 it was necessary to reconstruct everything in small stages, along other routes and with other products. In short, it represented the start of a new era.[13]

Equally for Antwerp, this was a period of fundamental change and reorientation. Its early annexation by France meant that the legal changes from the revolutionary period were quickly introduced into the Southern Netherlands. New manufacturing regions were also emerging, although at a slower pace and with less predictability than in Great Britain, which would result in Belgium becoming the first industrialized state on the Continent.[14] Far more

---

[11]At the turn of the eighteenth century Great Britain gained the lead over possible rivals in international trade. See Paul Bairoch, *Commerce extérieur et développement économique de l'Europe au 19e siècle* (Paris, 1976), 77. Imports were reduced to raw materials and food. The east-west axis was central in trading activities at the expense of several continental ports that traditionally concentrated on north-south commerce. See Ralph Davis, *The Industrial Revolution and British Overseas Trade* (Leicester, 1979), 13-15; Joost Jonker, *Merchants, Bankers, Middlemen: The Amsterdam Money Market during the First Half of the 19th Century* (Amsterdam, 1996), 32; and Robert Lee, "The Socio-economic and Demographic Characteristics of Port Cities: A Typology for Comparative Analysis?" *Urban History*, XXV, No. 2 (1998), 147-150.

[12]Erik Aerts and François Crouzet (eds.), *Economic Effects of the French Revolutionary and Napoleonic Wars* (Leuven, 1990); and Silvia Marzagalli, *"Les boulevards de la fraude:" Le négoce maritime et le Blocus continental, 1806-1813: Bordeaux, Hambourg, Livourne* (Villeneuve d'Ascq, 1999).

[13]Louis Bergeron, "Le négoce international de la France de la fin du XVIIIe au début du XIXe siècle: quelques remarques en guise de conclusion," in François M. Crouzet (ed.), *Le négoce international, XIIIe-Xxe siècles* (Paris, 1989), 200.

[14]For an overview, see Herman van der Wee, "The Industrial Revolution in Belgium," in Mikulas Teich and Roy Porter (eds.), *The Industrial Revolution in National Context: Europe and the USA* (Cambridge, 1996), 64-77; and Hilde Greefs,

important in terms of Antwerp's history, however, was the proclamation in 1795 of free navigation on the Scheldt, which heralded the end of the Dutch blockade that had blocked the port from the North Sea for more than two centuries. As a consequence, Antwerp was able to regain its position as the best-situated harbour in the Southern Netherlands and, thanks to the country's modernization process, to function as an important gateway for industries located in its immediate hinterland. Antwerp's competitive position was further strengthened by its excellent location for the transit trade to northern France, the Rhineland and Switzerland, and for facilitating maritime relations along an east-west axis to Britain and across the Atlantic. The fact that everything was "new" also meant that Antwerp offered businessmen some important advantages in terms of its international competitiveness with other ports. According to contemporaries, business transactions were less regulated than in other North Sea ports, such as Amsterdam and Rotterdam, which meant that cargo handling was both cheaper and faster than in nearby harbours.[15]

There is much empirical evidence to confirm the steady growth in port traffic following the reopening of the Scheldt. In only a few decades Antwerp was transformed from a regional textile centre into a flourishing international seaport and trading emporium. In 1800 Antwerp's role as a port city was still negligible, but by the 1840s it was ranked as the twelfth most important harbour in the world measured by the total tonnage of ships entering the port.[16]

The increase in maritime traffic after 1800 clearly confirms the importance of Antwerp's structural assets as a maritime gateway (see figure 1).[17] But

---

Bruno Blondé and Peter Clark, "The Growth of Urban Industrial Regions: Belgian Developments in Comparative Perspective, 1750-1850," in Jon Stobart and Neil Raven (eds.), *Towns, Regions and Industries: Urban and Industrial Change in the Midlands, c. 1700-1840* (Manchester, 2005), 210-227.

[15]The contemporary Willem De Clercq of the competing port of Amsterdam expressed it as follows: "In Antwerpen...is alles nog jong" ("In Antwerp, everything is still young"); Herman T. Colenbrander, *Gedenkstukken der algemeene geschiedenis van Nederland van 1795 tot 1841, Achtste deel: Regeering van Willem I. 1815-1825* ('s Gravenhage, 1915), 332. See also Greta Devos, "De Antwerpse naties tijdens de periode 1815-1940," in Greta Devos, Gustaaf Asaert and Fernand Suykens (eds.), *De Antwerpse naties: Zes eeuwen actief in stad en haven* (Tielt, 2004), 142.

[16]Paul Bairoch, "La Belgique dans le commerce international, 1830-1990," in Paul Klep and Eddy van Cauwenberghe (eds.), *Entrepreneurship and the Transformation of the Economy (10th-20th Centuries): Essays in Honour of Herman Van der Wee* (Leuven, 1994), 648-649.

[17]The following is based on an overview of port traffic in Antwerp as published by Veraghtert, "From Inland Port to International Port;" Lis, *Social Change*, 26-31; and Karel Jeuninckx, "De havenbeweging in de Franse en Hollandse periode," in

political instability and the threat of the renewed closure of the Scheldt seriously affected the realization of local ambitions and necessitated a flexible and adaptable approach to contemporary developments. The early revival was stifled by the Napoleon wars and the Continental Blockade (1806-1814), and deep-sea shipping came to a standstill during these years. Only smuggling and some inland and coastal shipping continued, but the international situation made these undertakings both dangerous and risky.[18]

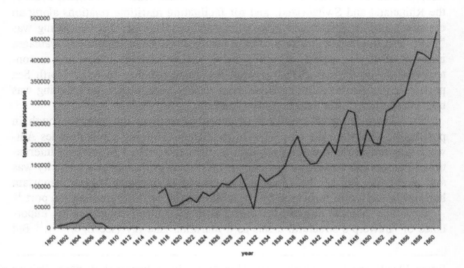

Figure 1:   Incoming Tonnage in Antwerp, 1800-1860 (Moorsom Tons)

Source: Karel Veraghtert, "From Inland Port to International Port, 1790-1914," in Gustaaf Asaert, *et al.* (eds.), *Antwerp: A Port for All Seasons* (Antwerp, 1986), 302; and Veraghtert, "De havenbeweging te Antwerpen tijdens de negentiende eeuw: Een kwantitatieve benadering" (Unpublished PhD thesis, University of Leuven, 1977), appendix XXV.

Karel Jeuninckx, *et al.* (eds.), *Bouwstoffen voor de geschiedenis van Antwerpen in de XIXde eeuw: Instellingen-Economie-Kultuur* (Antwerpen, 1964), 94-123.

[18]This is also proved by the police documents in Paris concerning smuggling in the Southern Netherlands; see Roger Dufraisse, "Contrebandiers Normands sur les bords du Rhin à l'époque Napoléonienne," in *L'Allemagne à l'époque Napoléonienne: Questions d'histoire politique, économique et sociale: Etudes de Roger Dufraisse réunies à l'occasion de son 70e anniversaire par l'Institut Historique Allemand de Paris* (Berlin, 1992), 209-211.

After the defeat of Napoleon and the union of the Southern and Northern Netherlands under King William I (1815-1830), commercial activities again flourished in the port. Especially during the 1820s, Antwerp underwent a rapid expansion of its port activities. The city fully exploited its advantageous location and profited from access to Dutch colonial trade; by 1829 Antwerp's share of Dutch colonial imports had risen to as much as fifty-five percent. Belgian independence in 1830 again disrupted port activities. The Dutch colonial markets were closed, and connections with the German hinterland became problematic, with the result that several merchants and shipowners moved elsewhere. The threat of a possible renewed closure of the Scheldt lasted until 1838, when the Dutch accepted the free traffic on the river in exchange for the payment of a substantial toll. But trading activity revived rapidly after the initial setbacks, and Antwerp increasingly exploited markets in both North and South America.

Like other port cities, Antwerp quickly became an attractive destination for immigrants seeking to exploit the new situation.[19] Before the reopening of the Scheldt, Antwerp seldom attracted foreign businessmen, and almost all its immigrants came from nearby provinces.[20] After 1795 there was a steady trickle of immigrant merchants from both within the country and abroad. Since it is impossible to obtain a comprehensive view of Antwerp's business community, my research has been confined to a sample of 234 businessmen active during the early nineteenth century. They were selected on the basis of a wide range of sources covering the period 1794-1825 which provided information on their financial capacity, social status and economic activity.[21] A distinction

---

[19]On the attractiveness of port cities for immigrants see, for example, Lee, "Socio-economic and Demographic Characteristics," 147-172; and Gordon Jackson, "Ports, 1700-1840," in Peter Clark (ed.), *The Cambridge Urban History of Britain. II: 1540-1840* (Cambridge, 2000), 703-731.

[20]Only a few mercantile houses in Westfalia specializing in the iron trade moved to Antwerp before the reopening of the river. Greta Devos and Hilde Greefs, "The German Presence in the Nineteenth Century," in Peter Marschalck (ed.), *Europa als Wanderungsziel: Ansiedlung und Integration von Deutschen im 19. Jahrhundert* (Osnabrück, 2000), 109.

[21]For the selection of the group, various sources were used: on the one hand, quantitative, mostly fiscal, records, such as the patent tax rolls or lists of the wealthiest citizens of the city compiled by local or provincial governments; on the other, sources with uncertain (mostly qualitative) criteria, such as the election lists for the Court of Commerce, known as the "Liste des négociants notables." Seven different sources were used in total, offering ten different lists of names, to select the important businessmen in the city. Patent taxation, installed by the French government to tax economic activity, has been used to obtain a clear view of their economic activities. See Hilde Greefs, "Zakenlieden in Antwerpen tijdens de eerste helft van de negentiende eeuw" (Unpublished PhD thesis, University of Antwerp, 2004), 24-38.

was made between businessmen who were born in Antwerp (128), migrants from the Southern Netherlands (forty-two) and immigrants from abroad (sixty-four, see table 1). Since there was no maritime trade in Antwerp during the eighteenth century, however, the analysis of the sample by place of birth is simply a way to provide a suitable point of departure for examining the port's subsequent development.[22]

Table 1
Geographic Origins of Antwerp's Businessmen by Place of Birth
(Absolute Numbers and Percent)

Geographic Origin (Birthplace)	Number (%)
Antwerp	128 (54.7)
Immigrants from Inside the Country	42 (17.9)
Immigrants from Abroad	64 (27.4)
German states	24
France	7
Denmark	1
Great Britain	11
Northern Netherlands	13
Spain	2
Sweden	1
Switzerland	3
United States of America	2

Source: Hilde Greefs, "Zakenlieden in Antwerpen tijdens de eerste helft van de negentiende eeuw" (Unpublished PhD thesis, University of Antwerp, 2004), appendix 1.

Almost half the businessmen in the sample were immigrants. Most foreigners were born in neighbouring territories, such as the "German states" (with a significant number coming from the Rhineland and other port towns), the Northern Netherlands and Great Britain. Businessmen from the Southern Netherlands also sought new possibilities in Antwerp, particularly those who had been born in towns and cities on the most important internal trade routes during the eighteenth century, such as Ostend, Bruges, Ghent, Louvain and

[22]Especially in nineteenth-century research, national sentiments sometimes seem to have dominatied the historiography. See, for example Beetemé, *Antwerpen*; and B.S. Chlepner, "L'étranger dans l'histoire économique de la Belgique," *Revue de l'Institut de Sociologie*, IX (1931), 695-734.

Liège.[23] Almost sixty-five percent of the foreigners had been born in an urban community or had moved to Antwerp via another town (the so-called "city-to-city flow"), although in many cases there is evidence of "port-to-port-migration," indicating that they were attracted by the commercial prospects of Antwerp as a port.[24] The dominance of stepwise migration patterns (either from city to city or port to port) demonstrates that most in-migrants were motivated by a search for the most suitable place for their commercial activities.

The move to Antwerp might also have been part of a strategy to adapt the structure of existing business networks to changing circumstances. The war between France and Britain, for example, obstructed trade routes and necessitated a reorientation of mercantile networks. The need to adapt business practices was reinforced by the closure of annual markets for the international exchange of goods, such as the Frankfurt Fair, and the loss of outlets and transit ports for colonial products, such as Bordeaux.[25] These factors encouraged merchants to reassess their market orientation, while changes in international trade offered some space for young, ambitious businessmen keen on travelling (as Stanley Chapman has illustrated in the case of Great Britain, where they settled in crucial trading nodes, working on commission and remaining in contact with trading companies in their home country).[26] In such a context, Antwerp was a well-situated, inexpensive and rising town and potentially an attractive base for operations. Evidence of chain (or step) migration, and collaborative arrangements between in-migrant businessmen with the same geographical origins, place of residence or family background, confirms that migration was rarely an individual matter.[27]

---

[23]It is difficult to speak of "foreigners" between 1796 and 1830 because of the different regimes: the French period (1796-1814), the period of the United Kingdom of the Netherlands under the reign of Willem I (1815-1830) and the Belgian period (from 1830 onwards). For this reason, the Belgian borders of 1830 were used as a criterion.

[24]Following Jan De Vries, *European Urbanization, 1500-1800* (London, 1984), 270-287, cities were defined as places with more than 10,000 inhabitants. Population figures for 1800 were used. For stepwise migration patterns to commercial centres, see Lynn Hollen Lees and Paul Hohenberg, "Population Flows in European Metropolitan Regions (1600-1850)," in Erik Aerts and Peter Clark (eds.), *Metropolitan Cities and Their Hinterlands in Early Modern Europe* (Leuven, 1990), 39.

[25]François Crouzet, "Wars, Blockade, and Economic Change in Europe, 1792-1815," *Journal of Economic History,* XXIV, No. 4 (1964), 567-588.

[26]Stanley Chapman, *Merchant Enterprise in Britain: From the Industrial Revolution to World War I* (Cambridge, 1992), 55-56; and Chapman, *The Rise of Merchant Banking* (London, 1984), 15, 51-56 and 68-70.

[27]The presence of relatives and friends facilitated the move to Antwerp; see Devos and Greefs, "German Presence." For example, Jean Martin Grisar, who moved

Immigrants and the Call of Maritime Trade

Since maritime trade was the driving force behind Antwerp's transition from a regional production centre to an international port, it is thus important to investigate who could profit the most from the reopening of the Scheldt. It is possible to discover which merchants were active in Antwerp by using data on patent taxes. These were introduced by the French authorities as a charge on independent economic professions. Information on ship arrivals was also utilized in the analysis in order to discover which merchants imported goods through the harbour.[28] This material was gathered by shipbrokers and provides information on ships arriving in Antwerp (according to their arrival date, place of origin, name of captain and flag), as well as details on the merchants who received the goods, the variety of products and the volume of freight.[29]

It was only possible to extract data from this extensive source material for five cross-sectional years: 1805 and 1810, when Antwerp was under French occupation; 1817 and 1827, when the port belonged to the United Kingdom of the Netherlands; and 1835, shortly after the Belgian Revolution

---

to Antwerp in 1802, was followed by his brother Charles, who moved to Antwerp *"pour y apprendre le commerce chez son frère négociant"* ("to learn the skills in the firm of his brother"); G. Gérard, "La famille Grisar à Anvers," *Recueil de l'office généalogique et héraldique de Belgique*, XII (1963), 71 and 90. Georges and Christian Kreglinger from Bielefeld showed their brother-in-law, Charles Frederik Scheibler from Monschau, and their cousin, Joseph Mathias Kreglinger, the way to Antwerp; Roland Baetens, "Het ontstaan en de groei van een familiale onderneming," in Baetens (ed.), *Spiegels van Mercurius. Plouvier & Kreglinger: Tweehonderd Jaar Handel en Maritiem Transport te Antwerpen* (Antwerpen, 1998), 25.

[28]The patent tax rolls for 1799-1842 are in Municipal Archives, Antwerp (MAA), Modern Archives (MA), 4789/1-86.

[29]*Ibid.*, Bib. 3400, *Arrivages*, 1816-1829; and Bib. 3399, *Annonces maritimes*, 1835. The source can to a certain extent be compared with the Customs Bills of Entry in Great Britain, although this information was gathered by the customs house. David M. Williams, "Liverpool Merchants and the Cotton Trade, 1820-1850," in John R. Harris (ed.), *Liverpool and Merseyside: Essays in the Economic and Social History of the Port and Its Hinterland* (London, 1969), 184-185, used this information to identify the cotton importers in Liverpool. For the French period, the ship arrivals published in "Etat des Bâtiments français et étrangers entrés au port d'Anvers," *Journal du Commerce d'Anvers* (Antwerpen, 1805 and 1810), were used. Marzagalli, *Les boulevards*, used comparable documents to reconstruct port traffic in Hamburg, Livorno and Bordeaux during the Continental Blockade. This source also contains information on imports (especially via inland navigation) from ports in the Northern Netherlands.

and the creation of an independent kingdom.[30] In 1805 port traffic had just revived, but this upward trend had been interrupted by 1810 due to the imposition of the Continental Blockade. As a result, Antwerp again became an inland port, highly dependent upon the Northern Netherlands for the supply of goods. Under the reign of William I (1815-1830) there was a period of commercial expansion, although 1817 was quite exceptional as a result of serious grain shortages in Europe and the overriding importance of grain traffic in the harbour. Furthermore, the market was flooded with British products which had been stockpiled during the Continental Blockade and subsequently dumped on the continental market at low prices.[31] An analysis of the data for 1817 will therefore reveal which groups were able to profit immediately from market instability. By contrast, the 1820s were much more stable, and port traffic peaked in 1827 due in part to the growing importance of intercontinental ship arrivals in Antwerp. The separation from the Northern Netherlands and the creation of the Belgian state in 1830 again led to instability, but data from 1835 will provide an insight into those businessmen who continued to trade despite the unfavourable conditions.

Data on ship arrivals cannot provide a complete picture of Antwerp's commercial activities, as no allowance can be made for the international transport of goods over land or the export of commodities. Moreover, it is extremely time consuming to reconstruct the exact volume and value of freight traffic because of the use of different measurements even for the same product. It is also difficult to establish whether a merchant was doing business on his own account or was acting on commission for other merchant houses, which would have resulted in a significantly different profit margin.[32] The main objective of this study, however, is to use the available data to establish which businessmen in the sample were involved in maritime trade. To achieve this objective, traders were split into three groups: merchants who were not involved in import activities through the harbour;[33] merchants who imported

---

[30]For an overview of trading activity during the sample years, see Veraghtert, "From Inland Port to International Port;" and Jeuninckx, "De havenbeweging in de Franse en Hollandse periode," 94-123.

[31]Robert Demoulin, *Guillaume Ier et la transformation économique des Provinces Belges (1815-1830)* (Liège, 1938), 123-124.

[32]It was common in mercantile circles to act partly as a commissioner and partly on one's own account, depending upon the different transactions and commodities involved. A good overview is offered by Joost Jonker and Keetie Sluyterman, *Thuis op de wereldmarkt: Nederlandse handelshuizen door de eeuwen heen* (Den Haag, 2000), 83-91. See also Chapman, *Merchant Enterprise*, 15, 68 and 133-136.

[33]No information was given if they were importing goods overland or were only involved in the local, regional or national distribution of imported commodities.

goods through the port but only received goods from harbours in the Northern Netherlands, which traditionally represented Antwerp's most important supply route during the period when the Scheldt was closed; and merchants who were involved in "real" maritime business or overseas trade (see table 2).

Table 2
Businessmen Active in Antwerp's Trade, 1796-1850,
By Place of Origin and Type of Commercial Activity

	Antwerpers	Immigrants Migrants from Inside the Country	Immigrants Immigrants from Abroad
Businessmen in the Sample N=234 (100%)	N=128 (100%)	N=42 (100%)	N=64 (100%)
Active in Trade N=208 (88.9%)	N=106 (82.8%)	N=41 (97.6%)	N=61 (95.3%)
Not Involved in Sea Trade N= 50 (24.0%)	40 (37.7%)	6 (14.6%)	4 (6.6%)
Only Importing through Ports in the Northern Netherlands N= 25 (12.0%)	16 (15.1%)	6 (14.6%)	3 (4.9%)
Involved in Sea Trade N= 133 (64.0%)	50 (47.2%)	29 (70.8%)	54 (88.5%)

Source: "Etat des Bâtiments français et étrangers entrés au port d'Anvers," *Journal du Commerce d'Anvers*, 1805 and 1810; Municipal Archives Antwerp (MAA), Bib. 3400, Arrivages, 1817 and 1827; and Bib. 3399, *Annonces maritimes*, 1835.

As far as in-migrant businessmen were concerned, the overall picture is clear: they came to Antwerp with a deliberate purpose to develop maritime trade. This was the case for 70.8 percent of immigrants from the Southern Netherlands and 88.5 percent of the foreigners in the sample. Furthermore, only a small proportion restricted their trading activities to importing goods from the Northern Netherlands or by land. By contrast, only 47.2 percent of the businessmen born in Antwerp imported goods through the harbour: most of them were not involved in sea trade or restricted their maritime relations to the Northern Netherlands. This suggests a high degree of path-dependency on the part of native-born Antwerpers who continued to rely on their traditional trading connections from the eighteenth century. A clearer picture of the relative importance of the different groups can be obtained from an analysis of the total number of shipments by merchant houses in each of the five cross-sectional sample years (see figure 2).[34]

---

[34]See appendix table 1 for absolute numbers and averages.

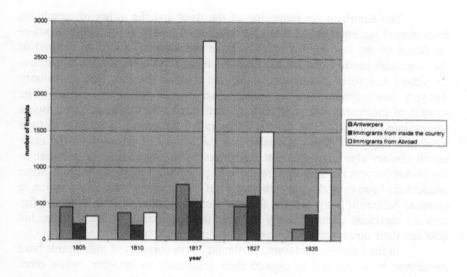

Figure 2: Number of Shipments Intended for the Selected Merchant Houses, 1805-1835

Source: See table 2.

The data, although rudimentary, illustrate the dominance of the foreign merchant houses in port traffic. Even though Antwerpers received more freight during the French period, foreigners on average ordered more. Moreover, a higher proportion of in-migrant businessmen, whether from the Southern Netherlands (32.3 percent) or abroad (48.4 percent), was actively involved in the maritime import trade compared to their native-born counterparts (21.5 percent). This suggests that Antwerp businessmen were not as interested or had greater difficulties participating in overseas trade after the reopening of the Scheldt. This changed dramatically, however, under the reign of William I. More than eighty percent of all traders active between 1815 and 1850 operated at an international level. But the most spectacular rise in the volume of business for any of the three groups was registered by foreign immigrants in 1817, when they dominated Antwerp's port traffic (both on average and in absolute terms). During the final two years (1827 and 1835) no fundamental changes occurred, and maritime trade remained firmly concentrated in the hands of in-migrants.

Explaining the Dominance of Immigrants in Maritime Trade

Port activities were dominated by immigrants, even though native-born Antwerp men were also attracted by the new opportunities offered by the reopening of the Scheldt. The reasons are not entirely clear but will be investigated in this essay.

The simultaneous reopening of the river and the influx of merchants from abroad has encouraged some historians of Antwerp to formulate hypotheses based on the key role of immigrants in international trade. At the end of the nineteenth century, Guillaume Beetemé remarked that foreigners in particular played key roles in maritime trade and stressed the fact that native-born Antwerp businessmen were not used to large-scale maritime business. The success of foreigners was explained by their business experience and network connections, which offered them a comparative advantage in relation to their local counterparts.[35] Other specialists on the history of Antwerp in the nineteenth century also suggested that foreigners were instrumental in demonstrating to Antwerpers the new opportunities to profit from maritime trade.[36] Some researchers have even doubted whether local businessmen were in a position to compete successfully against the foreign merchant houses.[37] The available figures on maritime trade certainly confirm the importance of immigrants, but how can their dominance in Antwerp's maritime trade be explained?

In the business literature, particular characteristics of immigrants have sometimes been stressed to explain their propensity to innovate, while other authors have emphasized the extent to which specific religions that emphasize rationality served as an ideal breeding ground for entrepreneurial success.[38] Research on the factors which determined whether "traditional" elites or "newcomers" profited from new business opportunities, particularly during periods of economic transformation, is not new, as the work on Amsterdam during the "Golden Age" between 1550 and 1630 demonstrates, and the available evidence suggests that economic success was often dependent upon the contribution of the business community and its ability to react to structural

---

[35]Beetemé, *Antwerpen*, II, 14.

[36]Demoulin, *Guillaume Ier*, 352-353; Jeuninckx, "De verhouding van de haven," 157; and Veraghtert, "From Inland Port to International Port," 311.

[37]Karel Degryse, *De Antwerpse fortuinen: kapitaalsaccumulatie, -investering en -rendement te Antwerpen in de 18de eeuw* (Antwerpen, 2005), 194.

[38]Werner Sombart, *Der Moderne Kapitalismus: Historisch-systematische Darstellung des gesamteuropäischen Wirtschaftslebens von seinen Anfängen bis zur Gegenwart* (2 vols., München, 1921), I, 884-889; and John E. Sawyer, "The Entrepreneur and the Social Order: France and the United States," in William Miller (ed.), *Men in Business: Essays in the History of Entrepreneurship* (Cambridge, MA, 1952), 7-22. The best-known proponent of the role of religion is Max Weber, who argued that the "Protestant ethic" was a breeding ground for capitalism; Max Weber, *The Protestant Ethic and the Spirit of Capitalism* (London, 1984), 47-48. See also Cor Trompetter, "On Entrepreneurship and Capitalism: Joseph Schumpeter and Max Weber on the Role of the Entrepreneur in Capitalist Development," *Economisch- en Sociaal-historisch Jaarboek*, LII (1989), 270-287.

change.[39] Research on the comparative entrepreneurial behaviour of newcomers and traditional elites has produced mixed results. While some scholars have concluded that newcomers were at the forefront in promoting innovation in international trade, others have stressed the relative importance of Amsterdam tradesmen or the fact that market conditions in the Dutch market had already evolved before the arrival of immigrants in a manner that facilitated the reorientation of trade and the spectacular growth in business activity.[40] But access to capital, business experience and network relations are frequently cited as key factors which can be used, either implicitly or explicitly, to explain differences in entrepreneurial behaviour.

Stanley Chapman's research on business behaviour in Great Britain during the nineteenth century suggests some important similarities. While foreign commission traders or agents with good contacts in their home countries tended to control Liverpool's imports of raw cotton and its export of British textiles, English businessmen dominated textile production and distribution in Great Britain.[41] In Le Havre, another expanding port in this period, the local business elite also feared competition in international trade from a growing group of foreigners.[42] Within the context of these wider international debates, the analysis will now focus on whether business experience, financial means or different network relations can explain the dominance of immigrants in Antwerp's maritime trade during the early years of the nineteenth century.

Business Experience and Financial Assets of Immigrants in Antwerp

To analyze whether immigrant businessmen were well prepared to do business in Antwerp, information was gathered on their professional careers, family backgrounds and business experiences at the moment when the Scheldt was

---

[39]For structural changes in the Amsterdam market see, for example, Jonathan I. Israel, *Dutch Primacy in World Trade, 1585-1740* (Oxford, 1989); and Jan De Vries and Ad van der Woude, *Nederland 1500-1815: De eerste ronde van moderne economische groei* (Amsterdam, 1995).

[40]For a recent study on the role of foreigners, see Oscar Gelderblom, *Zuid-Nederlandse kooplieden en de opkomst van de Amsterdamse stapelmarkt (1578-1630)* (Hilversum, 2000). For a comparison between natives and immigrants, see Clé Lesger, *Handel in Amsterdam ten tijde van de Opstand: Kooplieden, commerciële expansie en verandering in de ruimtelijke economie van de Nederlanden, ca. 1550-ca. 1630* (Hilversum, 2001).

[41]Chapman, *Merchant Enterprise*.

[42]Louis Bergeron, "Permanences et renouvellement du patronat," in Yves Lequin (ed.), *Histoire des français, 19e-20e siècles* (3 vols., Paris, 1984), II, 153-292.

reopened, as these represent some of the more tangible elements that could have played a part in facilitating their entrance into the world of business.

According to Jürgen Kocka, a family business environment can be viewed as an "ascribed advantage for the new generations to be used in market and competition processes of a very varying kind."[43] These advantages not only concerned the transfer of capital and knowledge but also the inculcation of attitudes and values, such as independence, accuracy and a willingness to work.[44] By following in the footsteps of relatives, businessmen could build up experience, gain personal access to partners and establish trustworthy relations with suppliers and clients. These contacts in turn generated trust, status and creditworthiness, critical factors in determining business success.[45] Family ties not only represented a source of capital, knowledge and labour but also served as a mechanism for the exchange of information on a basis of trust; they were therefore of critical importance in influencing a merchant's later career.[46]

Unfortunately, the professional backgrounds of immigrants are seldom easy to trace, particularly because many of them were only temporary residents in Antwerp. Their move to Antwerp cannot be described as an act of despair. Greta Devos, who has undertaken research on the port's German business community, has emphasized the distinction between businessmen who came to Antwerp to establish a branch of an existing firm and younger men who arrived to take up an apprenticeship.[47] In the case of those with responsi-

---

[43]Jürgen Kocka, "The Entrepreneur, the Family and Capitalism: Some Examples from the Early Phase of Industrialisation in Germany," in Harold C. Livesay (ed.), *Entrepreneurship and the Growth of Firms* (2 vols., Aldershot, 1995), II, 134.

[44]Because business education was still lacking at the beginning of the nineteenth century, researchers have stressed the importance of passing knowledge from father to son. See, for example, *ibid.*, 130-132; and Fritz Redlich, *Der Unternehmer: Wirtschafts- und Sozialgeschichtliche Studien* (Göttingen, 1964), 328.

[45]See, for example, Peter Mathias, "Strategies for Reducing Risk by Entrepreneurs in the Early Modern Period," in Clé Lesger and Leo Noordegraaf (eds.), *Entrepreneurs and Entrepreneurship in Early Modern Times: Merchants and Industrialists within the Orbit of the Dutch Staple Market* (Den Haag, 1995), 10-11; and Mary B. Rose, "The Family Firm in British Business, 1780-1914," in Maurice W. Kirby and Mary B. Rose (eds.), *Business Enterprise in Modern Britain: From the Eighteenth to the Twentieth Century* (London, 1994), 67.

[46]See, for example, Robert A. Pollak, "A Transaction Cost Approach to Families and Households," in Mary B. Rose (ed.), *Family Business* (Aldershot, 1995), 214.

[47]Greta Devos, "Inwijking en integratie van Duitse kooplieden te Antwerpen in de 19de eeuw," in Hugo Soly and Alfons K.L. Thijs (eds.), *Minderheden in Westeuropese steden (16de-20ste eeuw)* (Brussels, 1995), 138.

bility for setting up a new branch of an established firm, whether located in the Southern Netherlands (Belgium) or abroad, it is reasonable to assume that they were already embedded in business circles before moving to Antwerp. It also suggests that migration to Antwerp was part of a deliberate strategy to reinforce their economic activities.[48] The brothers Louis and Pierre De Bacques from Dunkerque, Jean Lodewijk and Ludwig Lemmé of Frankfurt-am-Main or the Van Der Hoeven brothers from Rotterdam acted in such a capacity. Others had already obtained their training in another port or commercial centre before moving to Antwerp or had worked abroad as merchants. Jean Mathias Gogel of Frankfurt-am-Main had grown up in a business family and worked in Göteborg, Stockholm and Stralsund before moving to Antwerp, while Jean Guillaume Rücker of Hamburg, Edmond and James Clegg of Manchester and Joshua Metcalf of Leeds had all been resident in London.[49] Most of these businessmen were in their thirties when they finally arrived in Antwerp.

But a number of young people also came to Antwerp: thirty-three foreign immigrants and fourteen migrants from within the country (51.6 and 34.1 percent of the total, respectively) were under the age of twenty-four when they arrived, often to take up an apprenticeship in either an established firm or with other in-migrant entrepreneurs. Apprenticeship offered an opportunity to acquire technical skills, but it was also important in terms of experience and recognized status; for these reasons it represented a good basis for the construction of commercial networks. Relatives, business partners or friends normally provided recommendations for an apprenticeship, and the system offered benefits for both parties. The master could reinforce his ties, while the apprentice obtained access to his master's local and extended business contacts, which often served at a later date as a starting point for the establishment of an independent firm.[50]

---

[48]As Stanley Chapman, *Merchant Enterprise*, 12, put it, "Merchant strategy was planned and controlled carefully by men of capital to extend their international trading networks."

[49]State Archives Antwerp (SAA), Antwerp Population Registers, 1800-1815 and 1815-1829.

[50]See, for example, Ida Bull, "Merchant Households and Their Networks in Eighteenth-Century Trondheim," *Continuity and Change*, XVII, No. 2 (2002), 213-232; and Marzagalli, *Les boulevards*, 41-43. Milja van Tielhof, *The "Mother of All Trades:" The Baltic Grain Trade in Amsterdam from the Late 16th to the Early 19th Century* (Leiden, 2002), 295 ff., shows the importance of travelling for the grain trade by the Amsterdam merchant Willem De Clercq. Apprenticeship in a foreign country was often used as a test for a new generation of businessmen; see Stanley Chapman, "The International Houses: The Continental Contribution to British Commerce, 1800-1860," *Journal of European Economic History*, VI, No. 1 (1977), 8-9.

David Parish, for example, acquired his initial training in his father's important merchant bank in Hamburg.[51] He came to Antwerp and worked with Gregorian Agie, who had been born in the French harbour town of Lorient. Agie started his career in the merchant house of Balguerie and Co. in Bordeaux and travelled to China under its authority.[52] The Antwerp firm of Parish, Agie and Co. took Jean Abraham and Guillaume Nottebohm, sons of a wealthy merchant in Bielefeld, as apprentices.[53] Once their apprenticeship was completed, the Nottebohm brothers started to trade on their own account. At a later date Jean and Albert Insinger of Amsterdam, sons of the merchant Herman Insinger, were also involved in the firm of Parish and Agie.[54] They were already known to David Parish because of his business ties with the merchant-bankers Hope and Co. of Amsterdam, which worked with the Insinger family.[55] Such relationships generated a complex web of spatial interconnections, particularly with relatives and business contacts in their home country or abroad. They provided significant advantages to immigrants who transferred their business activities to Antwerp or started their career as apprentices in the young port town.

Although some more experienced and older foreign traders migrated to Antwerp, many immigrants were young: some had yet to finish their apprenticeships or were at the start of their professional careers. As a consequence, the extent of their financial assets should not be overrated. Nonetheless, a few sources suggest that some in-migrants were able to rely on financial support or at least a modest starting capital. The grain trader Corneil Van Der Hoeven from Rotterdam, for example, founded a firm in Antwerp with an initial capital of 211,640.21 *francs*, two-thirds of which came from relatives in Rotterdam.[56] The capital possessed by the Kreglinger brothers was estimated at 42,328

---

[51]Richard Ehrenberg, *Das Haus Parish in Hamburg* (Jena, 1925), 2 and 82.

[52]Beetemé, *Antwerpen*, II, 15-17; and Augustin Thys, *Négociants et Industriels Anversois au siècle dernier d'après le journal "La presse"* (Antwerp, 1906), 3-4.

[53]"Nottebohm aus Bochum in Westfalen," *Deutsches Geschlechterbuch* (Limburg, 1962), 81-84.

[54]Insinger and Co. expanded rapidly during the Anglo-French War and is still active as a banking company in Amsterdam. See Frank J.A. Broeze, "A Challenge without Response: Holland and the Transpacific Route to East Asia after 1815," *Economisch- en Sociaal-Historisch Jaarboek*, XXXVIII (1975), 267; and Jonker and Sluyterman, *Thuis op de wereldmarkt*, 168.

[55]Marten G. Buist, *At spes non fracta. Hope & Co., 1770-1815: Merchant Bankers and Diplomats at Work* (Den Haag, 1974), 187 and 295-297.

[56]SAA, Notarial Records, 1045, E.A. Podor, no. 135, 23 May 1810.

francs when they arrived in Antwerp in 1797. Letters between the Kreglingers – Seybold Kreglinger in Karlsruhe, Christopher Kreglinger in Emmending and Theodor Friedrich Kreglinger in Paris – reveal that the young Kreglingers in Belgium constantly requested financial support. Sometimes they received money through the Bethmann Bank in Frankfurt, where Georg Kreglinger had almost certainly served his apprenticeship, while his brother Christian had worked as a young man in the bank of Gold and Co. in Amsterdam.[57]

Extensive involvement in international networks not only offered in-migrant merchants greater opportunities in the international commission trade but also enabled them to receive credit or other forms of financial support. Ridgway, Mertens and Co. and Parish, Agie and Co., for example, enjoyed monopoly positions in Antwerp's trade with North America in the early nineteenth century, but they cooperated closely with Baring Brothers, a firm of important merchant-bankers which specialized in commercial and financial transactions in the Atlantic trade. It is quite possible that the two Antwerp firms obtained financial support from Baring Brothers, which granted substantial credits (some of them without collateral) for continental houses engaging in trade with America.[58]

Although their starting capital was often quite modest, empirical evidence suggests that foreign merchant houses in Antwerp quickly managed to accumulate wealth. The book value of G. and C. Kreglinger in 1810 was 409,285 *francs*, but it was placed at approximately 600,000 *francs* according to a contemporary list of wealthy businessmen.[59] Regardless, the firm had managed to multiply its assets at least ten-fold in little more than a decade. The business capital of David Parish and Co. and Corneil Van Der Hoeven was estimated at between one and two million *francs* at the same time.[60] Nevertheless, because evidence relating to the starting capital of in-migrant merchants is limited, it is difficult to sustain the hypothesis that access to significant financial assets was critically important in explaining their relative success in international trade. Moreover, there was no lack of capital in Antwerp since the city was home to a significant number of wealthy inhabitants in search of lucrative investments. More than one-third of native-born businessmen in our sample belonged to Antwerp's financial and economic elite in the late eighteenth century, with average fortunes of more

---

[57]Private Archives, G. and C. Kreglinger, letters of 10 August, 24 August, 1 September and 11 September 1797; and Baetens, "Het ontstaan," 23 and 25-26.

[58]Ralph W. Hidy, *The House of Baring in American Trade and Finance: English Merchant Bankers at Work, 1763-1861* (Cambridge, MA, 1949), 138-139; and Chapman, *Rise of Merchant Banking*, 11 and 40.

[59]Baetens, "Het ontstaan," 25-26.

[60]Augustin Thys, "Commercants anversois en 1810," *Recueil des bulletins de la propriété publiés par le journal l'Escaut d'Anvers*, XXIV (1892), 60-68.

than 500,000 *francs*. In short, local businessmen also had considerable financial assets.[61]

Immigrants and Their Use of International Networks in Antwerp

It is also important to address the issue of whether differences in the scope, range or quality of networks affected the entrepreneurial attitudes and choices of native-born and in-migrant merchants. Webs of relations, based on contacts and business connections with other merchants or entrepreneurs, can be regarded as important "social capital" for international trade.[62] Relationships based on mutual trust were not only important in the private sphere but also could be useful in facilitating business arrangements. Economic transactions implied risks and important costs, such as the need to protect property rights, enforce contracts and gather information. In terms of economic theory, therefore, networks can be viewed as an efficient way to reduce the risks and costs involved in business transactions.[63]

Networks were particularly useful for gathering and verifying information. They were not only channels through which commodities or capital flowed but also mechanisms for the distribution of information, particularly at a time when fast and easy forms of communication (such as the telegraph) were not yet available.[64] Steamers were not in service for long-distance trade, and even regular sailing services were limited. The irregularities and uncertainties in business

---

[61]Members of the financial and economic elite in Antwerp during the eighteenth century are well known thanks to the research of Karel Degryse. He distinguished two categories: families with a capital of one million *francs* or more (the so-called "A families") and those with a capital between 500,000 and one million *francs* ("B families"). Of the selected Antwerp businessmen, fourteen belonged to an A family and twenty-three to a B family. Degryse, *De Antwerpse fortuinen*, appendices Ia and Ib.

[62]The term "social capital" is used by sociologists such as Robert Putnam and Pierre Bourdieu to refer to the existence of a wide range of social networks based on trust, family relations, authority and so on. For a critical overview of the use of this concept in history, see Dario Gaggio, "Do Social Historians Need Social Capital?" *Social History*, XXIX, No. 4 (2004), 499-513.

[63]For a comparison between neo-classical economic theory and socio-economics, see Etzione and Lawrence (eds.), *Socio-Economics*. For a "relational" view of economics, see Mark Granovetter, "Economic Action and Social Structure: The Problem of Embeddedness," *American Journal of Sociology*, XCI, No. 3 (1985), 481-510; and Mark C. Casson, "Entrepreneurial Networks in International Business," *Business and Economic History*, XXVI, No. 2 (1997), 811-823.

[64]Mark C. Casson, "Institutional Economics and Business History: A Way Forward?" *Business History*, XXXIX, No. 4 (1997), 150-153; and Jonathan Brown and Mary B. Rose, "Introduction," in Brown and Rose (eds.), *Entrepreneurship*, 2-3.

transactions could be more or less offset through the building and maintenance of networks. Indeed, personal webs helped to speed communication and reduce transaction costs. Moreover, networks were of fundamental importance in an uncertain business world for gathering and exchanging information about products and markets, economic and political developments, reliable agents and trustworthy businessmen.[65]

It was crucial to have contacts with the "right" people because, as Mark Casson has observed, "'Who you know' is often more important than 'what you know' because the people that you know can plug the gaps in what you know."[66] Sometimes the best persons on whom to rely were those with practical, technical or commercial knowledge at their disposal; in other cases it was sufficient to get in touch with people who knew a lot of other people, thereby facilitating interpersonal information flows. By using existing contacts or by accessing new business networks via letters of introduction, trust could be established and reputations built. Indeed, formal arrangements and institutional structures only provided partial protection because personal trust and reputation were critically important for guaranteeing the effectiveness of any business dealing.[67] Trust (the expectation that an agreement would be honoured) and reputation (based on the proven honesty of a business associate) continued to underpin commercial transactions and the maintenance of long-lasting relations among merchants. Entrepreneurs, who sometimes risked their lives and fortunes in business transactions, were not only concerned with maximizing their profits but also wanted to maintain their reputations. In a high-trust relationship, the risk of being cheated was markedly lower. A good reputation could be enhanced by cultivating social contacts, and a continuous investment of both time and money was necessary to maintain the utility of relationship networks. Respect, appreciation and respectability were only achieved within the framework of an intricate pattern of social relations which had been constructed in a conscious manner and often required careful manipulation and constant cultivation.[68]

---

[65]Gillian Cookson, "Family Firms and Business Networks: Textile Engineering in Yorkshire, 1780-1830," *Business History*, XXXIX, No. 1 (1997), 1-20; and Granovetter, "Economic Action and Social Structure."

[66]Casson, "Entrepreneurial Networks," 813.

[67]See, for example, Mathias, "Strategies for Reducing Risk," 5-24; and John Smail, "Credit, Risk, and Honor in Eighteenth Century Commerce," *Journal of British Studies*, XLIV, No. 2 (2005), 430-456.

[68]This relates to Pierre Bourdieu's theory that social capital is an individual matter; he insists on the importance of building and cultivating social relations. For the basics of this theory, see Pierre Bourdieu, "The Forms of Capital," in John G.

Antwerp is a particularly suitable place to assess the importance of network relationships within the business community. After all, Antwerp businessmen had been deprived of extensive international contacts because of the long-term closure of the Scheldt. An analysis of the spatial range and extent of business networks in this context will provide a means of examining the relevance of Beeteme's hypothesis that native-born business suffered from a lack of international contacts. Indeed, as far as international networks were concerned, it is entirely plausible that local businessmen were at a disadvantage compared to immigrants (including some merchants whose place of birth was elsewhere in the Southern Netherlands) who benefited from different geographic roots, family ties or had travelled or trained abroad.[69] It is highly unlikely that these in-migrants would have severed their external networks after their move to Antwerp.

Such an assumption is confirmed by the extensive correspondence between Georges and Christian Kreglinger in Antwerp and their brother Frederic Kreglinger in Paris. In a letter of 10 August 1797, Frederic promised his brothers to use all his power to help them. He sent by post information about products, prices and important suppliers, as well as news about the political situation in Prussia and France. He made every effort to facilitate the introduction of his younger brothers into an international trading web. He promised to write letters to "good friends," such as the partners in Von Emert, Gemuse and Co. in Bordeaux, and urged his brothers to contact trading companies in Bordeaux, Le Havre, Nantes, Bremen, Hamburg and Basel which held his firm in great esteem.[70] In many cases, therefore, foreign businessmen who came to Antwerp operated within an existing international web. Indeed, the potential benefits of these connections were often maximized following migration to Antwerp. Initially, the trade routes exploited by in-migrant merchants were directed towards cities and regions where they already had relatives, business contacts or friends. John Mathias Gogel, for example, originally came from a merchant family in Frankfurt but had lived elsewhere before moving to Antwerp. His business partner in Antwerp, Dietrich Lüni(n)g, was Swedish. The two probably became acquainted in Göteborg. In 1817 the firm Lüning, Gogel and Co. was the only trading company in Antwerp which dispatched ships on consignment and imported goods from Helsingborg, Halmstadt, Göteborg and Stockholm. Lüning became vice-consul for Norway and Sweden in Antwerp in 1821, which was a logical

---

Richardson (ed.), *Handbook of Theory and Research for the Sociology of Education* (New York, 1985), 249.

[69]See Devos and Greefs, "German Presence."

[70]Private Archives, G. and C. Kreglinger, letters of 10 and 24 August, and 1 and 11 September 1797.

consequence of his extensive trading contacts in Scandinavia and the reputation the firm enjoyed as a result of its trade in metals and timber.[71]

Good relations abroad also offered additional opportunities. For example, some immigrants were able to profit from market imbalances which affected the grain trade in 1816-1817. Foreigners with contacts in the Northern Netherlands and around the Baltic dominated grain imports into the harbour. In 1817, thirty merchant houses in the sample database were involved in the grain trade, but eighty percent of grain imports (from a total of 903 cargoes) were handled by four foreign firms: Adrian Saportas, Van Der Hoeven Brothers, Beerenbroeck and Riem and Nottebohm Brothers. The key figures in charge of these firms had all been born in the Northern Netherlands, traditionally an important staple market for grain, or had trained there.[72] A reverse market imbalance on the supply side affected the import of British textiles in the same years. As a result of the import ban on British products during the Continental Blockade, textiles had been stockpiled in Britain, but after 1814 these products were dumped on Continental markets at low prices.[73] British firms, working on commission, were responsible for the import and distribution of textiles on the Continent, including James Clegg and Brother from Manchester, Wilson and Co. from London, Joshua Metcalf from Leeds and Thompson and Co. from St. Andrews. They all specialized in textiles, and their Antwerp-based operations in 1817 facilitated a rapid distribution of these commodities on the Continent.

But at the start of their careers in Antwerp, these in-migrants had not established the necessary contacts to exploit the available opportunities across the full range of the port's trades. Some enjoyed advantages either with southern Europe (such as the Kreglinger family)[74] or northern Europe (like the Rückers of Hamburg), while others benefited from useful connections in the North American trade (Ridgway from Philadelphia or Clibborn from New York). As far as trade with South American ports such as Rio de Janeiro and Buenos Aires was con-

---

[71]R. Jung, *Die Frankfurter Familie Familie Gogel, 1576-1918* (Frankfurt, 1920), 32 and 37; MAA, Bib. 3400, *Arrivages*, 1817; SAA, PA, J 217/A, letter of 20 August 1821; Beetemé, *Antwerpen*, II, 81 and 86; and Greta Devos, "Die Firma Königs-Günther & Co.," 867.

[72]Adriaan Saportas was born in Amsterdam, while the brothers Jean and Corneille Vanderhoeven came from Rotterdam. The Prussian Frederik Riem stayed for years in Amsterdam, where he also married an Amsterdam girl. The Nottebohm brothers probably could rely on the contacts of David Parish in the Northern Netherlands.

[73]The Antwerp market was flooded with British manufacturers during this year; Demoulin, *Guillaume Ier*, 123-124.

[74]Georges Kreglinger lived in Livorno between 1791 and 1796 and worked for the firm Otto Franck and Co.; see Vincent Nolte, *Fifty Years in Both Hemispheres* (New York, 1854), 3-4.

cerned, there is no evidence of the existence of any trading networks, despite the fact that commerce with this region played a critical role in Antwerp's overall development in the nineteenth century. If new contacts as a rule were established through existing relations, then in-migrant merchants were once again advantaged. Merchants who received goods on consignment from North America, transported on American-flagged ships, later received freight from Asia or South America on similar vessels.[75] But although this is an excellent example of the cumulative benefits of relationship networks, it was certainly not the only possible course of action, as merchant shipowners from Ostend, Bruges and Ghent dispatched their vessels to South American ports with significant success and opened these important markets for Antwerp.[76] Although these businessmen already had some trading experience, it is clear that they were not able to rely on webs of international contacts to exploit the potential of this trade in its early stages of development.

The crux of the matter is whether it was really so difficult to build a reliable network of trustworthy international relations given the absence of any structural constraints which hindered access to international trade. Different forms of trading arrangements and collaboration agreements could be set up without too many legal, financial or technical problems. Furthermore, businessmen met each other regularly in Antwerp. A small number held office in the Chamber of Commerce, which instigated collective action and provided support for both nativeborn and foreign traders.[77] Merchants met each other in the port, at the stock exchange or in informal settings, such as the social and cultural clubs which were established in Antwerp during this period.[78] If they needed information – directly or indirectly – it could certainly be acquired locally.

Moreover, both foreign and native-born merchants were successful in re-establishing trading connections with London shortly after the lifting of the Continental Blockade, which suggests that contacts and networks could be quickly

---

[75]For example, the firms Ridgway, Mertens and Co. (later the firm Mertens, Mosselman and Co.) and Parish, Agie and Co. (later Agie and Insinger) acted as such.

[76]Mathias Joostens from Zoersel in the province of Antwerp, for example, sent his ships to Havana, Rio Grande and Rio de Janeiro. Ships of the firm Bisschop-Basteyns and N.J. De Cock (a cooperative venture between a Louvain merchant and a Ghent shipowner) went to Valparaiso, Havana and Matanzas.

[77]Ilja Van Damme, "De Antwerpse Kamer van Koophandel als publiekrechtelijke instelling, 1802-1871," in Greta Devos and Ilja Van Damme (eds.), *In de ban van Mercurius: Twee eeuwen Kamer van Koophandel en Nijverheid van Antwerpen-Waasland, 1802-2002* (Tielt, 2002), 23, 34-35, 234 and 237; and Greefs, "Zakenlieden," 343-347.

[78]Hilde Greefs, "Informele netwerken van de zakenelite in Antwerpen, 1796-1830," *De achttiende eeuw*, XXXIX, No. 2 (2007), 61-87.

rebuilt if this was in the best interests of a firm.[79] Conversely, not all foreign merchant houses were successful in adapting to changing market circumstances, as was evident in the case of the trade in colonial goods. This trade played a central role in Antwerp's port traffic, as it did at other European ports during the first half of the nineteenth century, but the most successful merchants in these trades were those who established direct connections with counterparts in the exporting ports. These men dominated trade in colonial goods in the 1820s, primarily because they had made the right strategic choices when markets were reopened following the fall of Napoleon.[80]

Yet many merchants, irrespective of their background, found it difficult to change their market orientation.[81] For example, during the French occupation a number of Antwerp merchants found it hard to break away from traditional trade via ports such as Rotterdam and Amsterdam, but even some of the foreign merchant houses failed to refocus their business activity from indirect to direct trading in colonial commodities. The traffic in colonial goods was substantial, but it was also a very competitive niche. Although it was never a monopoly, it was tightly controlled by a small group of merchant houses, which partly explains the departure of some foreign firms during the 1820s when trading conditions were relatively favourable.[82] While Antwerp businessmen sought other opportunities in finance or insurance, many foreigners left.[83] Another option was to change trade routes. Antwerp merchants, native-born and immigrants alike, tended to specialize in products from southern Europe, such as wine, oils and fruits; these trades

---

[79]Antwerp merchant houses, such as Egide Cenie, Egide De Backer et fils, Jean Bogaers fils and Jean François Vermoelen specialized in the import of colonial commodities via London.

[80]Greefs, "Zakenlieden," 236-242.

[81]Robert Wilson, for example, illustrates the difficulties of the wool merchants in Leeds to reorient their trade from the Continent to new markets in America. Robert G. Wilson, *Gentlemen Merchants. The Merchant Community in Leeds, 1700-1830* (New York, 1971), 60 and 95.

[82]In the sample of 1827, fifty-nine merchants, who were active in maritime trade in 1817 were missing; of this group, 28.8 percent (all foreigners) had left town. In the meanwhile, the average number of shipments for the remaining traders in the group rose; see appendix table 1.

[83]For a comparison in business behaviour between Antwerpers and immigrants in Antwerp, see Hilde Greefs, "De terugkeer van Mercurius: De divergerende keuzes van de zakenelite in Antwerpen en het belang van relatienetwerken na de heropening van de Schelde (1795-1850)," *Tijdschrift voor sociale en economische geschiedenis*, V, No. 2 (2008), 55-85.

were entirely separate from the highly competitive trade in colonial goods.[84] But local agents were required for trade in these products. Periods of economic pressure or political instability therefore led to different solutions: while some merchants decided to withdraw from Antwerp, others stayed and reoriented their business activities. International maritime trade was competitive but unstable. It attracted a lot of fortune hunters, but few were in it for the long haul, perhaps because it required flexibility and adaptability to changing circumstances.

Some Concluding Remarks

Thanks to the reopening of the Scheldt in 1795, Antwerp was able to regain its position in the early nineteenth century as the best-situated port in the Southern Netherlands. This essay has attempted to identify those merchants who were able to profit the most from the subsequent boom in maritime trade and to discus the factors which led to the dominance of immigrants in international trade. Antwerp is a useful testing ground for assessing the wider applicability of a number of hypotheses relating to the specific roles of "traditional" and "new elites" during periods of transition. Moreover, because of the absence of international maritime contacts during the eighteenth century, it provides a framework for reviewing the relative importance for business success of building and maintaining relationship networks, as highlighted in the recent literature on business behaviour. After the reopening of the Scheldt and the revival of international maritime trade, Antwerp's merchants, whether native-born or in-migrants, were faced with similar problems in developing connections to exploit the new opportunities.

Sample evidence on ship arrivals in Antwerp confirms the extent to which maritime trade during the first decades of the nineteenth century was dominated by immigrant merchants. Foreigners who moved to Antwerp early in the century were particularly successful in exploiting new trades. To reassess existing hypotheses relating to the history of Antwerp within the context of recent literature explaining differences in business behaviour, three factors were examined to explain the relative dominance of immigrants: business experience, financial assets and the extent of their networks The analysis indicates that the spatial extent of their commercial networks was a key factor in their success in maritime trade. Extensive links in their country of origin or elsewhere not only facilitated their integration into the commercial world of Antwerp but also reinforced the decision to base their operations there. To this extent, they initially enjoyed strategic advantages in international trade in comparison with the local business elite.

---

[84]An example was the Antwerp merchant Joseph Elsen, who specialized in the import of colonial goods from London in 1817. In the 1820s he reoriented his trading activities to southern Europe, specializing in the import of oils and wine. Another example is Godefroid de Vries (firm of the Widow Vermeylen), who specialized in imports from Messina in Sicily.

Confronted with competition from a constantly changing group of immigrants, Antwerp's native-born merchants at first shied away from extensive involvement in maritime trade. But during the first decades of the nineteenth century it became clear that the immigrant mercantile group was inherently too unstable to overwhelm the local elite completely. Maritime business remained risky and uncertain due to political and economic instability and required a great deal of flexibility on the part of the businessmen involved. While foreigners often left town, Antwerp businessmen sought new opportunities in "local" sectors, including trade-related industries and finance. A complementary relationship soon evolved: while foreign merchants resident in Antwerp exploited their international networks, native-born businessmen strengthened their links with the local and regional economies.[85] In pursuing these strategies, both groups acted with a clear economic logic by concentrating on activities in which they could realize the largest profits.

Appendix Table 1
Number of Shipments in Total (and on Average) Intended for Selected Merchant Houses, 1805-1835 (Absolute Numbers)

	Number of Freights in Total (on Average) Intended for the Selected Merchant Houses in Each Sample				
	1805	1810	1817	1827	1835
Number of Freights Intended for the Selected Merchant Houses (average)	1009 (17.1)	971 (13.9)	4052 (44.1)	2590 (56.3)	1471 (42.0)
For Antwerpers	455 (14.7)	381 (11.5)	776 (23.5)	473 (27.8)	159 (15.9)
For in-migrants from the Southern Netherlands (Belgium)	224 (12.4)	208 (10.4)	537 (24.4)	616 (47.3)	366 (33.3)
For Foreign Immigrants	330 (33.0)	382 (22.5)	2739 (74.0)	1501 (93.8)	946 (67.6)

Sources: "Etat des Bâtiments français et étrangers entrés au port d'Anvers," *Journal du Commerce d'Anvers* (Antwerpen, 1805 and 1810); SAA, Bib. 3400, *Arrivages*, 1817 and 1827; and Bib. 3399, *Annonces maritimes*, 1835.

---

[85]See Greefs, "De terugkeer."

Migrants, Merchants and Philanthropists: Hierarchies in Nineteenth-Century Greek Ports

Athanasios Gekas

Introduction

The growth and decline of nineteenth-century port cities has been the subject of considerable research in a comparative European context, and their role in European urban development has been established. Related research has also shown the roles of merchants as economic and social actors in Mediterranean ports.[1] This essay draws on research on the port of Corfu during the period of British rule (1815-1864) and on histories of other ports in the Greek kingdom, especially Patras, Syros (Ermoupoli) and Piraeus.[2] Most studies of these ports aspire to be comprehensive urban histories and focus on demography, social structure, port development and growth rather than issues of urban networks and hierarchies. Still, an examination of this literature shows that despite di-

---

[1] W.R. Lee, "The Socio-economic and Demographic Characteristics of Port Cities: A Typology for Comparative Analysis?" *Urban History*, XXV, No. 2 (1998), 147-172. For an earlier but very valuable historiographical essay on port cities, see Frank Broeze, "Port Cities: The Search for an Identity," *Journal of Urban History*, XI, No. 2 (1985), 209-225. Among the most ambitious research projects was the one proposed by Stuart Woolf in 1997 to compare Naples, Malaga, Lisbon, Oporto, Bordeaux, Copenhagen, Viipuri and Venice; the emphasis was placed on the role of the entrepreneur as defined by Schumpeter. The project attempted a shift from strictly economic and quantifiable factors of change to an emphasis on looking at how urban elites, especially merchants, responded to the decline of these European ports during the nineteenth century. Another important project relevant to this essay was carried out by the Fernand Braudel Center; some of the results were published in a special edition of its *Review*, XVI, No. 4 (1993).

[2] Vassilis Kardasis, *Syros: Crossroads of the Eastern Mediterranean* (1832-1857) (Athens, 1987, in Greek); Vasias Tsokopoulos, *Piraeus, 1835-1870: Introduction to the History of the Greek Manchester* (Athens, 1984, in Greek); Giannis Giannitsiotis, *The Social History of Piraeus: The Formation of the Bourgeoisie, 1860-1910* (Athens, 2006, in Greek); and Nikos Bakounakis, *Patra: A Greek Capital in the 19th Century* (Athens, 1995, in Greek). For the Ionian islands and their ports under British rule, see Athanasios Gekas, "The Commercial Bourgeoisie of the Ionian Islands under British rule, 1815-1864: Class Formation in a Semi-colonial Society" (Unpublished PhD thesis, University of Essex, 2004).

verse characteristics and differences in the timing of the process of elite formation, a similar methodology can advance our understanding of how networks of
power developed in all the ports. The diverse composition of the various Greek
ports due to in-migration is described first. The essay then demonstrates how
the synergy between merchants and state authorities – evident in the emergence
of commercial institutions – created new mercantile hierarchies. In addition to
those that derived from wealth, commercial activity and access to resources;
new networks were developed based upon factors such as the ability to raise
capital and to gain access to information. The last part of the essay examines
the role of merchants as philanthropists in response to real and perceived
threats to urban life.

Demographic and Cultural Characteristics of Port Cities

As Robert Lee has argued, "a key feature of the demographic development of
major port cities was a disproportionate dependency on in-migration."[3] The
examples of Ermoupoli, Piraeus and to some extent Corfu suggest that this was
true in Greece as well. The population growth of Ermoupoli – and in the period 1835-1870 of Piraeus as well – was a result of planned development, an
influx of refugees from Crete and rising fertility rates.[4] These were essentially
new towns. In-migration from other islands was due to the needs of the nascent
Greek economy, which was extremely dependent on ports for the export of
agricultural produce and the import of manufactured and other goods. The
settlers came from areas previously under Ottoman rule that were ravaged during the Greek War of Independence, and most were searching for a new beginning. Successive waves of refugees from the islands of Hydra, Psara and
Chios (whose destruction in 1822 was immortalised by Eugène Delacroix in a
famous painting) swelled the populations of Ermoupoli and Piraeus. The
French government, by protecting the Catholic population of Syros during the
war, also contributed significantly to this migrant flow.[5] Common origin was
instrumental in the creation of credit networks in Ermoupoli, as people from
the same island, especially Chios, cooperated and formed alliances. Overall,
human capital was extremely important for commercial growth in the cases of
both Ermoupoli and Piraeus. In 1821 Syros had a mere 150 inhabitants, but by
1828 it had risen to 13,805 and by 1853 to 19,981.[6] In Ermoupoli, however,

---

[3]Lee, "Socio-economic and Demographic Characteristics," 156.

[4]Tsokopoulos, *Piraeus*, 89.

[5]Violeta Hionidou, "Nineteenth-Century Urban Greek Households: The Case
of Hermoupolis, 1861-1879," *Continuity and Change*, XIV, No. 3 (1999), 403-427.

[6]Kardasis, *Syros*, 29 and 32-33.

both population and commercial growth slowed during the Crimean War. The port of Syros depended almost exclusively on the transit trade between the West and the East, and its merchant and shipping capital failed to diversify or adjust to the transition from sail to steam.[7] Following the same pattern of population growth, Piraeus grew from less than 200 people in 1835 to 1011 one year later and to 10,963 in 1870.[8] There was also inter-port migration, as many settlers moved permanently from Syros to Piraeus in 1835. This migrant flow was also due to the state's decision to make land available to the newcomers. The exodus of human capital from Chios had far-reaching consequences not only for the new Greek ports but also for the dispersal and subsequent success of Chiot businessmen.[9]

Migrants came to Patras mainly from the southern Ionian islands in the late eighteenth century and again after 1828 following the revival of the currant trade, although most were seasonal labourers. By contrast, many merchants who settled in the city came from the mainland (the Peloponnese).[10] Long-established commercial networks between Patras and the Ionian islands were developed further in the nineteenth century following the growth of Patras; the Ionian islands and Patras were to some extent integrated economically both by the transfer of capital (in the marine insurance sector, for example) and by currant exporters operating from the islands of Kefalonia and Zante, as well as from Patras.[11]

---

[7]It has been a while since the last monograph appeared on Ermoupoli, and any new work on the city's social structure would probably shed new light on its economic and social development.

[8]Michales Chouliarakis, *Geographical, Administrative and Population Evolution of Greece, 1821-1971* (3 vols., Athens 1973-1974), I, part B.

[9]Gelina Harlaftis, "Mapping the Greek Maritime Diaspora from the Early Eighteenth to the Late Twentieth Centuries," in Ina Baghdiantz McCabe, Gelina Harlaftis and Ioanna Pepelasis Minoglou (eds.), *Diaspora Entrepreneurial Networks: Four Centuries of History* (Oxford, 2005), 147-171.

[10]Bakounakis, *Patra*, 72-73.

[11]For the history of Greek-owned shipping and the "Chiot" and "Ionian" phases of this development, see Gelina Harlaftis, *A History of Greek-Owned Shipping: The Making of an International Tramp Fleet, 1830 to the Present Day* (London, 1996). For the transition from sail to steam in the shipping sector, see Vassilis Kardasis, *From Sail to Steam: Greek Merchant Shipping, 1858-1914* (Athens, 1993, in Greek). On the marine insurance companies, see Athanasios Gekas, "A Sector 'Most Beneficial to Commerce:' Marine Insurance Companies in Nineteenth-Century Greek Port Cities," *Entrepreneurial History Discussion Papers*, No. 1 (2008) (http://www.ehdp.net./p001/p001.pdf).

The influx of migrants from the Ottoman mainland contributed to the diversity of the port of Corfu and added to the immigrant population dating back to the arrival of the Sephardic Jews in the sixteenth century. Registers from Corfu Town in 1812 and 1818 provide a way to decipher early nineteenth-century migration patterns and commercial specialization. In these documents the *negozianti*, the principal wholesale merchants, were clearly distinguished from the *mercanti* (retailers) and the *bottegai* (shopkeepers).[12] Merchant-immigrants from Bordeaux and England were recorded as well as the Chiot firm of Theodoro Ralli and Company, a member of one of the most famous Greek commercial houses. When in 1819 the British Crown sold the town of Parga on the mainland opposite the port to a regional Ottoman notable, Ali Pasha, for £120,000, approximately 2000 refugees fled to Corfu, thereby reinforcing existing commercial networks in both the Adriatic and the Ottoman Empire. In later years the ethnic diversity of the merchant group was enriched by in-migrants from Epirus, other areas of the Ottoman Empire, the Italian states, Malta, Britain, Holland and even Switzerland.[13] During the period of British rule European merchants settled in Corfu to establish their own firms to act as agents for shipping companies or to engage in general trade, auctions and the provision of luxury goods and services (such as discounting bills) for the port's elite of British officers, foreign and local merchants and travellers. The founding of the Ionian Bank in 1840 further incorporated the Ionian ports into an imperial business network.[14] Foreign merchants involved in the import of British manufactured and colonial goods and the export of currants (in Kefalonia, Zante and Patras) also served as consuls for various states with regional commercial and trading interests. From the 1850s onwards, when Corfu, Patras, Syros and later Piraeus were linked with other ports in the Mediterranean by the expansion of steamship lines, foreign and local merchants also acted as commercial agents for these companies. A multiplicity of overlapping roles and commercial specializations were inherent characteristics of the merchant groups in the respective port cities.

---

[12]Istoriko Arheio Kerkyras (IAK), Town Population Register, 1812-1814, Executive, Police 1319; and Register of Corfu Merchants, Corfu 1818, Ionian State 232a. For a good definition of the terms *negozianti, mercanti* and *bottegai*, see Olga Katsiardi-Hering, *The Greek Merchant Colony of Trieste, 1750-1830* (2 vols., Athens, 1986), II, 393-408 (in Greek).

[13]Albert Mousson, *Corfu and Cephalonia: A Tour in 1858* (Athens, 1995), 41 (in Greek).

[14]Philip L. Cottrell, *The Ionian Bank: An Imperial Institution, 1839-1864* (Athens, 2007).

During the period of British rule many merchants who migrated to Corfu became naturalized Ionian subjects.[15] The privileged status of the Ionian islands as a British protectorate, and the position of Corfu as an important Adriatic port, induced migrant merchants to become Ionian nationals. The proximity of the island to Epirus and southern Italy explains the origin of most of the "foreigners" who requested Ionian citizenship. Approximately three-quarters of those petitioning for Ionian citizenship requested that Corfu be their political domicile, and a third of those whose occupation was recorded were merchants. There was a steady increase in naturalization petitions throughout the 1850s and a sharp decline in the early 1860s, suggesting a negative correlation between the trend in petitioning for citizenship and the unification of the islands with Greece after 1862.[16] As contemporaries noted, several important merchants were Jewish, which added to the diversity of the merchant group.[17] When in 1864 the Islands were united with Greece and formally adopted its constitution, which enfranchised all males above the age of twenty-one, forty percent of the Jews recorded in the electoral list were merchants, confirming the religious diversity of Corfu's mercantile class.[18]

But what does this tell us about urban hierarchies and business networks? While data on migration and the demographic characteristics of port cities provide a useful starting point for analyzing the profile of merchant communities, they cannot by themselves be used to construct overall interpretations about the formation of urban hierarchies. In order to answer questions relating to the role of merchants in the configuration of urban networks and hierarchies, we need also to examine institutions of urban governance, including commercial and philanthropic associations.

---

[15]From the early 1840s onwards the *Gazette*, the official newspaper of the Ionian state, published all naturalizations. The information included the petitioner's name, place of origin, occupation (in most cases) and place of domicile.

[16]The concentration of naturalized merchants in Corfu and Zante was striking: forty-nine, or fifty-five percent of the eighty-nine merchants naturalized, asked for political domicile in Corfu, while thirty-eight, or forty-two percent, chose Zante. That ninety-seven percent requested domicile in these two towns shows the indifference of the immigrant merchants to the towns of Argostoli and Lixuri in Kefalonia; *Ionian Islands Government Gazette (IIGG)*, 1840-1963.

[17]David T. Ansted, *The Ionian Islands in the Year 1863* (London, 1863), 14. For the history of the Jews in Corfu, see Sakis Gekas, "The Port Jews of Corfu and the 'Blood Libel' of 1891: A Tale of Many Centuries and of One Event," *Jewish Culture and History*, VII, Nos. 1-2 (2005), 171-196.

[18]The number of Jews in the retail trade included mostly peddlers (sixty of 113), while the shopkeepers were basically sellers of wines and spirits. A high percentage of the Jewish craftsmen were tailors (127 of 194).

Commercial Institutions, Merchant Networks and Hierarchies

An examination of urban governance allows comparisons among "city systems" that transcend old-style, class-based analyses of urban elites.[19] Urban institutions, broadly defined, gave the merchants agency, which in turn allowed them to create networks that advanced cooperation between themselves and intellectuals, professionals and some landowners who shared the modernizing projects promoted in all the ports. These institutions included municipal councils, sanitary committees, philanthropic associations and commercial organizations. Here we will focus not only on the commercial and philanthropic associations, especially the Exchange and the Chambers of Commerce, but also on new forms of business organization, such as joint-stock companies, which were instrumental in creating and maintaining business networks among those engaged in international trade. Through these commercial mechanisms, merchants in all ports acquired greater power by electing representatives and structuring hierarchies, while institutions such as the Exchange and the Chambers of Commerce became places where businessmen and government officials, whether from the central government in Athens or the British-controlled Ionian government in Corfu, could interact.

The Exchange and the Chamber of Commerce in the port of Corfu were founded in 1843 and 1851, respectively. The *Borsa* in the Ionian islands at the time was a place for both commercial and social interactions; merchants, as well as "proprietors" met in the Exchange building, read foreign newspapers and socialized. The Corfu Exchange was founded by local and foreign merchants as an outgrowth of the Society of Merchants, which dated from 1838 when the *Ionian Islands Government Gazette* announced its creation "following the example of the most eminent metropoles of Europe" as one of the "Establishments that signal the advanced pace of civilization." The newspaper congratulated the Society for "supplying themselves with abundant well-known newspapers of the most noble nations, not only to expand their commercial relationships but also to enrich and enlighten their knowledge, through this medium making our condition even better."[20] In Corfu, merchants and landowners were invited to subscribe to the Exchange by paying an annual contribution. This began the process of defining an "official" group of merchants, as opposed to the unofficial "Body of Merchants" (*Corpo di Negozianti*).[21] This

---

[19]John Smith, "Urban Elites c. 1830-1930 and Urban History," *Urban History*, XXVII, No. 2 (2000), 255-275.

[20]*IIGG*, 29 October/10 November 1838 and 12/24 April 1841.

[21]The three merchants of Corfu who notified the rest of the business community to register also took the initiative to devise the rules of operation for the Exchange; *ibid.*, 27 November 1843.

development, however, was not always smooth because there were significant differences and antagonisms within the merchant group. In 1851, for example, several merchants petitioned for the intervention of the High Commissioner, challenging the legitimacy of the group controlling the *Borsa* and asking for permission to form a Chamber of Commerce.[22] This process accelerated the emergence of new hierarchies among merchants with the registration and biennial publication of the "official" group of merchants in the state newspaper. As was the case in the development of the Exchange, foreign merchants, in particular Charles Ingat and Joseph Drazziger, were among the founders of the Chamber of Commerce in Patras. Another merchant, Hambourger from Baden, established the Commercial Association "Hermes" in 1868. In fact, the founding of the Commercial Association was very similar to the creation of an institutional framework in Corfu and was one of the few examples of cooperation between merchants and landowners.[23]

In Ermoupoli, the creation and control of the Chamber of Commerce reflected the agency of the Chios merchants, the most powerful "community" within the Syros merchant group. The Ermoupoli Chamber was the institution which articulated and represented the collective interests of the merchant "world" of the town, in particular against the centralizing and controlling tendencies of Athens; it also functioned as an advisory body in developing the government's commercial and shipping policies.[24] According to Papathanasopoulos, however, the establishment of the Chamber of Commerce in Ermoupoli and Patras (both in 1836) was due to state intervention designed ostensibly to create a climate conducive to business and was part of an overall reorganization of commercial structures within the Greek Kingdom.[25] What is clear is that the Chamber of Commerce served as a mechanism for the articulation of political demands by the Ermoupoli merchants. But relations with Athens were not always amicable. On several issues, such as the abolition of quarantine restrictions for ships arriving from the Ottoman Empire, the response from the capital was negative; on another occasion the Ermoupoli merchants objected to

---

[22]Great Britain, National Archives (TNA/PRO), Colonial Office (CO) 136/801, petition no. 1083, "Signor Inglessi: Differences between the Members of the *Borsa.*"

[23]Bakounakis, *Patra*, 76; and Christos Lyrintzis, *Society and Politics in Achaia of the 19th Century* (Athens,1991), 72 (in Greek).

[24]Kardasis, *Syros*, 37.

[25]N. Papathanasopoulos, *Greek Merchant Shipping: Evolution and Readjustment* (Athens, 1983), 51 (in Greek).

the "invasion" of the port's credit market by the National Bank of Greece.[26] This resistance to the centralizing tendencies of the central government is understandable given that Ermoupoli was the richest and most developed, both commercially and culturally, of the Greek ports during the first decades of Greek independence. Overall, the synergy between merchants and state authorities explain the establishment of various Chambers of Commerce. While the British Commissioners in Corfu consistently expressed a belief in economic and social progress through commerce and promoted innovations in that direction, the merchants of Ermoupoli were powerful enough to persuade the authorities in Athens of the need to establish their own commercial association.

In general, merchants were heavily involved in local politics and demonstrated a strong sense of local identity and urban affiliation. They therefore serve as a reminder of the limits to structural integration at a national level in the early years of the Greek kingdom. Merchants exercised political authority in individual ports as elected members of municipal councils. In Corfu, for instance, several merchants were elected to the municipal council in 1880.[27] But other forms of political action and organization, such as the direct articulation and promotion of common interests, advanced considerably the reputation, status and power of the merchants involved. Indeed, before the introduction of universal male suffrage in 1864 these forms of political action might have been more important than election to municipal office. Merchants in Corfu, for example, petitioned the British Commissioners on issues such as improvements in transport, the reduction of British import duties on Ionian products and the deregulation of the grain trade. Moreover, the actual process of petitioning government agencies fostered closer relations between the merchants and landowners who signed such requests. The pervasiveness of a liberal, free-trade perspective was clear in these petitions. Time and again the merchants emphasized the need to abolish the state body responsible for ensuring adequate grain supplies for the populace.[28] Although the merchants did not form a party in the Ionian Assembly, they were well organized as pressure groups based on either temporary or medium-term alliances which reflected their common interests. Petitions were an important means of articulating their concerns, as were articles in both local and official newspapers.

---

[26]Kardasis, *Syros*, 74.

[27]The merchants elected to the municipal council were A. Kefalas, S. Baldas, Papanicolas, Geromeriatis and G. Scarpas; *Rigas Feraeos*, 27 January 1880.

[28]On the grain trade, see TNA/PRO, CO 136/661, petition nos. 31 and 367; and CO 136/695, petition no. 105. On the issue of more frequent steamer communication, a demand put forward by "merchants and proprietors" from the islands of Zante and Kefallonia, see CO 136/777, petition no. 85, 3 April 1849.

In Piraeus, the pursuit of commercial interests, such as the demand to declare the city a free port, was channelled through the municipal council, which operated in a more organized fashion. This was a key element in the process of cementing social cohesion among the town's elite. Mercantile demands, however, originated essentially from a perceived collective need to assert the town's role as a separate entity; to this end, in 1840 the council rejected a proposal to merge with Athens.[29] The involvement of merchants in municipal politics reinforced the sense of a distinct urban identity among the Piraeus elite and reduced the significance of any differences. This sense of urban affiliation and local urban identity in Piraeus was markedly different from the situation in Patras, where incoming merchants were quickly incorporated into the urban elite, and Ermoupoli, where the newcomers sought to develop a sense of urbanity which was in sharp contrast to that of Athens.[30]

The business of merchants in all three ports became more homogeneous with the introduction of commercial legislation, the codification of commercial law and its application in the settlement of cases of insolvency and bankruptcy. This was a gradual process in Greece following the introduction of French commercial legislation during the Revolution in the 1820s and then again in 1836. Similarly, although the Ionian state did not officially adopt a commercial code until 1841, the process had actually begun in the early 1820s. The 1841 code, which was adjusted to reflect local commercial considerations, is evidence of an important process of institutional change. For example, the code in the Ionian Islands provided for the establishment of joint-stock companies and regulated mercantile activities by defining who was a merchant and what constituted a mercantile act.[31]

The introduction of the Ionian Commercial Code not only played an important role in defining credit networks and regulating more strictly the provision of credit but also led to the creation of new mercantile hierarchies. Merchants were now obliged to keep accounts that could be used, if necessary, to settle commercial disputes in the Commercial Courts. Prior to the implementation of the code, contemporaries claimed that not even wholesale merchants kept their books "properly," despite the fact that this was one of the ways of deciding when a merchant should be declared insolvent. It is clear from documents relating to cases of insolvency and bankruptcy that creditors enjoyed stronger rights after 1841: they were able to grant credit, control credit networks, claim outstanding debts through legal procedures and declare debtors

---

[29]Tsokopoulos, *Piraeus*, 135-136.

[30]Giannitsiotis, *Social History*, 311-312.

[31]*Commercial Code of the Ionian Islands* (Corfu, 1851, in Greek).

insolvent or bankrupt.[32] In other words, merchant-creditors were now able to determine the dominant code of business ethics by defining the key virtues and vices of contemporary business practice. They were thus able to assert considerable authority over their debtors in the various towns of the Ionian islands, where negotiations over credit were still conducted face-to-face, and the complexities of bureaucratic societies were still absent. While ethnicity and religion remained important criteria for advancing credit and providing financial support in cases of insolvency, there are no recorded cases where they influenced the decision of creditors to declare someone insolvent or bankrupt.[33]

Moreover, the merchants involved in controlling credit networks played an increasingly important role in regulating the settlement of commercial debts through their involvement in the judicial process and the Commercial Courts.[34] In 1856, "several merchants of Corfu" petitioned the state for a greater role in upholding and implementing existing commercial law.[35] The petition was successful, and in August 1857 the "Law Respecting the Appointment of Assessors in the Sittings of the Commercial Courts and Tribunals" was enacted. Merchants also acted as assessors elected by the Chamber in the judicial process of debt settlement and therefore in cases where they had personal business interests. Jewish merchants, however, were excluded, and in an attempt to redress this injustice eight Jewish merchants petitioned the High Commissioner to be admitted to appear before the Commercial Court as assessors.[36] By contrast, one of the most powerful merchants in the Ionian islands was not excluded, despite his status as an in-migrant. Ernest Toole, a currant

---

[32]IAK, Commercial Court, 347 and 349; and *IIGG*, 31 March 1856 and 2 September 1861.

[33]Bearing in mind the structure of the credit networks, where every debtor had several creditors, it took only one creditor to start the process of declaring insolvent any debtor who ceased his payments.

[34]The jurisdiction of the courts in settling commercial disputes was clearly specified in the Commercial Code.

[35]The index of petitions recorded that the merchants were "complaining against the administration of justice by the Commercial Courts in these Islands, for want of knowledge and experience on the part of the judges. And proposing that merchants should be elected as advisors in Commercial matters, as is done in all civilized countries. And beg his Excellency that a similar practice may be introduced in the Ionian States." TNA/PRO, CO 136/1056, petition no. 149.

[36]*Ibid.*, CO 136/857, petition no. 400, 8 December 1857. The petition, a rare piece of evidence of the self-perception of Jewish merchants *vis-à-vis* other Corfu traders, was successful.

exporter and, more important, the manager of the Kefalonia branch of the Ionian Bank, was duly elected to the post of assessor.[37]

Although there has been no similar research on any of the other Greek port cities, apart from the work of Vassilis Kardasis on credit, insurance and banking in Ermoupoli, analogous research into the records of other Commercial Courts is likely to be fruitful.[38] Research into the development of marine insurance and credit companies in the Ionian islands and Patras from the 1840s onwards can help to decipher the specific business strategies adopted by local merchants. The establishment of marine insurance firms as joint-stock companies was enabled by the commercial code. This new form of business organization was another example of institutional change and demonstrated the mercantile response to the changing business conditions. Correspondence between the Greek consul in Corfu and his superiors in Athens provides an insight into the business strategies adopted, which even involved the merging of Ionian and Greek insurance companies.[39] Most of the insurance companies in Patras were directly involved in the proposed merger, including the town's seven so-called "banks" which had benefited from significant capital investment by Corfu merchants. While it would be an exaggeration to talk about the emergence of a "national" insurance market, the extensive investment of Ionian capital in Ermoupoli and Patras indicates an up-to-date knowledge of business opportunities among merchants and investors not only in the two recipient port cities but also in Corfu.[40]

Investment was not only speculative but was also intended to divert capital away from traditional sectors, in particular agriculture, into shipping. The presence of Ionian investors in the Elliniki Atmoploia [Greek Steam Navigation Company], for example, both at its initial unsuccessful launch in Patras in 1853 and at Ermouploli in 1857, when the company was finally founded,

---

[37]As the economic crisis in the islands deepened in the 1840s, the Ionian Bank became increasingly involved in the liquidation of land for the debts of landowners and tenant farmers. This meant that Toole was involved in the process of declaring merchants and other borrowers of the bank insolvent and trying to reclaim part of the collateral.

[38]Giannitsiotis' work concerns a later period and in particular the economic crisis of the 1880s.

[39]IAK, Ionian Senate Documents, Royal Greek Consulate, 26, document 2842.

[40]The concentration of capital in these marine insurance companies and the coinciding geographical and business networks between Corfu (and to an extent the other Ionian islands) and Patras can be seen by the fact that twenty-eight percent of the shareholders in these companies come from or were based in Corfu, while sixty-five percent resided in Patras, the centre of the companies; see Gekas, "Sector."

demonstrates an overlap between local business interests and national sentiment. But it is still difficult to discern the key factors which determined contemporary investment strategies and business decisions. Scaltsounis, for example, a well-known figure in Greek economic thought, was the protagonist in an attempt to found an Ionian bank under the auspices of the National Bank of Greece. He was also the founder of the insurance bank "Arhangelos" in 1854 and a principal shareholder in more than one company (in 1868, for example, he owned 100 of the 379 shares in the "Odysseus" company).[41] The plan entailed the establishment of a competitor to the British-administered Ionian Bank and was designed to attract the number of merchants required by Ionian law as subscribers of the necessary capital.[42] While the first attempt failed, a more organised move to establish a bank in 1864 – a few days before the union with Greece officially took place – obtained the support of more than eighty merchants and landed proprietors in Corfu. This time, Paramithiotis, the agent of the National Bank of Greece in Corfu, proved to be more efficient than Scaltsounis had been a few years earlier, and the timing of the plan should not be overlooked in the search for factors which influenced business strategies.[43]

The published information on the insurance companies of the Ionian islands enables us to draw some tentative conclusions about the social identities of the shareholders. Particularly in the case of Ermoupoli, but also in Patras and Corfu (as well as Kefallonia and Ithaki, which are not considered in this essay), shipping was one of the most significant mechanisms leading to the emergence of new social strata. An analysis of the shareholding registers of Ionian companies clearly demonstrates the participation of diverse groups and the positive reception by urban communities of the business opportunities presented by the development of shipping and commerce. Moreover, small shareholders also responded positively to increased shipping activity, capital accumulation and the adoption of a new legal framework. In the 1850s in particular there was a widespread adoption by leading social groups in all three port cities of bourgeois values and aspirations, and the acceptance of a worldview based on accumulation, calculation and the belief that earning a profit entailed the assumption of risk. In a general context, the emergence of a vibrant insur-

---

[41]Nikos Vlassopoulos, *The Merchant Marine of the Ionian Islands, 1700-1864* (Athens, 1995, in Greek).

[42]Evangelos Prontzas, "The Ionian Bank, 'In Favour of Greece,'" unpublished draft, forthcoming (in Greek).

[43]Paramithiotis came from Ioannina, on the mainland opposite Corfu, and migrated to the port in the early years of the protectorate. He was involved in several business activities, including insurance and banking. These activities were quite profitable, as his will shows; IAK, Notaries 605b, Aspreas Notary Documents, M. Paramithiotis, will.

ance and banking sector had wider implications. In the case of Corfu, Ermoupoli and Patras (but not Piraeus), structural innovation in the tertiary sector marked a shift in their long-run development path from growth to relative decline, as the port cities lost their character as independent commercial centres and were increasingly subjected to the national economic priorities of an expanding Greek kingdom.

Philanthropy, Urban Networks and Hierarchies

The administration of philanthropy in Greek towns, as in other urban places in nineteenth-century Europe, assumed new forms when urban elites realized that poverty and other social problems had to be addressed in more organized ways, particularly as increased urbanization and the spread of disease rendered city populations extremely vulnerable. This was most evident in relation to the series of cholera outbreaks in the 1850s in Corfu, Piraeus (and Athens) and Ermoupoli. The outbreaks decimated the population and proved that the state authorities, whether in Greece as a whole or in Athens in particular, were unable to cope with such emergencies.[44] Disease continued to afflict Greek cities throughout the nineteenth century, with smallpox exacting a heavy toll in the 1880s not only in Piraeus and Athens but also in Corfu and Kefalonia. Under such conditions, it is not surprising that merchants played a critical role in responding to the crises. In Corfu, for example, the merchants established a subscription fund in 1855 to stem the tide of the cholera outbreak that almost certainly saved the town from social upheaval when doctors and the urban elite advocated the isolation of infected areas. The implementation of such a measure necessitated the isolation of all inhabitants who lived outside the city walls but earned their living in the port; this proposal was met with threats of violence. At this juncture, the merchants' committee stepped in, collected funds and maintained social peace by choosing the optimal solution.[45]

Philanthropic activity advanced the cohesion of urban networks among the middle classes in Greek port cities and created new social hierarchies. The successful articulation of collective interests among merchants and other members of the urban elite, including landowners, professionals and state officials, was ultimately dependent upon a convergence of ideology, plans and strategies relating to the organization and management of urban communities.

---

[44]For Athens, see Maria Korasidou, *The Miserables of Athens and Their Helpers: Poverty and Philanthropy in the Greek Capital in the 19th Century* (Athens, 1995, in Greek). For Ermoupoli, see Chistos Loukos, "Epidimia kai koinonia: I cholera stin Ermoupoli tis Syrou (1854)," *Mnemon*, XIV (1992), 49-69 (in Greek). For the Corfu cholera outbreak, see Athanasios Gekas "Institutions and Power in Corfu Town in the Mid-Nineteenth Century," *Istor*, XV (2007), 107-144 (in Greek).

[45]*Ibid.*

The initially timid but progressively more assertive involvement of merchants in urban politics towards the end of the nineteenth century testifies to an increasingly pragmatic approach to urban administration.[46] But the publication of membership lists and donations to charitable institutions highlighted the public relevance of philanthropy and the role of local subscribers. As a result, associational activity in all the ports in question increased the visibility and helped to reinforce the status of merchants, shipowners and other middle-class subscribers. For this reason, it may be useful to view the ports of the Greek kingdom and Corfu from the mid-nineteenth century onwards as sites where a "proto-civil" society first emerged as the middle classes asserted hegemony over the rest of the urban society.

In both Corfu and the Ionian state in general, philanthropic activity up until 1864 went hand-in-hand with the intensification of punitive measures by the state authorities. The municipal and state authorities became gradually less tolerant of beggars, vagrants and "idlers," especially in the case of young males. The creation of a poorhouse, and its funding and management by the Ladies' Benevolent Society, is a good example of the co-existence of punitive and philanthropic measures in the same initiative. At the same time, the state failed to provide for some groups who were particularly vulnerable, like people living on the margins of the town such as the Parga refugees in the Manduchi district. The petitions of the Manduchi inhabitants from the 1830s asking for improvements in their living conditions and for preventive measures to protect them from outbreaks of disease continued to be ignored, despite a visit by Commissioner Ward in 1852 which also failed to produce any results.

In Greek cities, especially Athens and Piraeus in the second half of the nineteenth century, new ideas about the treatment of the poor were developed with increasing support from the more active and wealthy citizens. A variety of motives – individual and collective, and public and private – determined the specific nature of these responses, which were also products of the need to maintain or gain social status and political power, particularly after 1864 with the introduction of universal male suffrage and votes for the poor. In Athens, the Eleimon Etairia [Benevolent Society] aimed at helping the poor but was equally concerned with "discovering" those who fraudulently pretended to be poor and in need.[47] In Corfu, such a process had been initiated in the 1830s, but it was subsequently managed in a more centralized and efficient manner under the direction of the state. The Corfu Poorhouse had been established by the government and had been responsible from the start for the registration of the local poor, although from the 1840s it had been funded by indi-

---

[46]The exception was Patras, where local merchants were more fragmented due to their diverse origins. In any case, their interests were not antagonistic to the political class to which they also lent funds. See Lyrintzis, *Society and Politics*, 106.

[47]Giannitsiotis, *Social History*, 278-279.

vidual subscriptions to the Ladies' Benevolent Society. In Piraeus and Athens, by contrast, the registration of the poor was initially advocated by the Eleimon Etairia. Thus, the process of questioning the real needs of beggars and vagabonds in Greek cities was initiated by middle-class individuals through their philanthropic associations, whereas in Corfu the Ionian authorities had been responsible for implementing a more restrictive and negative policy towards the poor, as was evident in the official acts against "vicious mendacity" since the 1830s. The British-influenced Ionian state was therefore more advanced in penalizing the poor and in adopting punitive treatment. In both cases, however, the growing concern of the urban elite of Corfu and Piraeus with real as well as perceived social problems was also the result of economic crises in the 1850s and 1880s, respectively. But there was an important difference between the two port cities. In Corfu, the merchants were more directly involved in responding to social issues: they played an important role in founding and administering charitable institutions and cooperated actively with the forces of law and order in line with the ideology and practice of the authorities. In Piraeus, by contrast, although factory owners were initially active in generating resources for the creation of an orphanage where young boys could learn a trade and thus form a new, well-trained and industrious working class, they later became indifferent and ceased to play a supportive role.[48] The spirit of educating the poor and transforming them from beggars to workers was most evident in the code of conduct of the orphanages in Piraeus and Ermoupoli in the second half of the nineteenth century, but these operated under the auspices of the local municipal council and philanthropic societies.[49]

The case of Piraeus corresponds to the typology of European port cities in which merchants and industrialists, as leading members of the bourgeoisie, preferred individual philanthropic activities rather than policies designed to address contemporary social problems through education and school-based technical training.[50] According to recent research, the Athens bourgeoisie aimed to confine the poor to the poorhouse, while the Piraeus factory owners preferred to leave the treatment of the poor to the police, which in many cases meant the expulsion of foreign immigrants from the city. This was also due to the fact that Piraeus was never short of either skilled or unskilled labour because of the upward trend in in-migration, particularly near the end of the

---

[48]*Ibid.*, 288.

[49]V. Theodorou, "Disciplinary Systems and Labour in Orphanages in the Second Half of the 19th Century," *Mnemon*, XXI (1999), 55-84 (in Greek); and Y. Kokkinakis, "Philanthropy, Technical Education and Labour Accidents in Piraeus in the Last Third of the 19th Century," *Mnemon*, XXI (1999), 85-108 (in Greek).

[50]Lee, "Socio-economic and Demographic Characteristics," 147-172; and Giannitsiotis, *Social History*, 294.

century. In Corfu, merchants and other members of the town's bourgeoisie chose to work with the state authorities to confine the registered poor to the poorhouse, where they could receive training, while attempting to penalize those who refused to comply. The comparison, however, remains incomplete because we know very little about the development of industry in Corfu except that it took place in the town's suburbs and that a small factory working class emerged towards the end of the century. Philanthropy in Corfu had a more institutional character and was channelled through various individual or collective, public or private mechanisms. What distinguished some merchants within the urban hierarchies of individual ports was their involvement in the introduction and operation of new institutions along British or Western European lines, ranging from the Savings Bank to philanthropic initiatives in Corfu during the outbreaks of cholera in the 1850s. Together with Ionian professionals, lawyers, doctors and members of the state administration, merchants acquired enhanced social standing through the administration of charitable and other urban institutions.

Concluding Comments

The dominant views of merchants in the historical literature characterize them as individual actors, primarily in the economic sphere, omitting their capacity for collective action through associations of urban governance. This essay has attempted to fill the gap by stressing that despite being immigrants, merchants in most ports played pivotal roles in both commercial and social life. They acquired a high profile through involvement in collective institutions, such as the Chambers of Commerce, and in philanthropic associations and initiatives, both in the Old Town of Corfu and the new ports of Piraeus and Ermoupoli. At the same time, the specific role of merchants can only be analyzed within a differentiated temporal framework which takes into account the social impact of growth (or, to a lesser extent, relative decline) in the four ports under consideration. While Patras was predominantly a centre for the export of currants and the import of goods from Corfu and Trieste, Ermoupoli (Syros) was the entrepôt of the Eastern Mediterranean and for the period 1830-1860 the most important Greek port. Yet the similarities between the ports of Corfu, Ermoupoli and Patras are not always evident, which suggests that future research on the history of nineteenth-century Greek ports needs to transcend the inherent limitations posed by analyzing a specific case study by focussing instead on a key set of variables in a number of ports, such as their commercial institutions, the formation of urban hierarchies and the emergence of a distinct merchant hegemonic elite.

Ultimately, the growth or decline of each port city determined its contemporary characteristics. The fluctuations of the international economy, particularly manifest in the case of Empoupoli, have been sufficiently (but not exhaustively) discussed in Kardasis' work.[51] But the history of this port is usually regarded as exceptional because of its meteoric yet short-lived growth. In a wider context, however, port development in Greece was determined by migration, trade patterns and the ability to maintain successful business networks. Regardless of the growth trajectory of individual ports, the emergence of new hierarchies in which merchants represented a central or dominant group was dependent on the establishment and effective control of commercial institutions, such as the Exchange, Chamber of Commerce, joint-stock banks and insurance companies and other credit networks. The adoption of a legislative framework for regulating commerce, together with other institutions of urban governance, was equally important. Furthermore, any project involving a comparative analysis of port cities in nineteenth-century Greece must include a wider set of variables, including the relative growth or decline of individual towns, political developments which determined the overall administrative framework of the port cities and the role of the state.

The growth or decline of individual ports, as well as the development of new urban hierarchies, was only partially dependent upon the fluctuations of the international economy and the impact of exogenous factors. Especially in the last quarter of the nineteenth century, when the world economy and the Mediterranean in particular entered a new phase of development, merchants in the ports discussed in this chapter were already developing distinct urban identities, particularly in terms of their relationships with Athens. Of course, the ports maintained their local identity and regional importance until the early twentieth century, but the centralizing tendencies of the Greek state and the development priorities of a national economy contributed to the decline of Patras, formerly the focal point for the export of currants, once the boom in this trade ended in the 1870s. Such an interpretation, however, is incomplete because it ignores other important developments, such as the hegemonic rise of the middle classes and the role of local merchants in this particular process. Thus, a comparative examination of local developments, such as the emergence of philanthropic activity in the four ports in question, suggests a different interpretation of long-run trends. Still, it is clear that additional research is required.

Economic growth (or relative decline) in all the ports in question, the ability of individual merchants to maximize their gains from trade through diversified commercial activity and the advent of new ideas relating to social progress and the organization of both urban space and society were among the most important factors which helped to mould merchants into a distinct class with common interests. During the period under consideration, merchants

---

[51]Kardasis, *Syros*. The issue of whether Ermoupoli's decline was as rapid as has been suggested awaits a thorough examination of Ermoupoli's economy and society after 1857, when Kardasis' study ends.

benefited from a convergence of socio-economic interests as a result of both short- and medium-term alliances which ultimately underpinned their hegemonic rule in their respective port cities. In contrast to an earlier historiography which prioritized "macro" sociological interpretations of the Greek state with a deliberate focus on the role of Athens, a more balanced interpretation of the historical cityscape of nineteenth-century Greece can only be achieved through a comparative study of port cities. Then it may be possible to formulate generalizations about trade, urban networks and hierarchies which are broad enough to include the particularities of each port city.

Port Cities, Diaspora Communities and Emerging Nationalism in the Ottoman Empire: Balkan Merchants in Odessa and Their Network in the Early Nineteenth Century

Oliver Schulz

Introduction and Methodological Remarks

Port cities are an interesting subject for historical studies due to their inherent cosmopolitan character, with a multitude of different communities living to- gether as a result of foreign trade and international trading contacts. These links led not only to the exchange of goods and money but also to the migra- tion of significant groups of people between different port cities. Odessa, in the present-day Ukraine, is a particularly attractive subject for an historical study because the migration and settlement of foreigners formed a deliberate part of Russian policy in the newly-conquered territories on the Black Sea shore in the late eighteenth century, when Catherine II founded the city on the spot of a former Tatar village.[1] My interest in the topic evolved during re- search for a PhD thesis on the intervention of the "European Concert" in the Greek War of Independence (1826-1832). To gain a full understanding of Rus- sian foreign policy in the Ottoman Empire in the late eighteenth and early nine- teenth century, and the emergence of Greek nationalism, a number of issues had to be taken into account, including Russian southward expansion to the Black Sea, settlement and population policy in *Novorossija* and the subsequent role of the Greek diaspora in Odessa and its contribution to the rise of a na- tional identity. In fact, the Greek diaspora set a pattern for other Orthodox Balkan people living under Ottoman domination. The Bulgarian merchants in Odessa in the early nineteenth century, who are unfortunately much less known and studied than their Greek "colleagues," will receive particular atten- tion here. Previous articles have already pointed out how the Bulgarian dias- pora in the nineteenth century modelled its own national movement on the Greek experience and often even participated in the Greek national movement against the Ottomans before emancipating itself from Greek tutelage in its fight for an independent Bulgarian state.

---

[1] For an overview of the history of Odessa, see Patricia Herlihy, *Odessa: A History, 1794-1914* (Cambridge, MA, 1986).

This essay cannot examine this question in detail on the basis of extensive archival research. It seeks instead to present a synthesis of this huge subject and to develop perspectives for future research. Before exploring the topic, however, it is necessary to make some methodological remarks about the study of the history of Odessa and its communities in the nineteenth century. As seductive as Odessa may appear as a research topic, there are several methodological difficulties which have to be kept in mind. The first is how to deal with the problem of statistical inaccuracy in the late eighteenth and early nineteenth century. Consular reports, for instance, which provide an overview of trade exchanges are far from complete, and there are missing years, as for instance in the case of the French archives. On the one hand, the early period, such as the years 1816-1821, is well documented, with tables listing all the ships arriving in and leaving Odessa during each year, as well as their "nationality," crew and goods. On the other hand, information for later years is very incomplete. In addition to these problems, the French consuls acknowledged that accurate information on different types of goods was difficult to obtain because many merchant houses had no desire to reveal all the details of their commercial activity.

There are also problems in relation to population statistics. It is already well known that Odessa grew rapidly. Between 1840 and 1851, its population increased by more than twenty-eight percent, from 68,765 to 96,443 inhabitants, while the number of registered merchants rose by 77.4 percent, from 3199 to 5676. In 1856 the number of inhabitants finally surpassed 100,000, and Odessa had grown into one of the most important cities in the Russian Empire. The Russian author Skal'kovskij estimated that about 25,000 inhabitants lived from trade, but porters and other persons involved in the transport system have to be added to this figure. Finally, in 1897 a census was taken in the entire Russian Empire. Despite well-known methodological reservations and the fact that it was carried out after the period currently under examination, its figures are not without interest. Individuals were enumerated on the basis of their mother tongue, and Odessa's total population was recorded as 343,479. This included 193,254 Russians (50.78 percent of the total), 21,526 Ukrainians (5.66 percent), 123,686 Jews (32.5 percent) and 5013 Greeks (1.32 percent). Unfortunately, these figures say little about the origins of the inhabitants, as many non-Russians were Russified during the nineteenth century. Moreover, "mixed" marriages between Russians and Balkan Christians had also taken place because both communities adhered to the Orthodox religion. Finally, the fact that the census listed about 3000 Greek men and only about 1800 women suggests that many of these Greek men were simply short-term residents. Authors such as Skal'kovskij based their estimates on the category of "nationality" or religion, and it is very difficult to determine the actual number of Greeks. In 1845, the newspaper *Odesskij Vestnik* published figures that claimed that sixty-six to seventy-seven merchants in Odessa were foreigners, apart from the Russian merchant Novikov. As early as 1817 the ten richest Greek merchants had a fortune of ten million *roubles*, and ten years later these companies, including the Serafino, Iannopulo, Marazli and Paleologos families, belonged to the richest trading companies in the Russian Empire.[2]

This methodological problem is exacerbated by the fact that the "Greeks" themselves did not constitute a monolithic bloc but were a rather heterogeneous group which included many non-Greeks from the Balkans. But due to their Orthodox religion they were classified as "Greeks," i.e., Orthodox Christians from the Ottoman Empire who were subject to the "Greek" Patriarchate of Constantinople. The Bulgarians were just one example of this classification, which did not take into account the concept of "nationality" in the modern sense. The fact that this religious connotation continued to prevail for a long period during the nineteenth century was reflected in the fact that the Russian consul in Galaţi (in present-day Romania), where the Bulgarian merchant Vasil Aprilov lived after leaving Odessa, still referred to him as a "Greek from Nežin" (*Nežinskij Grek*) even after his death in 1847 when pro-Bulgarian agitation fostered by Aprilov and his friends had already started.[3]

In this respect, the Greeks in Odessa, and in Russia in general, were not an isolated case, as documents from other European cities with a "Greek population" confirm. A list of "Greek" merchants in Vienna in the late eighteenth century, for instance, contains several apparently Bulgarian merchants who were active in the Austrian capital, such as Vulko Danith from Philippopolis in "Macedonia," Elias Radovan from Raslok in the "Kingdom of Bulgaria," Christoph Nicolovitz from Sophia in "Macedonia" and Peter Nicolaus from Nissa in the "Kingdom of Bulgaria." This source reveals another problem: the imprecision and changing meaning of geographical terms and boundaries on the Balkan Peninsula. For instance, the merchant from Philippopolis (present-day Plovdiv on the Thracian plain in Bulgaria) was said to have come from "Macedonia," and the merchant from Razlog in "Macedonia" (a town which is part of present-day Bulgarian Pirin Macedonia) came from "Bulgaria." It was reported that the merchant Nicolaus from Nissa came from Bulgaria, although the city of Niš is today a part of eastern Serbia.[4] These examples reveal the underlying difficulty in analyzing the history of "Greek" diasporas or of any diaspora community from the Balkans, not only in Odessa. To complicate things, Vasil Aprilov, who was sent from Bucharest to Kronstadt

---

[2]*Ibid.*, 91-92 and 242.

[3]For the Russian consul's comment, see Ilija Konev, "Vasil Aprilov i bŭlgarsko-ruskite kulturni vzaimootnošenija," *Istoričeski Pregled*, XXX, No. 2 (1974), 69-78.

[4]Polychronis K. Enepekides, *Griechische Handelsgesellschaften und Kaufleute in Wien aus dem Jahre 1766* (Thessaloniki, 1959), 26-40.

by his Brother Christofor to attend the high school *Honterus-Gymnasium* there, was referred to as "Vaszille Aprilow Orphanus e natione Servica oriundus." In this period, it was not uncommon to identify Bulgarians living abroad as Serbs because the foreign authorities were in most cases not able to distinguish between the different South Slavic peoples whose languages and cultures must have appeared to them to be the same. Another example of this practice from Kronstadt in Transylvania was Ioan Ioanovič from Veliko Tŭrnovo, who in the documents was also referred to as a "Serbian merchant."[5] Nor is it surprising that the names of the Bulgarian merchants in present-day Romania often appeared in a Romanian or a Romanized form, such as Paraschiva Hagi Ghețu, whose family came from Svištov on the Danube, or Dobre George from Veliko Tŭrnovo. Such a phenomenon emphasizes the extent to which individuals were assigned multiple identities in documentary evidence, depending on its specific purpose, in a context where multilingualism was common, and future studies will need to take this into account.[6]

The Preliminaries: Russian Expansion to the Black Sea and Greek Settlement in Novorossija

As a result of the advance of Russian armies into the Black Sea region during the Russo-Ottoman wars in the late eighteenth century, a vast territorial complex was annexed by the Russian Empire. Russian policy in the following decades aimed at the consolidation of these territories and played a prominent role in Russian economic and strategic considerations.[7] Within the context of Russia's strategy, Novorossija was intended to consolidate the Russian border against possible Ottoman attacks and to provide the Russian economy with an outlet, particularly for raw materials and agricultural products. The foundation of the port city of Odessa in 1794 has to be seen in the context of these interests, as a key element in Russia's overall strategy involved the settlement of colonists not only from the Russian Empire, but also from Germany or the

---

[5]Stojan Maslev, "V.E. Aprilov v Brašov," *Istoričeski Pregled*, XVIII, No. 1 (1962), 76-77.

[6]Cornelia Papacostea-Danielopolu, "La compagnie grecque de Brașov: La lutte pour la conservation des pivilèges (1777-1850)," *Revue des Etudes Sud-Est européennes*, XII, No. 1 (1974), 74.

[7]It is not possible to analyze Imperial Russian foreign policy in the Balkans in detail. See Barbara Jelavich, *Russia's Balkan Entanglements, 1806-1914* (Cambridge, 1991); I.S. Dostjan, *Rossija i balkanskij vopros: Iz istorii russko-balkanskich političeskich svjazej v pervoj treti XIX v.* (Moskva, 1972); and Ivo J. Lederer, "Russia and the Balkans," in Lederer (ed.), *Russian Foreign Policy: Essays in Historical Perspective* (New Haven, 1962), 417-451.

Balkan Peninsula. In the latter case, a considerable part of the Christian population was desperate to flee Ottoman rule and was attracted by the prospect of land and property in Novorossija or by the economic potential of an involvement in developing Russian foreign trade.[8]

Foreign trade, which was carried out through several port cities on the Black Sea, such as Odessa, Kerč' and Taganrog, was of particular interest to Greeks from the Ottoman Empire. This group had benefited from Anglo-French commercial rivalry in the Mediterranean and dominated the foreign trade of the Ottoman Empire. From a Russian perspective, they were the commercial experts the Russians needed in order to develop the economic potential of the new provinces. Moreover, they were Orthodox Christians and well connected in Ottoman politics and society. A considerable number of Greeks were already in Russia's service as diplomats, in government administration or the army, so that they could serve Russian interests in the Ottoman Empire as well.[9] These Greeks in the Russian administration, in particular the diplomats, played a very important role in the formulation of Russian policy in the Balkans. A politician such as Ioannis Kapodistrias, who served as Secretary of State for Foreign Affairs under Alexander I, had direct access to the tsar and was in a good position to influence decision making. He demonstrated a very clear anti-Ottoman stance in his comments, which reflected a strong sense of Greek patriotism among the Greek diaspora in Russia, but he turned down the offer to become the head of the secret revolutionary organization *Filiki Eteria*. The discourse which dominated the Greek community in Russia in the eighteenth and early nineteenth century was also largely shaped by popular legends, myths and an oral tradition which circulated in Greek circles in Russia. According to the publication *Agathangelos* by the Athos monk Theokletos Polyeides, the Greeks were to be liberated from the Ottomans by a "tall and fair-haired people from the North," which clearly implied that the Russians were destined to play a key role in securing their freedom, while in an Orthodox reading the Russian Tsar Peter I was depicted as an instrument of Providence, a link with the Byzantine past and a prerequisite for victory over the "Latin West."[10]

---

[8]For the early phase of the settlement policy, see Roger Bartlett, *Human Capital: The Settlement of Foreigners in Russia, 1762-1804* (Cambridge, 1979). For the colonists from Germany and the Balkan Peninsula, see Detlef Brandes, *Von den Zaren adoptiert: Die deutschen Kolonisten und Balkansiedler in Neuruβland und Bessarabien 1751-1914* (München, 1993).

[9]See Nicholas Charles Pappas, *Greeks in Russian Military Service in the Late Eighteenth and Early Nineteenth Centuries* (Thessaloniki, 1991).

[10]Theokletos Polyeides (c.1690–c.1759) initially came from Adrianople. The history of the *Agathangelos* and its reception are treated by John Nicolopoulos, "From

Unfortunately, a glance at the historiography on the Greeks in Russia reveals that most of this chapter in the history of the Russian Empire has still to be written, as Greek historians have very often approached the topic with a national and pedagogic purpose.[11] Moreover, it is important to note that Greek settlement in Russia was not confined to the reign of Catherine II, nor to Southern Ukraine and the city of Odessa. In fact, there had already been Greek colonies in Moscow and in Nežin (present-day Ukraine) at the time of the Muscovite Empire.[12] The influx of Greeks in the late eighteenth and early nineteenth century was not exclusively concentrated in Odessa, as Greek people were to be found on the entire Black Sea shore, specifically in the Mariupol' area and in the Caucasus.[13] On the other hand, although Russian research on *Novorossija* in general and Odessa in particular has already covered some central aspects of the development of foreign trade, the multi-ethnic character of the region has either been accorded insufficient attention or has been interpreted in terms of Marxist ideology. Apart from these ideological constraints, however, Russian historiography contains valuable information on Odessa and *Novorossija* and thus constitutes an important first step for further research in this field.[14]

Agathangelos to the Megale Idea: Russia and the Emergence of Greek Nationalism," *Balkan Studies*, XXVI, No. 1 (1985), 41-56.

[11]As an introduction to the topic, and for relevant bibliographical references and archival holdings, see Konstantinos K. Papoulidis, "Oi Ellines tis Rosias ton 19o kai stis arches tou 20ou aiona," *Valkanika Symmeikta*, IV (1992), 109-140.

[12]See Ekkehard Kraft, *Moskaus griechisches Jahrhundert: Russisch-griechische Beziehungen und metabyzantinischer Einfluß, 1619-1694* (Stuttgart, 1995); and Edgar Hösch, "Die Nežiner Griechen," *Forschungen zur osteuropäischen Geschichte*, LII (1996), 57-68.

[13]See Apostolos Karpozilos, "The Greeks in Russia (Pages from the Political and Cultural History of Pontian and Mariupol Greeks in Southern Russia)," *Archeion Pontou*, XLVII (1996-1997), 16-39; and Ekkehard Kraft, "Die griechische Emigration aus dem Osmanischen Reich in den Kaukasus," in Raoul Motika and Michael Ursinus (eds.), *Kaukasien zwischen Osmanischem Reich und Iran 1555-1914* (Wiesbaden, 2000), 69-86.

[14]See G.L. Arš, "Grečeskaja emigracija v Rossiju v konce XVIII-načala XIX v.," *Sovetskaja ètnografija*, No. 3 (1969), 85-95. For the history of *Novorossija* in general, see E.I. Družinina, *Južnaja Ukraina v 1800-1825 gg.* (Moskva, 1970); and Družinina, *Južnaja Ukraina v period krizisa feodalizma 1825-1860 gg.* (Moskva, 1981). On foreign trade, see V.A. Zolotov, *Vnešnjaja torgovlja Južnoj Rossii v pervoj polovine XIX veka* (Rostov, 963). Soviet research has underlined the link between Russian policy in *Novorossija* in terms of settlement and foreign trade, on the one hand, and Russian foreign policy relative to "Eastern Question" on the other hand. As Rus-

To understand why the Russian government encouraged the immigration of Greek merchants to *Novorossija* in general and to Odessa in particular, it is necessary to go back to developments in Ottoman foreign trade in the eighteenth and early nineteenth centuries.[15] The main development before the nineteenth century was the emergence of a group of merchants among the Orthodox population on the Balkan Peninsula which not only dominated trade in the Balkans but also established a commercial network throughout Europe. They were to be found in Constantinople and in important port cities, such as Smyrna or Thessaloniki, but also on the Aegean Islands, such as Chios, which played an important role in east-west trade between Smyrna and the ports of Marseilles and Livorno.[16] These Orthodox merchants were Ottoman, Habsburg or Russian subjects and organized imports and exports to and from the Ottoman Empire. They also settled in Nežin in Russia, Leipzig, Vienna, Livorno and Naples, and they established branches in Western Europe so that Mediterranean trade could be linked to the Atlantic. In this context, other important factors facilitated their increasing dominance of trade, including the progressive decay of Ottoman power in the Balkans as well as the wars of the eighteenth century with their effects on the Mediterranean. During the Seven Years' War, for instance, Greek merchants seized the opportunity to replace French traders, while during the Revolutionary wars they organized the shipping of grain to Marseilles. Anglo-French rivalry in the Mediterranean, with piracy on both sides, also contributed to the increased use of Greek ships to carry goods which reinforced the dominant position of Greek merchants in these trades.

Structural changes in the Ottoman Empire also gave birth to new social groups among the Orthodox population of the Balkan Peninsula. The abolition of the janissary corps and the establishment of a regular Ottoman army

sian exports from Odessa had to pass through the Straits, a link between the two political questions is evident. See A.V. Fadeev, *Rossija i vostočnyj krizis 20-ch godov XIX veka* (Moskva, 1958).

[15]For a good introduction, see Daniel Panzac, "International and Domestic Maritime Trade in the Ottoman Empire during the Eighteenth Century," *International Journal of Middle East Studies*, XXIV, No. 2 (1992), 189-206.

[16]On Chios, see Daniel Panzac, "L'escale de Chio: un observatoire privilégié de l'activité maritime en Mer Egée au XVIIIe siècle," *Histoire, économie et société*, No. 4 (1985), 541-561. On Smyrna, see Elena Frangakis-Syrett, "Izmir – An International Port in the Eastern Mediterranean in the Eighteenth Century (1695-1820)," in *Economies méditerranéennes. Equilibres et intercommunications XIIIe-XIXe siècles* (2 vols., Athènes, 1985), I, 107-128. On Thessaloniki, see Konstantin A. Vakalopoulos, "Commercial Development and Economic Importance of the Port of Thessaloniki from the Late Eighteenth Century to 1856," in Apostolos E. Vakalopoulos, Konstantinos D. Svolopoulos and Béla Király (eds.), *Southeast European Maritime Commerce and Naval Policies from the Mid-Eighteenth Century to 1914* (Boulder, CO, 1988), 301-320.

created new market opportunities, specifically in feeding and equipping the troops. In the Bulgarian lands this resulted in increased sheep-raising and production of cloth for the army.[17] The accumulation of wealth due to these business activities resulted in the appearance of new notables and the further extension of trade, as this new group created a new market for goods and commodities imported from Western Europe.[18] There was an increasing commercial exchange with traders in Leipzig and significant imports of Leipzig cloth, following the import into the Danubian Principalities from the early eighteenth century onwards of textiles from Aix-la-Chapelle, Verviers and Vervins. The Russian fur trade with the Ottoman Empire was also largely organized by Balkan merchants and led to the creation of a trading triangle between Ottoman cities and towns (Constantinople/Uzundžovo, Ioannina and the fur-making community of Kastoria in present-day Greek Macedonia), the German states and Russian commercial centres in Nežin, Kiev and Moscow. Greek merchants had established branches in Western Europe from a relatively early date, as in Amsterdam where the Dutch government in 1730 had granted Greek, Jewish and Armenian traders rights equal to those of Dutch merchants. Furthermore, the "nautical islands" of Hydra, Spetsai and Psara played an important role in trade, for example in the transport of wine from the Aegean Islands to Russia and of grain from the Balkans, Anatolia, the Danubian Principalities and southern Russia (Ukraine) to the Aegean Islands, Naples and Marseilles.[19]

A new opportunity for extending these commercial activities was created at the end of the Russo-Ottoman War (1768-1774) with the conclusion of the Peace of Küçük Kaynarca (Malka Kajnardža in present-day Bulgaria). This treaty not only defined the territory to be ceded by the Ottomans but also opened up the Black Sea, which had hitherto been an "Ottoman lake," to foreign commerce.[20] The Russians wanted to modernize their country by deploy-

----

[17]Virginia Paskaleva, "Contribution aux relations commerciales des provinces balkaniques de l'Empire ottoman avec les Etats européens au cours du XVIIIe et la première moitié du XIXe siècle," *Etudes historiques à l'occasion du VIe Congrès international des études slaves Prague* (4 vols., Sofia, 1968), IV, 265-292.

[18]Richard J. Crampton, *A Concise History of Bulgaria* (Cambridge, 2005), 56-57.

[19]See Traian Stoianovich, "The Conquering Balkan Orthodox Merchant," *Journal of Economic History*, XX, No. 2 (1960), 234-313.

[20]The French translation of the Treaty of Küçük Kaynarca is printed in Clive Parry (ed.), *Consolidated Treaty Series, Vol. XLV* (New York 1969), 368-385. The importance of this treaty in political and economic terms is assessed by Ivan Pŭrvev, "Russia, Orthodoxy in the Ottoman Empire and the Peace of Kuchuk Kainardja 1774," *Bulgarian Historical Review*, XVIII, No. 1 (1990), 20-30; and I.S. Dostjan, "Značenija

ing a range of measures, including the development of foreign trade, but the country did not possess a developed merchant marine of its own or the necessary commercial expertise. Under such circumstances, the Russian authorities increasingly turned to Greek merchants due to their dominant role in Mediterranean trade and their connections with Europe. As a "mobile diaspora group" *par excellence*, they could be entrusted with the organization of Russian foreign trade. Their settlement in *Novorossija* reflected a characteristic feature of the Russian Empire at this time, namely the idea of an "inter-ethnic division of labour," which meant that certain functions or areas of economic and social life were covered by non-Russian groups if the Russians themselves could not assume responsibility for the task.[21]

The exact nature of trade exchanges can be deduced from consular reports for the port of Odessa, at least for the years for which these sources are complete. In 1816, for instance, the majority of ships sailing under the Russian flag had Greek crews, but this became a major problem for Russian foreign trade in the Black Sea area in 1821 when the Greek War of Independence erupted; the Ottoman authorities stopped these ships at the Straits and refused to deliver the required documents for further passage. The dominance of Russian-flagged ships, and thus of Greek foreign commerce in Odessa, was evident in a report on the ships arriving in the port during the first three months of 1816. Out of a total of eighty-one vessels, forty-four sailed under the Russian flag and eleven under the Ottoman flag, again, in most cases, with Greek crews. Unfortunately, insufficient care was taken to differentiate between the port of origin and the final destination of these ships and often the documents only referred to Constantinople, even if the vessels continued to a port in the Mediterranean or Western Europe. Although this is an additional methodological problem for analyzing the exchange of goods between Odessa and other European ports, the reports contain invaluable information on goods transported and provide a basis for reconstructing a typical pattern of exchange. Whereas exports from Odessa were clearly dominated by wheat, imports were essentially products which could not be grown or produced in Russia, such as fruits (lemons, oranges, dried fruits, etc.), coffee, tobacco, wine (from the Greek island of Santorini and elsewhere) or Oriental pastries (in particular, *halva* from the Ottoman Empire). The ports in the Black Sea which were mentioned in this source were Izmail, Sozopol, Varna or Nesebŭr, which had important Greek merchant communities as well.[22]

Kjučuk-Kainardžijskogo dogovora 1774 g.v politike Rossii na Balkanach konca XVIII i XIX vv.," *Etudes balkaniques*, XI (1975), 97-107.

[21]Andreas Kappeler, *Rußland als Vielvölkerreich* (München, 2001), 108-121.

[22]Cf. Archives du Ministère des Affaires Etrangères Paris, Correspondance consulaire et commerciale Odessa, II, Doriot to French State Department, 31 December

In the late eighteenth and early nineteenth century, the term "Greek" did not define an ethnic group but referred to the Orthodox religion; it therefore included Aromanians (Orthodox) Albanians and Bulgarians, as well. As these groups did not have an autochthonous church organization, this not only facilitated Hellenization but meant that Greek played an important role in the eastern and the central areas of the Balkans as the language of business, culture and education. Due to the gradual decline of Ottoman power and the subsequent insecurity in its territories, settlement abroad became increasingly attractive for Orthodox merchants from the Ottoman Empire. The companies they established were organized around their own families, which meant that family members could be found in different countries where they organized branches of the firms. This family business structure was important for the success of the Balkan merchants because it reduced costs by eliminating the need for brokers. With the foundation of Odessa in 1794, the centre of trade activities in Russia shifted from traditional locations, such as Moscow, Kiev and Nežin, to *Novorossija*, and particularly to the new port city. Odessa grew rapidly and was to become one of the major cities of the Russian Empire. From a population of about 7500 in 1800, the city exceeded 100,000 by mid-century and reached 656,000 by 1915. Exports grew in a similar fashion. In the period 1801-1805 imports and exports amounted to four million silver *roubles* per year, but this figure rose to thirty-five million by 1856-1860 and to 103 million by 1911-1913. Odessa's growth and commercial importance were enhanced by the establishment of the free port in 1819 and the creation of a sort of monopoly in the export of Russian wheat.[23]

It is of course impossible to consider all the merchant families with a Balkan background in Odessa who played important roles in its trade in the early nineteenth century.[24] In the Greek case, it is sufficient to focus on two typical examples – the Rallis and Rodokanakis families – who originated from

---

1816. Izmail lay in the Russian province of Bessarabia, conquered in 1812. The Greek community of this town played a prominent role in the Greek War of Independence. For Bessarabia and the Greek insurrection in 1821, see I.F. Iovva, *Bessarabija i grečeskoe nacional'no-osvoboditel'noe dviženie* (Kišinev, 1974).

[23]The history of the urbanization process in the Imperial era is covered by Frederick W. Skinner, "Trends in Planning Practices: The Building of Odessa, 1794-1917," in Michael F. Hamm (ed.), *The City in Russian History* (Lexington, KY, 1976), 139-159.

[24]An overview can be found in Viron Karidis, "A Greek Mercantile *Paroikia*: Odessa, 1774-1829," in Richard Clogg (ed.), *Balkan Society in the Age of Greek Independence* (London, 1981), 111-136.

the island of Chios.[25] The Rallis had started business in Smyrna and were active in Constantinople. In 1815, Pandia and Augustus Rallis joined Iannis and Eustratios Petrocochino to found the Ralli Argenti Company in Marseilles, with a second branch in Constantinople (the Petrocochino and Argenti Company). In 1818, Iannis and Stratis Rallis, who had been active in Livorno, went to London to found another branch. They traded in silk and cotton from Persia and Anatolia via Smyrna and Constantinople and exported British cloth and French silk to the eastern Mediterranean. They subsequently founded the company Ralli and Petrocochino in London in 1823 and began to import wheat from the Black Sea. They established a branch in Odessa for this purpose, and a member of the family was later even appointed American consul in the city. The Rodokanakis Company had branches in Smyrna, Constantinople, Marseilles, the Italian ports, the Netherlands and London, and traded in Russian wheat, British cloth, French silk, cotton, wool, olive oil, other Ottoman foodstuffs and raw materials, as well as specie.[26] George Rodokanakis (born in Chios in 1795), whose elder brother Peter had been hanged by the Ottomans during the "Turkish atrocities" in Chios in 1822, continued the family tradition, while his younger brothers went to the major European port cities. Theodore Rodokanakis went to Odessa in 1819, another brother organized the family's trade activities on the Aegean island of Syros and George's nephew Paul went to Marseilles, where he was head of the Chamber of Commerce and Industry for some time.

The Rallis and Rodokanakis families reveal two important features. First, the Greek diaspora in Odessa was part of a much broader commercial network all over Europe and participated in the developing trade of Western goods and Ottoman raw materials and foodstuffs. Second, these Greek merchants benefited from the fact that they had already acquired the Ottoman *berat*, which enabled them to be active in international trade. It is interesting to note that as early as the beginning of the nineteenth century, a considerable

---

[25]Several members of the Rallis and Rodokanakis families in Odessa are mentioned in Konstantinos Amantos, "To emporion ton Chion pro tou 1821," *Deltion tis istorikis kai ethnologikis eterias tis Ellados*, XII (1957-1958), 180-181. Moreover, the author points out the links of the Chiot merchant community all over Europe, with branches in Trieste, Livorno, Vienna, Marseilles, Amsterdam, London, Odessa, Taganrog and Moscow. For a concise overview, see Patricia Herlihy, "Greek Merchants in Odessa in the Nineteenth Century," *Harvard Ukrainian Studies*, III, No. 4 (1979-1980), 399-420.

[26]The growing trade between Western Europe and the Ottoman Empire has been analyzed in terms of the integration of the Ottoman economy into a global framework of exchange. See Immanuel Wallerstein, Hale Decdeli and Reşat Kasaba, "The Incorporation of the Ottoman State into the World Economy," in Huri İslamoğlu-İnan (ed.), *The Ottoman Empire and the World Economy* (Cambridge, 1987), 88-97.

part of British trade with the eastern Mediterranean was no longer organized
by the Levant Company, which theoretically had a monopoly, due to the fact
that Greek merchants could offer lower prices for the transport of goods. Not
only did Greek merchants gain a prominent position in various sectors of trade
in the Mediterranean, but the foundation of Odessa also allowed them to extend the range of their activities and rapidly to obtain a monopoly in the export
of Russian wheat.[27]

The merchants' flexibility was revealed when the Russo-Ottoman War
(1828-1829) ended and the Treaty of Adrianople ended the heyday of commerce in Odessa. The trading places in Wallachia and Moldavia (Brăila and
Galaţi) were already integrated into the overall scheme of European trade and
exchange, and many foreign merchants now moved there. The importance of
Odessa declined distinctly after the Crimean War, due to the consequences of
the war itself and the abolition of serfdom in Russia under Alexander II, which
changed the framework for wheat exports. Many Greek merchants left the city
to establish new companies abroad. This was also true for the Bulgarian merchants, who will be introduced later in this study: Vasil Aprilov, for example,
moved before to Galaţi, which became a major port city on the Danube, with
trading contacts all over Europe and several merchant communities.[28]

Sponsoring Cultural Activities and Education: The Transition to National Agitation

The Greek diaspora not only concentrated on commercial activities but also
contributed to the rise of a Greek national movement and thus indirectly to the
establishment of an independent Greek state in the nineteenth century. This
was possible because the merchants invested part of their wealth in education
and thus renewed interest in Greek history and culture. Later in the nineteenth
century, the Rodokanakis family, for instance, sponsored a high school for
girls in Odessa (1871).[29] But the Greek merchants not only financed schools in

---

[27]See Elena Frangakis-Syrett, "Greek Mercantile Activities in the Eastern
Mediterranean, 1780-1820," *Balkan Studies*, XXVIII, No. 1 (1987), 73-86; and John
R. Lampe and Marvin R. Jackson, *Balkan Economic History, 1550-1950: From Imperial Borderlands to Developing Nations* (Bloomington, IN, 1982), 31-32. A *berat* was
an Ottoman charter granting rights and privileges. The names of the Greek merchants
from the Rallis and Rodokanakis families can be found in various forms in the literature
and the sources. Here they are given in their English form.

[28]Paskaleva, "Contribution aux relations commerciales," 276.

[29]Following Miroslav Hroch's classical model, they can thus be classified as
representatives of the first phase in the process of building national consciousness, i.e.,
the cultural and literary contribution. See Miroslav Hroch, *Die Vorkämpfer der nation-*

Odessa, such as the "Greek Commercial Gymnasium" founded in 1817, where a strong sense of Greek cultural patriotism was taught by teachers like Konstantinos Vardalachos (1775-1830), but also contributed to the construction of a Greek theatre in 1814 and of hospitals.[30] Furthermore, they gave grants to Greek students so that they could study in Western and Central Europe. This meant that Greeks came into immediate contact with Western ideas of the Enlightenment, as mariners and merchants in port cities in Western Europe, students abroad or due to the temporary presence of French troops on the Ionian Islands during the Revolutionary wars. The Western Enlightenment combined with specifically Greek features, such as Orthodoxy, as a defining factor of "Greekness" and helped to form the modern national consciousness of the Greeks.[31]

This phenomenon was not restricted to the Odessa merchants but applied to Greek merchants in Russia in general, who were very interested in education and culture in Ottoman Greece. The merchants who were active in the diaspora in Russia also maintained strong ties with their region of origin. The merchant Z. Kaplanis from Ioannina donated his fortune to several educational projects in Epirus, such as the Kaplanis School in Ioannina. Other important contributors were the Zosimos brothers in Nežin (later Moscow). They not only provided schools in Ottoman Greece with Western texts and scientific instruments but also financed the publication of Greek Bibles and knew Adamantios Korais, who promoted the idea of an independent Greece.[32] Moreover,

---

alen Bewegung bei den kleinen Völkern Europas: Eine vergleichende Analyse zur gesellschaftlichen Schichtung der patriotischen Gruppen (Praha, 1968). On the Rodokanakis' high school, see F.K. Iannitsi, "Grečeskaja diaspora na juge Rossii: Dejatel'nost' semej Mesaksudi (Kerč') i Rodokanaki (Odessa) (XIX-načalo XX v.)," *Vestnik Moskovskogo Universiteta. Serija VIII: Istorija,* IV (1998), 69-76.

[30]For the history of this school, see G.L. Arš, "Grečeskoe kommerčeskoe učilišče Odessy v 1817-1830 gg.," in *Obščestvennye i kul'turnye svjazi narodov SSSR i Balkan XVIII-XX vv.* (Moskva, 1967), 31-62.

[31]On the specific character of nationalism among the Balkan peoples, as compared to Western nationalism, and the role of Orthodoxy in the process of nation-building, see Paschalis M. Kitromilides, "'Imagined Communities' and the Origins of the National Question in the Balkans," *European History Quarterly,* XIX, No. 2 (1989), 149-194; and Emmanuel Turczynski, "The Role of the Orthodox Church in Adapting and Transforming the Western Enlightenment in Southeastern Europe," *East European Quarterly,* IX, No. 4 (1975), 415-440.

[32]For the role of Epirote merchants, see L. Vranousi and B. Sphyroeras, "From the Turkish Conquest to the Beginning of the Nineteenth Century," in M.B. Sakellariou (ed.), *Epirus: 4000 years of Greek History and Civilization* (Athens, 1997), 240-269.

Greek merchants from Russia supported the philanthropic organization *Philomuseos Eteria* ("Society of the Friends of the Muses"), founded in Vienna in 1821. In the same year three Greek merchants from Odessa founded the secret organization *Filiki Eteria* ("Society of Friends"), which aimed at a more active struggle against the Ottomans and the creation of an independent Greece. This organization was established at the beginning of the outbreak of the Greek War of Independence in 1821 and was supported financially by merchants such as Ioannis Amvrosios, who had already contributed to the foundation of the "Commercial Gymnasium" in Odessa, and Dimitrios Inglezis, a prominent Greek notable in Odessa.[33]

This general tendency was reinforced by simultaneous developments among other Balkan peoples. This was true, for example, of the Bulgarians: their diaspora community in Odessa was quite important, and their activities largely mirrored those of the Greeks.[34] Like the Greeks, the Bulgarian merchants kept strong ties with their native regions and towns, in particular with Gabrovo (in the centre of present-day Bulgaria), which reflected the economic development of the Ottoman Empire and its trade in the late eighteenth and

---

[33]See Theophilus C. Prousis, "The Greeks of Russia and the Greek Awakening, 1774-1821," *Balkan Studies*, XXVIII, No. 2 (1987), 259-280; and Prousis, "Dēmētrios S. Inglezēs: Greek Merchant and City Leader of Odessa," *Slavic Review*, L, No. 3 (1991), 672-679. On the Filiki Eteria, see G.L. Arš, *Tajnoe obščestvo "Filiki Eterija"* (Moskva, 1965). For the Aid Committee in Odessa, see G.M. Pjatigorskij, "Dejatel'nost' Odesskoj grečeskoj vspomogatel'noj kommissii v 1821-1831 gg. (Po materialam Gosudarstvennogo archiva Odesskoj Obl.)," in *Balkanskie narody i evropejskie pravitelstva v XVIII – načale XIX v.* (Moskva, 1982), 135-152. The Greek War of Independence adversely affected trade carried out via Odessa, as ships sailing under the Russian flag with Greek sailors were systematically stopped by the Ottoman authorities at the Straits. Normally, the cargo was confiscated and the Greek crew ill-treated. See Archives du Ministère des Affaires Etrangères, Paris, Correspondance consulaire et commerciale Constantinople, LXXXI, La Tour Maubourg to Montmorency, Constantinople, 9 March, 1822. The commander of the city (*gradonačal'nik*) complained about the negative impact of Ottoman reprisals on trading companies in Odessa. See note of A.D. Gur'ev, c. 22 May/3 June 1823, as printed in *Vnešnjaja politika Rossii XIX i načala XX veka. Dokumenty Rossijskogo Ministerstva Inostrannych Del*, Second ser., V (Moskva, 1982), no. 51, 118-122. After the naval battle of Navarino, the Ottoman authorities decreed an embargo against Russian, British and French ships which severely affected trade in Odessa. See Great Britain, National Archives (TNA/PRO), Foreign Office (FO), CLXVI, Yeames to Dudley, Odessa, 1/13 November 1827, attachment to Disbrowe to Dudley, St. Petersburg, 9/21 November 1827.

[34]For Bulgarian emigration to Russia, see St. Dojnov, "Bulgarische Emigranten in Rußland (zweite Hälfte des 18. Jahrhunderts)," *Bulgarian Historical Review*, XXVII, Nos. 1-2 (1999), 48-71.

early nineteenth century.[35] Among the Gabrovo merchants in Odessa were the brothers Nikifor and Vasil Aprilov, and the Palauzov brothers, Vasil N. Rašeev and Spyridon Stomonjakov. Later in the century merchants from Karlovo, Plovdiv, Kazanlŭk, Varna and other Bulgarian places also moved to Odessa, which subsequently became a centre of Bulgarian emigration. These merchants, who as Orthodox Christians from the Ottoman Empire were referred to as "Greeks," possessed a commercial network with extensive connections to European trade. A considerable number of Bulgarian merchants settled in Wallachia and Moldavia (in Bucarest, Galaţi and Brăila), as well as in Kronstadt in Habsburg Transylvania (Braşov in present-day Romania), while Constantinople was another important centre for Bulgarian merchants. Odessa was an attractive trading centre for Bulgarian foreign commerce because it was situated on the coast not far from the Danube; it therefore offered good opportunities for trade between Russia, the Ottoman Empire and Central Europe. Bulgarian merchants in Gabrovo imported hides, wool, fish, caviar and butter from Odessa, and an important part of this trade was carried out via Constantinople or on the Danube, where Bulgarian merchants in Svištov established the link. Moreover, Gabrovo merchants imported wool from Smyrna and Gallipoli and re-exported it to Bucharest, Braşov, Budapest and Vienna, where they knew fellow merchants with whom they formed a commercial network.[36] Another example of Odessa's integration into this European commercial network was the trade in Bulgarian handicrafts in the first half of the nineteenth century. The typical carpets (*kilim*) from the area of Čiprovci in northwestern Bulgaria were sent to Constantinople, Thessaloniki, Bucharest, Kronstadt or Odessa, and the silk produced in Trjavna in the Stara Planina Mountains was sold in Moscow, Adrianople, Constantinople and at the fair in Uzundžovo.[37]

---

[35]Marxist historiography has interpreted this process as a transition from "feudalism," associated with the Ottoman period, to capitalism, associated with the creation of independent states in the Balkans. See Nikolaj Todorov, "Sur quelques aspects du passage du féodalisme au capitalisme dans les territoires balkaniques de l'Empire ottoman," *Revue des Etudes Sud-Est Européennes*, I, Nos. 1-2 (1963), 103-136.

[36]See Daniela Coneva, "Vasil N. Rašeev i tŭrgovskite vrŭzki na Gabrovo s Odesa prez XIX v.," *Istoričeski Pregled*, LV, Nos. 1-2 (1999), 176-184. On foreign and domestic trade in the Bulgarian lands in this period, see the short summary by Ivan Sakazov, *Bulgarische Wirtschaftsgeschichte* (Leipzig, 1929), 245-264. Further examples of these trading contacts (e.g., a merchant in the 1780s named Daskalov from Trjavna who dealt with suitcases and sent them from Nevrokop and the Uzundžovo fair to Moscow) are given by Arno Mehlan, "Mittel- und Westeuropa und die Balkan-Jahresmärkte zur Türkenzeit," *Südostforschungen*, III (1938), 69-120.

[37]See S. Yaneva, "La structure par branches, la répartition territoriale et le volume de la production artisanale bulgare dans les terres situées entre le Danube et le

The case of the Bulgarians and their definition by contemporaries as "Greeks" reveals the role of social mobility in the acculturation of ethnic groups which still occupied a particular position within the division of labour in the first half of the nineteenth century. At a later stage, this phenomenon highlighted the importance of social factors for the process of creating a national identity. The terms "Serb" and "Bulgar," for instance, initially referred to the rural population, whereas migration to the city and the achievement of middle-class status automatically meant strong Hellenization. In this context, the foundation of Serbian and Bulgarian schools as a component of the nation-building process led to a slow transformation of the Serbian and Bulgarian ethnic groups into separate nations.[38]

The most prominent Gabrovo merchant in Odessa was undoubtedly Vasil Evstatiev Aprilov (1789-1847), who played a central role in promoting Bulgarian education and indirectly in the development of a national consciousness among the nineteenth-century Bulgarian population.[39] As an orphan, Aprilov had been looked after by his brothers; he had attended various schools, including a Greek school in Moscow, and had moved to Odessa on account of its favourable business opportunities. Due to his education and occupation he was largely Hellenized and, like other Bulgarians, was a member of the *Filiki Eteria*. It was only later that he started being interested in the language and history of Bulgaria. Earlier research pointed out that Bulgarians were not only members of the *Filiki Eteria* but also actively supported the Greek insurrection, including such prominent examples as Dimitŭr Mustakov in Bucharest, Anton Ivanov Kamburov in Kronstadt and Nikolaj Stanov from Koprivštica, who had become an important merchant in Adrianople and supported the Greek insurgents financially. Moreover, weapons and gunpowder

---

mont Balkan au cours des années 30 à 50 du XIXe siècle," *Bulgarian Historical Review*, XVII, No. 4 (1989), 15-29.

[38]Victor Roudometof, "From Rum Millet to Greek Nation: Enlightenment, Secularisation, and National Identity in Ottoman Balkan Society, 1453-1821," *Journal of Modern Greek Studies*, XVI, No. 1 (1998), 13-14. For the dissolution of Orthodox unity as a consequence of nation-building processes in the Ottoman Balkans, see Ekkehard Kraft, "Von der *Rum Milleti* zur Nationalkirche. Die orthodoxe Kirche in Südosteuropa im Zeitalter des Nationalismus," *Jahrbücher für Geschichte Osteuropas*, LI (2003), 392-408. Ottoman domination had dissolved the difference between religion and nationality which was a prerequisite for the acculturation processes between different Orthodox Balkan peoples. See Peter F. Sugar, "External and Domestic Roots of Eastern European Nationalism," in Sugar and Ivo J. Lederer (eds.), *Nationalism in Eastern Europe* (Seattle, 1969), 32-33.

[39]For a biographical outline, see M. Arnaudov, *V.E. Aprilov. Život, dejnost, sǎvremennici* (Sofija, 1935).

for the Greek War of Independence were stored at several places in Bulgaria.[40] After Greek independence had been achieved and recognized by the European powers, Aprilov and his fellow merchants revealed a new orientation with the promotion of the idea of education in Bulgarian as an indispensable supplement to the prevailing instruction in Greek. They were interested in the creation of an independent Bulgarian church and became the fathers of the "Bulgarian Renaissance" (*Bŭlgarskoto Vŭzraždane*), which preceded the creation of an independent Bulgarian state in the second half of the nineteenth century. Certain researchers even think that Aprilov's return to his roots stemmed from his reading of Paisij Hilendarski's "Slavobulgarian history." This text from the second half of the eighteenth century had been written by a monk from Mount Athos and is considered to be the founding document of modern Bulgarian historiography and a major contribution to Bulgarian national identity. As the document, however, was not printed until after the early nineteenth century and was only circulated in manuscript copies, it is not at all certain that Aprilov had had access to the text. Irrespective of whether he read Paisij or not, Aprilov sponsored the first modern Bulgarian school in Gabrovo, which opened in 1835 and served as a model for future schools in Bulgaria.[41]

Bulgarian Merchants, Their Balkan Network and the Foundation of the Bulgarian School in Gabrovo

In their joint effort to promote education in Bulgarian, the Bulgarian merchants were able to benefit from their extensive network throughout Europe to raise funds and solve practical problems. As in the Greek example, the merchants reinvested a part of their fortunes in cultural activities and took an active part in them. In 1824, for instance, a Bulgarian literary society was founded in Kronstadt, which was to deal with the standardization of Bulgarian spelling and the creation of a literary language. The merchants, who played a major role in this society and who were also active in the book trade, were Anton Ivanovič Kamburroglu from Sliven, who had been established in Kronstadt before 1795, the millionaire Hadži Jordan Hadži Genovič from Bucharest and Vasil Neno-

---

[40]Cf. Nikolaj Todorov and Veselin Trajkov, "L'insurrection grecque de 1821-1829 et les Bulgares," *Etudes balkaniques*, VII, No. 1 (1971), 10-11. For Mustakov, cf. Nikolaj Todorov, *Filiki Eterija i bŭlgarite* (Sofija, 1965).

[41]The fact that Aprilov was initially largely Hellenized can be seen in the fact that even his letters dealing with the idea of education and of creating a Bulgarian school in his native town of Gabrovo were written in Greek. Some of these letters, which he and his fellow merchant Nikolaj Stepanov Palauzov sent to the metropolite of Tŭrnovo or to the monk Neofit Rilski, are printed in Ivan Snegarov, "Materiali za istorijata na bŭlgarskata prosveta prez Vŭzraždaneto," *Izvestija na Archivnija Institut*, I (1957), 199-265.

vič. Nenovič, who came from a merchant family in Svištov on the Danube with trading contacts to Vienna and Bucharest, had been educated in Greek, as was typical. His example reveals the importance of personal contacts and networks in structuring merchants' circles. Vasil Nenovič had attended the Prince's Academy in Bucharest, where the Greek Konstantinos Vardalachos had been a teacher, before his transfer to the Greek Commercial High School in Odessa. Furthermore, Vardalachos had left Wallachia and lived in Kronstadt between 1821 and 1824 as a refugee after the Greek War of Independence had begun. A very important contact for Bulgarian education and the formation of national consciousness was thus established at this time by the merchants in Kronstadt. The educationalist Petŭr Beron, who was to publish the book *Riben bukvar* which was to be used to teach the Bulgarian language, had attended the Prince's Academy in Bucharest as well and lived in Kronstadt at the same time as Vardalachos. Beron based his own pedagogical approach on the Lancaster method, which required older pupils to support and teach the younger ones. He had become acquainted with this method due to direct contact with Vardalachos, who had used it in his classes: it was also to be adopted in the school in Gabrovo financed by Aprilov and other merchants.[42]

As in the Greek case, the activities of Aprilov and the other Bulgarian merchants in Odessa in establishing a school in Gabrovo underline the importance of personal acquaintances and networks. Vasil Aprilov and Nikolaj Palauzov wrote to the Gabrovo merchants in Bucharest, including Teodosij P. Jovčev, Kelifarov, the Mustakovi brothers and the Bakaloglu family, to raise funds for the future school in Gabrovo. It is also interesting to note that the Greek Theodore Rodokanakis was also one of the donors, which underlines the fact that in this early stage the cultural and educational activities of various Balkan peoples did not yet follow the nationalist patterns of later periods and that the forerunners of the national movements of different Balkan groups were

---

[42]See Pirin Boiagiev, "La société littéraire bulgare de Braşov (1824-1826)," *Revue des Etudes Sud-Est européennes*, XVI, Nos. 3-4 (1978), 553-568. Beron was not only Hellenized but also worked as a Greek teacher in Kronstadt, where the merchant Anton Ivanovič from Sliven hired him to teach Greek to his children. See Stojan Maslev, "Vasil N. Nenovič und Petŭr Beron in Braşov," *Bulgarian Historical Review*, XXI, No. 4 (1993), 49-50. The Sliven merchants came from a place which was very important for international trade in the Ottoman Empire because of the fair held there. One of the merchants, Ivan Dobrovolski, showed how a network of relatives and friends were an integral part of the individual career pattern. Dobrovolski started in his father's business, but after 1830 he was employed by the Odessa merchant Paraškeva Nikolau and later on by his uncle Dimitŭr Hadži Kostov in Constantinople. See I. Rusev, "The Bulgarian Commercial Companies during the National Revival Period: An Economic History of the Town of Sliven," *Bulgarian Historical Review*, XXI, No. 1 (1993), 54-93. Note the form of the merchant's name as "Kamburov" with a Bulgarian ending and as "Kamburroglu" with a Turkish ending depending on which sources are used.

not in open conflict. Other donors who subsequently contributed to the school in Gabrovo came from all over the Bulgarian lands, such as Najden Krŭstjov from Adrianople and the Metropolitan of Veliko Tŭrnovo. The importance of personal networks was evident again when books had to be printed for the Gabrovo School. As there was no Bulgarian printing press in Gabrovo, books such as the "Bulgarian grammar" (*Bolgarska grammatika*) were printed free of charge in Kragujevac in Serbia due to the personal connections of the Mustakov family with a member of the court of the Serbian Prince Miloš Obrenović's. The Mustakov family, who had come to Bucharest shortly before 1797 when Ivan Hadži Nikolaj Mustakov and Hadži Velč'o Mustakov settled there, played a decisive role in printing the book. They knew Aprilov and Bakaloglu because they had also lived in Bucharest. And one of Ioan Hadži Nikolaj Mustakov's five sons, Nikifor Mustakov, lived in the Curtea Veche district and thus in the same quarter as Vasil Aprilov. Dimitrie Mustakov looked after the estates which the Serbian prince Miloš Obrenović owned in Wallachia; this was important in the 1830s when he was finally able to organize the printing of the book in Serbia.[43] Furthermore, this type of personal connection was useful again when the teacher for the Gabrovo School had to be chosen. The monk Neofit Rilski, who had already worked as a teacher in Samokov, was chosen jointly by the Metropolitan of Tŭrnovo and the Mustakovi brothers in Bucharest. After Neofit had started teaching in Gabrovo, Aprilov's support from Odessa continued, and in 1836 he sent teaching materials to his native town.[44] The importance of the Gabrovo school in the process of Bulgarian nation-building is underlined by the fact that it not only had pupils who later became teachers throughout the Bulgarian lands but that it also set the teaching standard for other schools in Koprivštica, Panagjurište, Kazanlŭk, Sofia, Kotel and Kalofer.[45]

---

[43]Constantin N. Velichi, *La contribution de l'émigration bulgare de Valachie à la renaissance politique et culturelle du peuple bulgare (1762-1850)* (Bucarest, 1970), 78-79. For the Mustakovs' activities in book printing, see N. Žečev, "Bucarest comme centre culturel des Bulgares au cours de la Renaissance (XVIIIe-XIXe siècle)," *Bulgarian Historical Review*, XX, Nos. 1-2 (1992), 28-43.

[44]The central role of Christian Balkan merchants and their financial support for nation-building in the Balkans in general is emphasized by Charles Jelavich and Barbara Jelavich, *The Establishment of the Balkan National States, 1804-1920* (Seattle, 1977), 15.

[45]See Rumjana Radkova, "Prinosŭt na Neofit Rilski za razvitieto na kulturno-prosvetnoto dviženie prez Vŭzraždaneto," *Istoričeski Pregled*, XXXI, No. 4 (1975), 67-76; and Petŭr Končev, *Iz obštestvenoto i kulturno minalo na Gabrovo. Istoričeski prinosi* (Gabrovo, 1929; reprint, Gabrovo, 1996), 390-415.

Conclusion

Despite considerable methodological difficulties, Odessa is a very rewarding case study for future research on the link between foreign trade, diaspora communities and nascent nationalism in their countries of origin, an approach which combines economic history with the history of migrations and its socio-cultural effects. The Bulgarian and Greek communities are just two examples, while the Jews or Armenians would be other interesting case studies. The same observation is true for other port cities on the Black Sea which are less known but in no way less interesting, such as Taganrog, Kerč' or Izmail in the Russian Empire; Varna, Sozopol and Nesebŭr in present-day Bulgaria; or Constantinople or Trabzon in present-day Turkey. The present study has merely been able to point out some individual links between members of the different communities in these port cities as a precursor to a larger analysis.

Both the Greek and the Bulgarian diasporas played similar roles in the process of nation-building and, according to Hroch, correspond to the first step in this process, namely the emerging awareness of a national identity which was not necessarily in fierce opposition with other emergent national identities. By contrast, the second step was marked by the construction of a distinct and separate identity, which was transformed in the third and last step into a mass phenomenon in the modern sense. Educational projects aiming at alphabetization and language training were a decisive part of this strategy. In this process of rising national consciousness, Odessa was part of a larger framework which comprised other diaspora merchant communities throughout Europe; hence the need for extensive research on this question. It will be important to assess how many members of the community took a more active stance and subsequently chose to fight against the Ottomans for Bulgarian independence. The Bulgarian students at "Novorossijsk University" in Odessa in the second half of the nineteenth century, or the Bulgarian merchant N.M. Toškov who financed the Bulgarian liberation movement, are only two examples of this phenomenon.[46]

On the other hand, certain Greek merchants in Odessa showed a pattern which was totally opposed to a more active stance in the fight for national independence and the transition to the next step in national agitation. The Rallis family is a classic example of the subsequent assimilation of Greek families who stayed in Odessa, even when the business opportunities which had made them rich in the early nineteenth century had diminished. Stefan Rallis, for instance, became a member of the city's *Duma* in the 1860s. His twin sons, Peter and Paul, studied law at "Novorossijsk University" in Odessa. Peter Rallis then became an officer in the Imperial Guard in St. Petersburg, and by

---

[46]Guido Hausmann, *Universität und städtische Gesellschaft in Odessa, 1865-1917: Soziale und nationale Selbstorganisation an der Peripherie des Zarenreiches* (Stuttgart, 1998), 142-150.

1910 Paul Rallis was the President of the Odessa Discount Bank. A similar pattern was exhibited by the Rodokanakis family. Theodore Rodokanakis had married a woman from the Mavrokordatos family, which was one of the most important Greek families in the Ottoman Empire. His son Pericles continued the business activities with his father in various fields, such as textile production, brewing, leather manufacturing and shipping. Later, he was even co-opted into the nobility of the Russian Empire. Finally, Peter Ambrosevič Mavrokordato (whose name already had a Russian form with the father's name "Ambrosevič" and who was probably a relative) was President of the Historical and Archaeological Society in Odessa in 1910 and thus a notable in late Imperial Odessa. The significance of this acculturation and assimilation into contemporary Russian society, and the interesting question of identity in the multi-ethnic setting of Imperial Russia, are crucial issues which will have to be analyzed in future research.[47]

---

[47]Herlihy, *Odessa*, 258-259.

Combining Business and Pleasure?
Cotton Brokers in the Liverpool Business
Community in the Late Nineteenth Century[1]

Sari Mäenpää

> "A first-class merchant does not burden his life with a multitude of details, and is always seemingly in leisure, while intent upon great issues."[2]

Liverpool's established trans-Atlantic trading skills and its proximity to the Lancashire cotton manufacturing industry made it one of the most important ports in Europe by the late nineteenth century. By 1850 Liverpool handled eighty-five percent of Britain's cotton imports – the greatest trans-oceanic trade in the world at the time – and dominated its exports. By this period Liverpool had also become, and remains, the leader in the world cotton market.[3] As the volume of trade increased, a group of specialist cotton brokers emerged.[4] Since prices in the cotton trade were extremely volatile, many men preferred to spread their risks, which put the new specialist brokers in an important position as intermediaries.[5] Previous historical research on this topic

---

[1]This essay draws heavily on the database compiled by the Mercantile Liverpool Project (MLP), funded by the Leverhulme Trust, English Heritage, the P.H. Holt Trust and Liverpool City Council's World Heritage Site Office. The project was based in the School of History at the University of Liverpool.

[2]Samuel Smith, *My Life-Work* (London, 1902), 36.

[3]This is despite the fact that virtually no actual cotton physically passes through the port today. Nonetheless, cotton around the world is traded "to Liverpool Rules" through the Liverpool Cotton Association.

[4]Sydney J. Chapman, *The Lancashire Cotton Industry: A Study in Economic Development* (Manchester, 1904), 113.

[5]William H. Hubbard, *Cotton and the Cotton Market* (New York, 1923), includes two chapters on the Liverpool cotton trade (288-306). In Thomas Ellison, *The Cotton Trade of Great Britain, Including a History of the Liverpool Cotton Market and the Liverpool Cotton Brokers' Association* (London, 1886; reprint, London, 1968), part II is devoted entirely to the Liverpool cotton market. See also Nigel Hall, "The Liver-

has concentrated mainly on the trade, with the result that relatively little is known about the cotton brokers as individuals.[6] Speculation, the effects of events such as the American Civil War and the hazards inherent in the shipping of an easily damaged (and inflammable) cargo like cotton made it an extremely risky business. Extensive networks were required to keep a close eye on fluctuating prices. What demands did this trading environment make on the people involved with what was often a highly speculative trade?

This essay concentrates primarily on cotton brokers and their lives in a large port city. The core nominal data – basically, a list of people who called themselves cotton brokers – were derived from local trade directories (colloquially known as *Gore's*, after John Gore, who published them from 1766 onwards). This information was correlated with census material to reconstruct the Liverpool cotton broker community between 1850 and 1901. Almost 700 brokers and their firms and partnerships have been drawn from a much larger database.[7] In addition, qualitative source material, such as obituaries, biographies and autobiographies, has been used to shed light on their lifestyles.

The second main aim of this study is to explore the attitudes of these men (and the occasional woman who infiltrated their ranks)[8] to an underlying dichotomy: the relationship between work and leisure. Was trading a way of life, a vocation or simply a means to make a profit? Was some higher moral value attached to trade, or did a businessman's real ambitions lie elsewhere? What values were assigned to commerce as a career? The urban environment, some sectors of it awash with money, provided a playground for an elite, some of whose members regarded the urban setting as somewhat degrading.

---

pool Cotton Market: Britain's First Futures Market," *Transactions of the Historic Society of Lancashire and Cheshire*, CXLIX (2000) 99-118. David M. Williams, "Liverpool Merchants and the Cotton Trade 1820-1850," in John R. Harris (ed.), *Liverpool and Merseyside: Essays in the Economic and Social History of the Port and Its Hinterland* (London, 1969) 182-211, has studied cotton merchants in the pre-1850 period. See also Francis E. Hyde, Bradbury B. Parkinson and Sheila Marriner, "The Cotton Broker and the Rise of the Liverpool Cotton Market," *Economic History Review*, New ser., VIII, No. 1 (1955), 75-83.

[6]Graeme J. Milne, *Trade and Traders in Mid-Victorian Liverpool* (Liverpool, 2000), 49. Hall, "Liverpool Cotton Market," 99, has also emphasized the central role of brokers in the Liverpool cotton market; see also Hyde, Parkinson and Marriner, "Cotton Broker," 76.

[7]This was constructed as part of the Mercantile Liverpool Project, A simple search for "cotton broker" produced 1320 hits.

[8]Peter Boult, a broker with Shand Higson and Co., was recorded in the 1881 census as head of a household which included his twenty-four-year-old daughter, Jessie, also described as a cotton broker.

What was the mercantile elite's outlook on an expanding, exceedingly work-based city that was said to have benefited greatly from its civic pride?

Cotton Brokers in the Liverpool Business Community

This study examined three sample years – 1851, 1882 and 1902 – in which a total of over 600 cotton-broking firms listed themselves in Liverpool trade directories. The firms represented around five percent of all the trades in Liverpool, including the registered merchants' and brokers' firms (see table 1). In addition, some companies were involved in cotton as a secondary trade, as were many others on a temporary basis. Hundreds of non-specialist merchants or brokers might dabble in cotton when they thought it might be profitable, and the boundaries between merchants and brokers could also be fluid.

Table 1
Number of Cotton Broking Firms in Liverpool, 1851-1902

	1851	1882	1902
Cotton-Broking Firms	125	275	211
All Broking Firms	658	1568	1463
All Firms	2259	5166	5574
% of Brokers	19.0	17.5	14.4
% of All Firms	5.5	5.3	3.8

Source: Liverpool Trade Directories, 1851, 1882 and 1902.

The 1851 Liverpool trade directory reveals that cotton traders often acted as shipowners or ship's agents, but in the following decades shipowning ceased to be a secondary trade as the demands of increasing capital intensity reinforced its specialist status. The relative importance of secondary trades is difficult to judge on the basis of trade directories, but census enumerators' books, which allowed an individual to list only one occupation, normally recorded the occupation by which an individual could best be described. Overall, cotton brokers appear to have had surprisingly few complementary trades compared to other businessmen. Indeed, seventy-one percent of those who listed themselves as cotton brokers in the trade directories were also enumerated as brokers in the censuses, which suggests that this was the main or only source of income for most. In 1851, however, approximately one-third of the cotton traders also acted as cotton dealers, but this combination seems to have been discontinued by the early twentieth century, when about fifteen percent of the cotton brokers had moved into cotton merchanting as a second source of income (see figure 1). By this time, general broking and cotton merchanting had replaced dealing as the most common source of additional income, although produce brokerage became increasingly important. In addition, cotton brokers tended to specialize regionally, importing cotton either from America, Egypt or India, and the available evidence suggests that there was a general trend towards regional and commodity specialization in cotton trading as well.

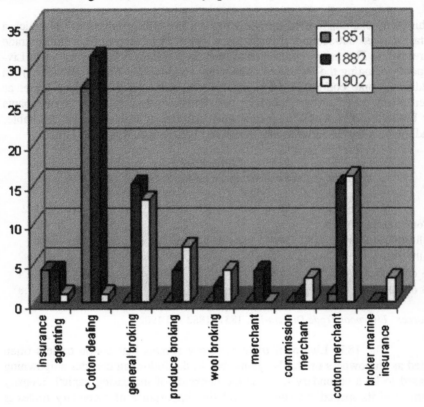

Figure 1:   Secondary Trades of Liverpool Cotton Brokers, 1851-1902

Sources: See table 1.

Although some notable firms remained stable over many decades, in general business mortality was high among cotton broking firms, which indicates either problems of succession or an extremely volatile trading environment. Fewer than two percent of the companies listed as cotton brokers in 1851 were still in business at the end of the century. This calls into question the popular image of the sound, old family firm, as the majority was clearly neither sound nor old. But it is sometimes difficult to judge the longevity of firms, as partnerships were frequently created, extended or disbanded and often changed their names when a partner retired. Often the survival of these firms depended on sons taking over, but the database suggests that most were lucky if they succeeded in securing kinship succession for more than two subsequent generations.[9] James Stock, for example, established the firm of James Stock and Co.; his son John succeeded him and in turn left a large fortune to *his* son. James Stock's grandson, however, was not interested in business, preferring instead the "position of a country gentleman" and later entered Parliament. Despite family discontinuity, George Henry Brown and his niece continued to trade under the Stock family name, which presumably had some value as a brand name which evoked an established trading relationship.

A good deal of research has been done on the role played by inmigrants in the growth of Liverpool, much of it conveniently summarized in Colin G. Pooley's contribution to John Belchem, *Liverpool 800* (Liverpool, 2007). While such work makes clear the great importance of in-migrants, gives figures on their origins and provides a wealth of "mini-biographies" of such prominent men as William Brown, it does not quantify these people by occupation, which would enable a separate consideration of the merchants. Fortunately, the Mercantile Liverpool Project (MLP) database does.

The composition of Liverpool's cotton-broker community reflected its close trading links with other prominent markets. Most brokers were English-born, but twenty percent was born elsewhere. There was a noticeable German, American, Brazilian and Egyptian presence in Liverpool due to the central positions of these countries in the international cotton trade as either producers or intermediaries. Liverpool had especially close connections with the New York and Bremen cotton exchanges; in 1881, for example, six percent of Liverpool cotton brokers had been born in the US. Some in-migrant brokers adopted a deliberate strategy of marrying a local woman whose father had business and social ties in Liverpool as a means of integrating into the merchant community. The census data confirm this strategy: migrant cotton brokers frequently married local women, although such marital patterns often reflected the fact that these brokers generally came to Merseyside at a relatively young age to complete their apprenticeships. In most cases, they would have been able to marry only after starting their own business. It was no coincidence that this stage in a new broker's career occurred at the same time that his contacts "back home" might have become useful to a prospective father-in-law. The available evidence also points to another prevalent inclusion strategy:

---

[9]On kinship succession and inheritance in family firms, see especially Alastair Owens, "Inheritance and the Life-Cycle of Family Firms in the Early Industrial Revolution," *Business History,* XLIV, No. 1 (2002), 21-46; and Andrea Colli, Paloma Fernandez Perez and Mary B. Rose, "National Determinants of Family Firm Development? Family Firms in Britain, Spain, and Italy in the Nineteenth and Twentieth Centuries," *Enterprise and Society*, IV, No. 1 (2003), 28-64.

membership in the congregation of a local (usually dissenting) church.[10] Samuel Smith, for example, became closely connected with other Scottish merchants by attending the Canning Street Presbyterian Church, and in particular the literary Presbyterian Canning Street Society, from whose members he received "boundless hospitality."[11] The Holts and Rathbones, both of which were involved, *inter alia*, with cotton broking, were among the most respected families in the city and had for several generations been active in the Unitarian Church, a denomination famous for the close ties among its members, both in business and marriage. The local congregation, first at the Renshaw Street Chapel and finally at the present building in Ullet Road, had an almost legendary reputation for charitable work, although the change of premises was clearly connected with the development of fashionable residential districts favoured by the merchant class.

Liverpool also had a wealthy and influential Scottish merchant community which was united by membership in a Presbyterian Church or a golf club; most Scottish merchants belonged to one or both of these circles. Scots cotton brokers were an important minority: their proportion varied from four to seven percent, but peaked in the 1880s. Perhaps due to an interest in their national game, many other cotton brokers felt it necessary to join a golf club; reputedly, these were places where many business deals were done. The Irish-born had an even higher presence among brokers in the early period: in 1851 they comprised over nine percent, although by the end of the period this group had virtually disappeared. The other prominent mid-nineteenth century group had migrated from such important cotton manufacturing districts as Manchester, Oldham and Bolton, but they rightly perceived that their prospects of mercantile success were greater in Liverpool. They, too, faded away towards the end of the century. By contrast, few brokers were of Welsh origin. Despite extensive in-migration and the development of a network centred on a large number (peaking at nineteen) of Welsh chapels, the Liverpool Welsh concentrated mainly on construction, property development and coastal shipping.[12]

Entering Business

Samuel Smith can serve as a near-perfect case study of a successful Liverpool cotton broker not only because he wrote an excellent autobiography but also

---

[10]B. Guinness Orchard, *Liverpool's Legion of Honour* (Birkenhead, 1893), 42.

[11]Smith, *My Life-Work*, 15.

[12]This is not to say that there were *no* Welsh-born brokers in Liverpool. Hugh Hughes, for example, a principal in Hugh Hughes and Co., had his office in Exchange Street East but was born in Anglesey.

because his career fits within our time frame. Born in Kirkudbright in 1836, he came to Liverpool in 1853 and was apprenticed to a firm of cotton brokers. At the outset he was mainly given routine work in the counting house, tasks he found "degrading" and "wearisome beyond measure." He was a member of the Canning Street Presbyterian Church, which stood in the then-mercantile residential heartland of what is today known as the Georgian Quarter. Soon, however, he began soon to make friends through literary and debating societies, and in 1857 he joined the Liverpool Philomathic Society (a debating society), which greatly helped him in the art of speaking. Through the Society he met members of the local commercial "aristocracy," such as Sir James Picton and Sir Arthur and Sir William Forwood.[13] In 1857 he was promoted to head of the salesroom, which meant that he had to go out "on Change." Physically, the "Change" was the large flagged area between the Town Hall and the Exchange where cotton brokers (among others) assembled in the afternoon to consummate deals face-to-face; to be "known on change" was an indication of status, and for a while much of young Samuel's time was spent on the flags. When that stage in his career progression was complete, he left Liverpool in 1860 for a tour of America to learn about "the other end" of the trade. After eleven months abroad he returned to start his own business at the age of just twenty-four. Soon thereafter he became increasingly engaged first in religious and then in philanthropic work. In 1870 he bought a country house in Windermere and a son was born; soon afterwards, he was elected to the Town Council and, still only forty years of age, to the Presidency of the Liverpool Chamber of Commerce. In 1883 he was elected a Liberal MP for Liverpool. In 1898 his only son, Gordon, died, and he built the Gordon Smith Institute for Seamen to commemorate him.[14] What is illuminating about his "public life" is how early it started: at the age of thirty-four he had been in independent business for only a decade yet was already able to divert some of his time and energy away from the daily need to make money.

William Forwood, another cotton broker, followed a career path similar to that of Samuel Smith. He went to a secondary school in Nottinghamshire, but despite being talented in mathematics he never attended university. His father was already in business in Liverpool and felt that university

---

[13]James Allanson Picton (1805-1889) was an architect best known for his authoritative (and still useful) *Memorials of Liverpool* (London, 1873). He was the driving force behind the establishment of the Liverpool Library and Museum, serving as its first Chairman from 1851 until his death. The Forwood brothers were contemporaries of Samuel Smith, already on their way to being commercial and political heavyweights. Both were shipowners rather than merchants, but by 1880 they held such prominent places "in public life" that they could have had little time for anything else.

[14]A handsome red brick building which still survives, albeit now converted to offices.

training would spoil him for business, since more education than necessary was regarded as "unsettling."[15] After a trip to Australia and South America he entered his father's office and became a partner in 1862 when his father retired. Forwood also joined the Philomathic Society and became President in 1868 at the age of twenty-eight. This was followed by a wide range of other public positions, such as the presidency of the Chamber of Commerce in 1871; in 1880 he was elected Mayor of Liverpool.

Cotton brokers normally received a classical education at least to the secondary school level. According to Samuel Smith, a businessman should receive just the right amount of education - not too much and not too little. In fact, Smith regarded too much university training and "minute-scholarship" as being of little value for a merchant. On the contrary, the head of a firm needed the skills of "a statesman, an economist, and a financier, as well as a merchant, which required good judgement."

Notwithstanding the short duration of most cotton-broking "dynasties," a commercial career was often "inherited" from an older male relative. The 1851 data show that twenty percent of all cotton brokers' households contained a resident son who was either a cotton apprentice, a cotton clerk or a cotton broker, which indicates a strong tendency to inherit the father's career. Indeed, there was often more than one: in 1881, John Bateson, Chairman of the Liverpool Cotton Brokers' Association (LCBA), resided in Wavertree. Living with him were not just the five servants (as befit his status) but his elder son, aged twenty-eight and a cotton broker, and his younger son, who was a cotton broker's clerk. The resolution of the apparent paradox, of course, is that the young men did not necessarily go into their father's firms when they "came out of their time" at the end of an apprenticeship. But when they did so, it had several advantages: the father could help the son start his career by providing business expertise and contacts in various business networks.

Since boys began their careers between the ages of fourteen and sixteen, an apprenticeship was often served with someone known to the family. Indeed, young cotton apprentices would often live in the broker's household. After five or six years, a young man might take a post as a clerk or, if exceptionally talented or lucky, go straight into a partnership. It would normally take about nine years from starting an apprenticeship to founding a business or entering an established partnership. This often happened about the age of twenty-four, when starting a business also meant becoming an adult. This also tended to coincide with marriage, the establishment of a household and the assumption of more responsible positions in public clubs and associations.[16]

---

[15]William B. Forwood, *Some Recollections of a Busy Life, Being the Reminiscences of a Liverpool Merchant, 1840-1910* (Liverpool, 1910), 20-21.

[16]The fact that it was often a young man's trade is not without exceptions. In 1881 William Greenhalgh was thirty-eight and living in unfashionable Everton with

Escaping the Urban

Liverpool, as many cities, enjoyed an unprecedented level of in-migration from the early nineteenth century onwards. In consequence, poor people looking for work inhabited the urban area close to the docks. In the 1850s most brokers still lived in an area now known as the Liverpool "city centre."[17] But by then the wealthier residents, including some cotton brokers, had already started to escape to the developing suburbs. Even in the few cases where business and the family home were still located under the same roof, individual merchants began to acquire an additional residence in the more rural settings of South Liverpool and increasingly on the other side of the Mersey.[18]

By the 1850s about a fifth of the brokers lived across the river in Birkenhead or New Brighton, although their residences tended to be situated relatively close to the coast due to inadequate transport. It was already possible to commute conveniently to Liverpool everyday except Sunday, when ferry service was less frequent.[19] Most mercantile businesses were located relatively close to home, which allowed the men to arrive on horseback or even on foot, and parts of East Liverpool, such as Fairfield and West Derby, were still popular because they were served by horse buses and trams, which were both respectable and expensive compared with their later counterparts.[20]

By the early 1880s, the spatial dispersion of cotton brokers' residences was far greater, as individual families relocated to more isolated locales around Liverpool and the Wirral (on the other side of the Mersey). During this period Liverpool's population grew substantially, and wealthy residents were increasingly drawn to the suburbs to escape pollution and overcrowding; the merchant elite now generally avoided the central urban area as a place of residence. As a result, Liverpool's wealthy merchants tended to con-

---

nine children and no servants (clearly one of life's losers). The 1912 trade directory gives his home address as Blundellsands, one of the elite residential areas of the time. Was this a fortuitous inheritance, or was Greenhalgh a late developer held back by an excess of procreation?

[17]The distribution of wealth and poverty within and surrounding the town is studied in Richard Lawton and Colin G. Pooley, *The Social Geography of Merseyside in the Nineteenth Century* (Liverpool, 1976).

[18]The MLP database links nineteenth-century addresses with present-day port codes, which makes it possible to track merchant mobility quite accurately.

[19]Smith, *My Life-Work*, 15. The lack of Sunday transport to Liverpool from the opposite side of the Mersey was the main reason he founded a church in Egremont.

[20]For a meticulously detailed account, see J.B. Horne and T.B. Maund, *Liverpool Transport* (5 vols., London, 1975-1991), I.

gregate in exclusive areas where poor people (apart from servants) were completely absent. The area inhabited by the wealthy commercial class had spread
considerably in thirty years: there were significant clusters of cotton brokers to
the north of Liverpool in Bootle, Waterloo, Blundellsands and Crosby following the opening of the railway from Liverpool to Southport in 1851. Central
Liverpool was practically emptied of cotton brokers' residences: in 1881 only
ten percent of the families lived in the town centre. By this time, the increasing preference for suburban residence had been reinforced by the development
of large-scale parks   around Liverpool, the most exclusive of which were
Prince's Park (laid out between 1842 and 1844) and Sefton Park (opened in
1872). Toxteth Park Ward, especially Sefton Park and Prince's Avenue, became the place to live for the Liverpool business community, including many
cotton brokers, and the southern part of Liverpool was particularly popular
among foreign merchants. The most well-off cotton merchants, such as the
Branckers and Holts, lived in this area. John Brancker, Justice of the Peace
and Chairman of the Mersey Docks and Harbour Board (MD&HB), 1890-
1899, lived in Greenbank Road, while Robert Holt, a member of the famous
Unitarian family and a son of a cotton broker, lived in Ullet Road.

By 1901, the majority of brokers had moved further from the city
centre to sparsely-populated districts on the other side of the Mersey and further away along the northern coast. A number of families, especially if they
still resided in Liverpool, often had a summer house in Wales or the Lake
District. Out-migration from Liverpool continued in the early twentieth century, although southern Liverpool, especially around Sefton Park, retained its
popularity as a residential suburb. While there were only a few cotton brokers
still living within Liverpool's civic boundaries, three-quarters of these lived in
the southern parts around Sefton Park. To the north, on the other hand, migration had continued beyond Bootle and Litherland, which had been spoiled by
the northward extension of the Dock Estate and the noxious industries (including a tannery and a tar distiller) which tended to cluster around it.

The exodus of cotton brokers and wealthy merchants from the inner
city continued; a suburban residence, country house or even a domicile abroad
offered an escape from the noise, pollution, slums and the poor which represented all that the commercial elite despised. Cotton broker Samuel Smith, for
example, described Liverpool in his autobiography as "grimy."[21] When Liverpool expanded, the Holt family in 1877 moved to Sefton Park, and then further away to Mossley Hill. They had previously lived in Edge Lane in eastern
Liverpool, which in the early nineteenth century had still been relatively un-
touched countryside. As Anne Holt wrote in the family diary in 1861,

---

[21]Smith, *My Life-Work*, 21.

One feels more and more than ever how completely this neighbourhood is becoming incorporated in the town and losing all the quietness and freshness of air it once had. The new parade ground at Mount Vernon and the general military ardour of the townsfolk adding greatly to the natural noises of the situation.[22]

An increasing segregation of work and home, as well as more time spent commuting, had consequences for business practices and culture. Graeme Milne has argued that the adoption of office telephones was caused by the increasing distance between business and home, which made it too troublesome for businessmen to commute daily. Telephones therefore became an important tool to control employees and to monitor activities in the office.[23] The growing distance between workplace and home arguably led to an increased distinction between public and private lives, as well as greater separation within the merchant community between women and men. Eleanor Gordon and Gwyneth Nair have shown that despite gentrification, the middle-class family was not cut off from the wider world and that the home remained "intimately linked with production and sociability."[24] Much of the area into which the merchants moved was unsullied countryside which was seen as a haven from the hustle and bustle of a stressful business life. In Liverpool, the dispersion of residences across an increasingly wide area also meant that the precise location of the home became an important determinant of social status. Perhaps for this reason, there was a decline in charitable commitment in Liverpool by the early twentieth century and a development of alternative clubs and societies in the suburbs. Middle-class families increasingly lived in isolation from each other, and the Mersey became a dividing line in social life, especially in the evenings and weekends, despite regular ferry transport. Relatively long distances affected the socializing and visiting patterns of these families, and contemporary diaries reveal that dinner guests often stayed overnight or over the weekend.[25] Geographic origins and denominational affiliations were often

---

[22]Liverpool Record Office (LRO), 920 DUR 1/4, Holt Family Diary, 11 August 1861.

[23]Graeme J. Milne, "British Business and the Telephone, 1878-1911," *Business History*, LXIX, No. 2 (2007), 163-185.

[24]Eleanor Gordon and Gwyneth Nair, *Public Lives: Women, Family and Society in Victorian Britain* (New Haven, 2003), 6.

[25]See, for example, Margaret Ismay's diaries from the early 1880s (National Maritime Museum [NMM], ISM/9-11). She lived in Crosby, in North Liverpool by the Mersey, and often had overnight guests due to lack of transport. For example, on 10

important criteria affecting residential patterns: immigrants from Scotland, for example, tended to move to places with an existing Presbyterian community and church. Unitarians often chose to live close to each other and adjacent to their chapels, which were important bases for social, cultural and charitable activities. By the 1890s leading Unitarian families, such as the Holts, Rathbones, Mellys, Booths and Muspratts, who formed a close-knit alliance of friendship and marriage, had all built their homes in Ullet Road, where the new chapel was built between 1896 and 1899. Escape to the country was facilitated by improvements to the public transport network, which was increasingly used by businessmen and their families, although private coaches were still used extensively even in the late nineteenth century since many families lived in locations outside the immediate reach of public transport.[26] Elite women regularly used public transport, especially the omnibus, unless they had a coachman available for their personal use. Even in the 1850s it was still common for Liverpool businessmen to walk to their offices or go on horseback, but by the start of the twentieth century the trip to and from work took an increasing part of a businessman's day and often had to be done by coach.[27] This had certain consequences for business practices, as well as for family life, because an increasing number of social activities in business circles were concentrated at lunchtime or immediately after work, with free time spent outside the city at home or at yacht clubs, golf courses or cricket grounds.

The Office World

Despite spreading their residences further away from urban Liverpool, the workplaces of cotton brokers remained in the town centre. Most of their offices were situated in a relatively small area in the business district near the waterfront and the Exchange in buildings that often had a separate sample room or warehouse downstairs. As a rule, each broker or firm would occupy one office and sometimes a separate salesroom in the same building. Larger firms would have a general office and a separate salesroom for each article of trade. Brancker, Boxwell and Co. was a notable Liverpool firm engaged in

---

January 1881 she wrote: "Had a dinner party. The Mayor and Mr. Forwood, Mr. and Mrs. Dale, Barrows, Hobsons and Herbert Jones dined with us. Mr. and Mrs. Dale remained the night."

[26]Many large households employed a coachman, though only the Earles appear to have had two.

[27]By 1900, however, the motor car was beginning to appear. Early models, including some made in Liverpool, were fragile and unreliable, but by 1907 the Rolls-Royce Silver Ghost brought fine engineering standards to the market, transforming the motoring experience, though only for the rich.

cotton-, produce- and general broking, as well as merchanting. As a consequence, it occupied three separate offices in the Exchange: a general office, a general salesroom and a separate cotton salesroom. Offices were generally small, and business was often conducted either outside the Exchange "on the flags" or in cafes or private clubs. Especially before the arrival of the telephone, the office was mainly an administrative base where the clerks toiled and the post arrived. The salesroom, where the samples were viewed, was probably not a place where a partner would spend much time. The overall impression is that a partner was seldom office-based to the same extent as an apprentice or a clerk, especially in the period before developments in telecommunications. Samuel Smith, a Liverpool cotton broker and later an MP, wrote in his memoirs that "[i]n all weathers, cold and wet, winter and summer, we stood outside, sometimes under the sheltering arches when the rain and cold were unendurable."[28] Contrary evidence, however, was given a few years later by B. Guinness Orchard, who wrote about Liverpool millionaire William Brown that "[a] merchant of high and assured status need not go looking for others; he sits in his office and they call upon him; while the details of running-about work devolve upon the heads of departments."[29]

Evidence from biographies suggests that partners often had distinct responsibilities within a firm. Robert Rankin, a partner in the firm of Rankin, Gilmour and Co., spent most of his time in the office. According to John Rankin's memoirs,

> Mr. Rankin, except when the Dock Board called for him, was always at the office, initiating and directing, seeing and knowing almost intuitively what was going on...G.W. Houghton [another partner] devoted himself so far as his share of correspondence permitted, to work on the flags.[30]

A partner's work generally involved fewer routine tasks, since his role was to act as a representative to the outside world. Due to the speculative nature of business, a cotton brokers' work was socially interactive, with the workplace also serving as a venue for this. The concept of a "place of work" was flexible, and available evidence suggests that merchants were relatively mobile. Many "business hours" were spent either reading newspapers in places like the Exchange Reading Room, the Palatine Club and the Athenaeum; standing

---

[28]Smith, *My Life-Work*, 16.

[29]Orchard, *Liverpool's Legion of Honour*, 212.

[30]John Rankin, *A History of Our Firm* (Liverpool, 1921). Rankin was the third generation of his family to serve on the Board.

outside on the flags; or lunching in one of the clubs located in the business district. Therefore, it is difficult to define which part of their daily activities was regarded as business and which as pleasure. Moreover, leisure and the manner in which it was enjoyed was also an opportunity to create and consolidate "friendships." The Liverpool Philomathic Society, for example, clearly fulfilled the important need for "the good feeling which it creates among its members towards each other – a feeling not confined within the walks of this society, but carried into the more active and general scenes of life."[31] The manner in which leisure was utilized also affected wider issues of inclusivity and reputation, as membership in some institutions was proof of success, wealth and social standing. Indeed, an essential part of middle-class masculinity was to "be somebody," a public person whose status was constructed and reinforced through active attendance at civic processions and meetings of voluntary societies and trade associations.[32]

Public Work or Public Leisure?

Becoming a partner also meant accepting the responsibilities of an economically independent citizen, a position which was a prerequisite for being taken seriously in the public arena. Salaried employees were seldom included in the membership lists of voluntary associations unless they were of great importance, such as the Town Clerk or (towards the end of the period) one of the new breed of salaried "chief executives," such as Harold Sanderson, the General Manager of the White Star Line. In general, the importance of partnership status still extended far beyond the confines of the "change."

As a businessman's career progressed, either by obtaining a more senior position in his firm or going into business on his own, an increasing proportion of his time was spent in networking. It was a very social lifestyle, and an appropriate public image was of central importance for a businessman. A proper British merchant was an all-around figure, "a truly great man, honourable, far-sighted, enterprising, yet withal prudent and cautious; simple in his life, and temperate in all things." For Samuel Smith, "trustworthiness" and "honour" were the most important qualities of a businessman.[33]

A businessman's judgment was tested in the public arena. James Smith, Samuel's brother, became a cotton broker and was deeply engaged in

---

[31]James Kidman, *A Philomathic Retrospect: Inaugural Address Delivered at the Opening of the Seventy-fifth (Diamond) Session of the Liverpool Philomathic Society, 27 September 1899* (Liverpool, 1899), 137.

[32]Catherine Hall, *White, Male and Middle Class: Explorations in Feminism and History* (New York, 1992), 17.

[33]Smith, *My Life-Work*, 36.

social, political and charitable activities outside his immediate business focus. The wide array of public activities in which cotton brokers were involved indicates that financial success was not the only symbol of achievement. On the contrary, social prestige seems to have been a more important motive for their actions in the urban arena. The evidence in obituaries also points to the existence of a dual career path: a man would have his first career as a businessman and after enough money was made and the leadership succession sorted out, he would retire, either in part or in whole, from his business and start a second career in politics and philanthropy. The amazing amount of energy required was well illustrated by the career of James Smith.

James went into partnership with his brother and Edward Edwards in 1864 at the age of twenty-three. He later became a director of Lloyd's Bank and the London and Lancashire Fire Insurance Company, as well as a director of the LCBA and a member of the Liverpool Chamber of Commerce. Despite his commercial responsibilities, he soon became involved in politics as President of the Wirral Liberal Association, President of the Wallasey Central Liberal Club and a member of the Liverpool Reform Club. He was also engaged in the Presbyterian Church, giving substantial funds to build a new church and financially assisting the upkeep of a mission hall in Egremont. In the 1880s he became involved in the municipal affairs of Wallasey and was chosen as a member of various county council committees. He provided two public recreation parks in Cheshire and was appointed a Justice of the Peace for both Wirral and Dumfriesshire, where he had a country residence. He supported various charities in Wallasey, including the YMCA, local hospitals and the Liverpool and District Temperance Union. After his brother's death he also assumed the presidency of the Seamen's Friendly Society. In addition, he was a keen sportsman and devoted much time to cricket as captain of the New Brighton Cricket Club and curled, fished and shot at his country house in Scotland. Adrian Jarvis' study of the members of the MD&HB suggests that such a spread of activities was by no means unique.[34]

Successful cotton brokers, such as Francis Reynolds, were keen on being seen as good charity men. Reynolds was a member of the St. Mary's Young Men's Society and funded the Home for Catholic Friendless Youths. Others, such as John Sheppard, became actively engaged in civic life. In 1874 he became a member of the Garston Local Board and eventually its Chairman from 1879 to 1882, and in 1889 he became a representative on the Lancashire County Council. The Conservative Owen Williams represented St. Paul's Ward on the Liverpool City Council and was a member of the Lancashire County Council for the Toxteth Division. At the same time, he was deputy

---

[34]See Adrian Jarvis, "The Members of the Mersey Docks and Harbour Board and Their Way of Doing Business," *International Journal of Maritime History*, VI, No. 1 (1994), 123-139.

chairman of the State Fire Insurance Company and a director of the Great North of Scotland Railway.

Apart from active involvement in formal associations, a position of leadership in the LCBA was also regarded as an important mark of merit. The most successful businessmen, apart from holding several interlocking directorships, were members of various associations and active in municipal life. For example, Sir Helenus Robertson became a partner of the firm Finlay, Lawrence and Lance at the age of twenty-four. He became the first President of the LCBA and later was elected Chairman of the MD&HB (1911-1919). He retired from business in 1883 to devote "himself to his public duties and to commercial activities on a wider scale as a director of various public companies." He held a number of directorships, including in the Liverpool Commercial Bank and the Bank of Liverpool, and was a member of the Alpine Club.

Liverpool cotton brokers held an impressive number of positions of trust, mostly within the urban area. Their contact networks extended from the city council to charitable bodies and interlocking directorships. For example, Alexander Theodore Brown was a nephew and partner of George Henry Brown in the firm James Stock and Co. He actively supported the development of Liverpool University and was a member of the Liverpool Literature and Philosophical Society. He wrote a history of the Liverpool Royal Institution School and published a book on Liverpool architecture. He was also President of the Liverpool Athenaeum, a keen cyclist and a member of the Wayfarers Club. Danson Cunningham of the firm of Cunningham and Henshaw was another eminent cotton broker with at least nine people working for him at the time of his death. He was a director of the LCBA (1898) and held several interlocking directorships in the Royal Insurance Company and the Liverpool Warehouse Construction Company; he was also a member of the New York and New Orleans cotton exchanges and the MD&HB (1895-1915). If this was not enough, he was a member of the Liverpool Cricket Club, the Liverpool Racquette Club and the Seamen's Orphanage.

Business as a Measure of Success

Cotton brokers had access to wide-ranging networks of information and influence through membership in both formal and informal associations, although family and fellow churchgoers were often preferred as sources of market information, a theme which emerges in many other places in this volume. Such information was a major asset which could be enhanced by work "in public life." Charitable work and municipal activities provided social status and enhanced public reputation. Although successful cotton brokers regarded charity as a moral obligation, their involvement served first and foremost as a means to legitimize their positions within the local elite.[35]

Vying with the magistracy as the most prestigious "appointment" for a second career "in public life" was election to the MD&HB.[36] Membership, or even better the rare honour of chairmanship, brought perhaps the highest status among brokers. The business reputation of the merchant enhanced that of the Board and *vice versa*. The MD&HB was an extremely powerful organization entrusted with the annual expenditure of considerable sums of what was in effect public money without the normal restrictions (including being voted off) which governed members of the Corporation or the various Poor Law bodies. Only the Special Auditor stood between the payers of the port's dues and major defalcation, a situation which marked a rather special degree of trust. At any time just short of half the twenty-eight members were usually merchants or brokers (most of the rest were shipowners), and within that group the cotton men usually predominated.

The available biographies suggest, however, that the ultimate aim of a "typical" businessman was a public career, preferably as an MP. Many businessmen tended to follow a dual career path. For example, William Ratbone VI was a politically ambitious cotton broker who became famous for his philanthropic work. He was elected a Liberal MP for Liverpool in 1868 and sat for the city until 1880; subsequently, he was returned as MP for Carnarvonshire from 1881 to 1885 and for North Carnarvonshire from 1885 to 1895. A second career in public life, as was the case with Samuel and James Smith, often began in their forties or fifties, so that business success only seemed to serve as a means to an end, bringing in the money and providing the initial basis for social prestige. A successful business career, which provided an independent status, was essential to prove your ability in the public arena, even if a political career remained the real ambition of many of these men. In 1898, for instance, Samuel Smith took his son Gordon into his business in the hope that he would continue his name and influence in Liverpool. He was hoping for an eventual Parliamentary career for his son but admitted that he "was desirous that he should have practical knowledge of business life, which is in many ways the best apprenticeship for public service."[37]

---

[35]Peter Shapely, "Urban Charity, Class Relations and Social Cohesion: Charitable Responses to the Cotton Famine," *Urban History*, XXVIII, No. 1 (2001), 49.

[36]The two were not, of course, mutually exclusive: of the first 100 men elected to the Board, thirty-seven also served as magistrates. See Jarvis, "Members."

[37]Smith, *My Life-Work*, 414. As we have seen, this plan was thwarted by his son's premature demise.

The Victorian work ethic pointed towards a notion of trade as less honourable than some other occupations.[38] This might have provided a motivation for businessmen to try to gain social prestige in other arenas. This was well illustrated by B. Guinness Orchard in his collective biography of Liverpool's merchant elite where he argued against the idea of the inherent immorality of trade:

> Trade is not in itself immoral, nor is immorality general among traders, nor are they at bottom less honourable, less anxious to live on a high level, less sensitive to the opinions of their fellows than these critics whose comparative freedom from temptation is largely due to the wealth amassed by businessmen; while among the various motives which spin men on to become wealthy not the weakest is a craving to retire from commercial life into other scenes where, perhaps, they will be more able to respect themselves...Notorious immorality is much against a man's commercial success; in public it ruins him.[39]

Conclusion

According to the available evidence, it is often difficult to delineate work from leisure in the lives of Liverpool's cotton brokers.[40] An early (perhaps enforced) career choice and work in a family firm might have had a negative effect in terms of the work satisfaction for successive generations. In addition, the volatile nature of business might have created a need for a safety net. A questionable social status bolstered by contemporary notions of the immorality of trade might have caused a businessman to seek social prestige elsewhere. The underlying notion that trade lacked social prestige seems to have been true, at least to some extent, since the most successful cotton brokers had wider goals than simply business success and profit making. In this sense, social prestige was almost as important as the accumulation of capital. "Lei-

---

[38]Peter D. Anthony, *The Ideology of Work* (London, 1977), 42; Rosemary Deem, "Leisure, Work and Unemployment: Old Traditions and New Boundaries," in Deem and Graeme Salaman (eds.), *Work, Culture and Society* (Milton Keynes, 1985), 180-181; and Richard Grassby, *The Business Community of Seventeenth-Century England* (Cambridge, 1995), 51.

[39]Orchard, *Liverpool's Legion of Honour*, x.

[40]Sociologists have faced difficulties in defining the concepts of work, nonwork and leisure. See, for example, Keith Grint, *The Sociology of Work: An Introduction* (Cambridge, 1991), 11 and 23.

sure" implied a preference for rural pursuits based around a private family summer house, whereas work retained an explicit urban and public focus. For businessmen, the city was a place where fortunes were made and personal ambitions hopefully fulfilled, but the urban environment also provided a web of contacts and a political playground from which to retire to the suburbs in order to enjoy a much-envied imitation of the lifestyle of the country gentry, once money from trade had provided the means to achieve this objective. Their miniature stately homes in Allerton or Oxton boasted not only large houses with many servants but also such accoutrements as coach houses and large grounds to which access was controlled by a manned lodge at the gate. For successful cotton brokers, like the elite merchant community in general, urban space had increasingly become a place where leadership qualities were tested and social and political ambitions were realized.

Printed and bound by CPI Group (UK) Ltd, Croydon, CR0 4YY

16/04/2025

14658574-0005